Lecture Notes in Computer Science   12064

Sandra Burri Gram-Hansen ·
Tanja Svarre Jonasen · Cees Midden (Eds.)

Persuasive Technology

Designing for Future Change

15th International Conference on Persuasive
Technology, PERSUASIVE 2020
Aalborg, Denmark, April 20–23, 2020
Proceedings

 Springer

Editors
Sandra Burri Gram-Hansen 🆔
Aalborg University
Aalborg, Denmark

Tanja Svarre Jonasen 🆔
Aalborg University
Aalborg, Denmark

Cees Midden
Eindhoven University of Technology
Eindhoven, The Netherlands

ISSN 0302-9743   ISSN 1611-3349 (electronic)
Lecture Notes in Computer Science
ISBN 978-3-030-45711-2   ISBN 978-3-030-45712-9 (eBook)
https://doi.org/10.1007/978-3-030-45712-9

LNCS Sublibrary: SL3 – Information Systems and Applications, incl. Internet/Web, and HCI

This Springer imprint is published by the registered company Springer Nature Switzerland AG
The registered company address is: Gewerbestrasse 11, 6330 Cham, Switzerland

Preface

Persuasive Technology (PT) is a vibrant interdisciplinary research field focusing on the design, development, and evaluation of interactive technologies. PT aims at changing people's attitudes or behaviors through persuasion and social influence, but with strong considerations regarding transparency and ethics. The 15th International Conference on Persuasive Technologies and Persuasive Design (Persuasive 2020) brought together international researchers and practitioners from industry and academia who are working in the field of behavior design and persuasive technologies. As a community, we aim at enriching people's lives in various domains such as health, safety, and the environment – by supporting their personal goals to change their behavior.

The Persuasive conference series is the leading venue to meet and discuss cutting-edge theoretical and methodological perspectives and to present recent insights from practice and research. The conference provides a venue for networking between researchers and practitioners from all corners of the world, and has in previous years been held in exciting places such as Chicago, USA; Padua, Italy; Linköping, Sweden; Oulu, Finland; Sydney, Australia; and Waterloo, Canada.

Persuasive 2020 was the 15th edition in this conference series, and was hosted during April 20–23, 2020, by Aalborg University in Denmark. Aalborg University was proud to be the first university in the world to host the conference for the second time, having also been co-host of the Persuasive 2010 conference which took place in Copenhagen. For Persuasive 2020, particular attention was directed towards creating bridges and networks between researchers and practitioners, and towards sustainability and green initiatives. This focus is closely related to Aalborg city's role as a European Sustainable City, and its early involvement in international charters for sustainability.

On April 20, a Doctoral Consortium on Persuasive Technologies was held as part of the pre-conference activities. The consortium was organized and facilitated by leading international researchers in the field, and comprised an opportunity for PhD students to network as well as gain valuable feedback on their work. On April 21, the program combined interactive workshops with ground-breaking tutorials. The included workshops comprised a program which highlighted both academia and real wold practice, and provided participants the opportunity to be inspired by both sides. On April 22 and 23, the main conference took place with six single track sessions including oral presentations of accepted academic papers. The program furthermore included two keynotes as well as a poster and demo session.

This volume contains the accepted papers presented during the main conference. The included papers were reviewed by a board of experts in the field, in a double-blind review process. Papers were selected for publication and presentation at the conference based on the review process. Overall, 46 reviewers were randomly assigned to the papers excluding all and any conflicts of interest. Each review combined a rating of the paper along with a detailed textual review, which not only provided the program chairs with significant insight concerning the individual submissions, but also ensured that the authors were provided with high-quality feedback and recommendations for their final versions of their paper.

The Program Committee carefully assessed all reviews and all comments made by the reviewers, and based on this the final list of papers to be presented at the conference was comprised. 56 papers were included in the review process and 18 papers were accepted, compliant with an acceptance rate of 32%.

Apart from the papers accepted and presented at the conference, adjunct proceedings were also published, in order to include those papers related to poster presentations, demos, doctoral consortium, as well as tutorial and workshop descriptions. The success of this conference was in every way dependent of the support of the Persuasive Technology Society, and in particular the people who actively contributed with publications or as reviewers for the different submission types. As already mentioned, the Persuasive conference series is to a great extent an event which facilitates knowledge sharing and collaboration across nationalities and across different research areas. We as editors are grateful to have had the pleasure of creating the 2020 bridge between academia and practice – and between friends around the world.

April 2020

Sandra Burri Gram-Hansen
Tanja Svarre Jonasen
Cees Midden

Organization

General Chair

Lykke, Marianne   Aalborg University, Denmark

Organizing Chair

Hyldgaard, Charlotte   Aalborg University, Denmark

Program Chairs

Burri Gram-Hansen, Sandra   Aalborg University, Denmark
Midden, Cees   Eindhoven University of Technology, The Netherlands
Jonasen, Tanja Svarre   Aalborg University, Denmark

Workshop and Tutorial Chair

Skov, Mette   Aalborg University, Denmark

Poster and Demo Chair

Burri Gram-Hansen, Sandra   Aalborg University, Denmark

Doctoral Consortium Chairs

Brogaard Bertel, Lykke   Aalborg University, Denmark
Hasle, Per Frederik Vilhelm   University of Copenhagen, Denmark
Oinas-Kukkonen, Harri   University of Oulu, Finland

Industri Chair

Larsen, Thilde Møller   House of Energy, Denmark

Digital Media Chair

Damyanov, Denis Nikolaev   Aalborg University, Denmark

Program Committee Members

Ali, Raian   Bournemouth University, UK
Arakawa, Yutaka   Nara Institute of Science and Technology, Japan
Baghaei, Nilufar   Otago Polytechnic, New Zealand

Berkovsky, Shlomo	Macquarie University, Australia
Brinkman, Willem-Paul	Delft University of Technology, The Netherlands
Burri Gram-Hansen, Sandra	Aalborg University, Denmark
Chittaro, Luca	HCI Lab, University of Udine, Italy
Corbett, Jacqueline	Laval University, Canada
Damyanov, Denis	Aalborg University, Denmark
Davis, Janet	Whitman College, USA
De Vries, Peter	University of Twente, The Netherlands
Felfernig, Alexander	Graz University of Technology, Austria
Gretzel, Ulrike	University of Southern California, USA
Ham, Jaap	Eindhoven University of Technology, The Netherlands
Hasle, Per Frederik Vilhelm	University of Copenhagen, Denmark
Kaipainen, Kirsikka	Tampere University, Finland
Kegel, Roeland	University of Twente, The Netherlands
Kekkonen, Markku ·	University of Oulu, Finland
Kelders, Saskia	University of Twente, The Netherlands
Klaassen, Randy	University of Twente, The Netherlands
Langrial, Sitwat	Namal Institute Pakistan
MacTavish, Tom	IIT Institute of Design, USA
Meschtscherjakov, Alexander	University of Salzburg, Austria
Midden, Cees	Eindhoven University of Technology, The Netherlands
Oduor, Michael	University of Oulu, Finland
Ogie, Robert	University of Wollongong, Australia
Oinas-Kukkonen, Harri	University of Oulu, Finland
Orji, Rita	Dalhousie University, Canada
Schmidt-Kraepelin, Manuel	Karlsruhe Institute of Technology, Germany
Schueller, Stephen	University of California, Irvine, USA
Shevchuk, Nataliya	University of Oulu, Finland
Spagnolli, Anna	University of Padova, Italy
Jonasen, Tanja Svarre	Aalborg University, Denmark
Tikka, Piiastiina	University of Oulu, Finland
Tondello, Gustavo	University of Waterloo, Canada
Tscheligi, Manfred	University of Salzburg, Austria
Van Gemert-Pijnen, Lisette	University of Twente, The Netherlands
Van Rompey, Thomas	University of Twente, The Netherlands
Vassileva, Julita	University of Saskatchewan, Canada
Vlahu-Gjorgievska, Elena	University of Wollongong, Australia
Win, Khin Than	University of Wollongong, Australia
Yetim, Fahri	FOM University of Applied Sciences, Germany

Department of Communication and Psychology, Aalborg University, Denmark

Aalborg University is .a dynamic and innovative research and educational institution with an active commitment to international cooperation. The university offers education and research within the fields of natural sciences, social sciences, humanities, technical, and health sciences. Since its establishment in 1974, AAU has been characterized by a problem-based and project-oriented teaching method (PBL) – also called the Aalborg Model, and by extensive collaboration with the surrounding society. Despite the fact that AAU is a fairly young university, it is already ranking among the best and most acknowledged international universities in the world.

The Department of Communication and Psychology is a large, interdisciplinary department at Aalborg University. The department's research and teaching activities are directed towards designing and putting into practice processes and products that improve or expand people's ability to participate in communicative contexts. The foundation of the department is humanistic, and our activities therefore focus on people and the relationships between people, organizations, society, media, and technologies.

Contents

Methodological and Theoretical Perspectives on Persuasive Design

On the Impact of the Application Domain on Users' Susceptibility to the Six Weapons of Influence

Alaa Alslaity$^{(\boxtimes)}$ and Thomas Tran

University of Ottawa, Ottawa, ON K1N 6N5, Canada
aalsl005@uottawa.ca, ttran@eecs.uottawa.ca

Abstract. Persuasive technology is gaining increasing attention nowadays. Researchers have proposed several approaches to support technology with persuasive capabilities inspired originally from the domain of social sciences. Cialdini's six persuasive principles, known as the "six weapons of influence," is an example of such techniques that are widely deployed in the persuasive technology domain. However, the literature lacks studies that asses the relationship between the domain, in which a persuasive technology is applied, and how the former is actually affecting the degree of persuasion achieved by Cialdini's six persuasive principles. To bridge this gap, we investigate the effect of the application domain on users' susceptibility to Cialdini's principles. Two application domains were considered, namely an e-commerce recommender system and a movie recommender system. A within-subject study is conducted, and a total of 107 responses were collected. The results show that when using the same persuasive technique, the nature of the application domain affects the way users got persuaded by that technique. Hence, our findings suggest that the application area, as a contextual dimension, is an important factor that should be taken into consideration when designing persuasive systems.

Keywords: Cialdini's persuasive strategies · Persuasive recommender system · Persuasive Technology

1 Introduction

Persuasion can be defined as *"a symbolic process in which communicators try to convince other people to change their attitudes or behaviors regarding an issue through the transmission of a message in an atmosphere of free choice."* [1]. Over the last decades, persuasive-related research has been conducted in social sciences as well as in other related fields such as marketing, healthcare, law, education, etc. [2]. In fact, persuasive communication can shape or impact humans' decision making in different settings, including, but not limited to, the market, the courtroom, or the family [2].

Recently, persuasiveness has been introduced to Computer Information Technology (CIT) area. The increased research in this direction has led to a new research and application area named *Persuasive Technology* (PT) [3]. The essence of PT is that a particular

© Springer Nature Switzerland AG 2020
S. B. Gram-Hansen et al. (Eds.): PERSUASIVE 2020, LNCS 12064, pp. 3–15, 2020.
https://doi.org/10.1007/978-3-030-45712-9_1

technology can be used as a means of persuasion that aims to convince users to behave in a desired way [3]. PT has been introduced into different application areas, such as healthcare (e.g., to motivate users toward healthy behavior), education (e.g., to motivate students to complete their tasks), and lifestyle (e.g., encourage users to follow green routes). Also, persuasion has been recently augmented to other applications, which are not persuasive by nature, such as Recommender System (RS) [4].

In the literature, there is a consensus that persuasion solutions cannot be considered as a "one-size-fits-all" approach. For this, recent research in PT has been directed towards personalizing PTs [3], where the personalization was mainly based on users' characteristics. In particular, researchers studied the impact of users' characteristics (e.g., age, gender, and cognitive ability) on their susceptibility to persuasive strategies. The Communication-Persuasion Paradigm [5], however, stated that the extent to which a message influences its receiver depends on four factors, namely (1) characteristics of the source (i.e., the message sender), (2) the message, (3) characteristics of the destination (or the receiver of the message), and (4) the context. That is, user's characteristics are only one of four factors that impact persuasion. Hence, it is insufficient to tailor persuasion based on users' characteristics only.

Having said that, this paper aims to investigate the effect of the *context* as another impacting factor. In particular, this paper investigates the effect of the application domain on users' acceptance of Cialdini's six weapons of influence (discussed in Sect. 2.1). To do so, we choose Recommender System (RS) as an application domain, and we conducted a within-subjects study on users of two different domains, e-commerce RS and a Movie RS.

Our results revealed that the same persuasive strategy, when used in two or more different application domains, would have different impacts on the same user. Our results, hence, suggest that the context in which the application is deployed plays an important role in affecting users' susceptibility to persuasive techniques. Thus, the application context should be taken into consideration when designing persuasive applications.

The rest of this paper is organized as follows: Sect. 2 discusses background concepts and related work. Section 3 provides details about our study and methodology. Sections 4 and 5 illustrates and discussed the results of the study. Finally, the paper is concluded in Sect. 6.

2   Background and Related Work

This section provides a brief background about the six weapons of influence and discusses the state-of-the-art related work.

2.1   The Six Weapons of Influence

There is a wide variety of persuasion means in the literature. Social scientists proposed various taxonomies of persuasive strategies, such as the 40 strategies that have been described by Fogg [6], over 100 groups suggested by Kellermann and Tim [7], and the six principles *of Cialdini* [8]. The latter is the focus of this paper.

The six principles of Cialdini (a.k.a., the six weapons of influence)[1] have been widely used in the literature, and they have been verified as general persuasive principles [9]. The idea of these principles is that there is no magical strategy that can influence all people, and hence, people can be convinced in different ways. These principles are:

1. *Authority*: "People defer to experts." People are more inclined to accept recommendations made by a legitimate authority.
2. *Commitment*: "People align with their clear commitment." People tend to commit to their previous or reported opinion or behavior.
3. *Social Proof* (Consensus): "People follow the lead of similar others." Usually, people tend to do what others do. So, people are most likely to accept recommendations if they are aware that others have accepted as well.
4. *Liking*: "People like others who like them." People are most likely inclined to accept requests that are made by somebody we like.
5. *Reciprocity*: "People repay in kind." People tend to return a favour. So, humans are more inclined to follow recommendations that are made by a person to whom the receiver is in debt.
6. *Scarcity*: "People want more of what they can have less of." People consider whatever is scare as more valuable.

2.2 Related Work

This section discusses the research on the Cialdini six principles, and how the persuasiveness of these principles can be affected by various factors.

Oyibo et al. [10] conducted a study that investigates Nigerians' susceptibility to the six principles of Cialdini. The study also investigated if gender has any impact on the responses. The results show that Nigerians are susceptible to all principles but at different levels. Specifically, the level of susceptibility to the six principles was ordered, from the highest to the lowest, as follows: Commitment, Reciprocity, Authority, Liking, Consensus, and Scarcity. The study also concluded that *gender* plays a role in participants' responses, with males found to be more susceptible to Commitment and Authority than females.

In another study, Oyibo et al. [11] investigated wither the personality of users who came from different cultural backgrounds would affect the level of persuasion of different strategies. The study provided a comparative analysis of the Nigerians' susceptibility to persuasive strategies compared to Canadians. A study of 248 total responds (88 Nigerians and 196 Canadians) was conducted. The results revealed that the susceptibility of Nigerians is different than the Canadians for all strategies except for Commitment strategy. In particular, Authority and Scarcity were found to be the most effective on Nigerians. On the other hand, Reciprocity, Liking, and Social Proof were the most effective on Canadians.

---

[1] The "Six weapons of influence" and the "six principles of Cialdini" are used interchangeably in this paper.

Gkika and Lekakos [12] investigated the impact of implementing the six weapons of influence on users' intention to use a recommendation. The paper suggested an explanation to represent each strategy. A user study was conducted where users were revealed with recommendations, along with six different explanations. Then users were asked to evaluate the extent to which each explanation may change their mind to watch the recommended movie. The results showed that, in general, incorporating persuasive explanations to recommendations that are close to users' preferences would affect their behavior in terms of accepting/rejecting recommended items.

As an extension to Gkika and Lekakos' study [12], Sofia et al. [9] investigated the influence of persuasive strategies on users' intention to use a recommended item if it is preferred to the user. Particularly, the authors discussed the six weapons of influence in conjunction with users' personalities; Similar to the previous study, the persuasive strategies were also incorporated into the systems as explanations along with the recommended items. The results indicated that all strategies positively affect users' acceptance of the recommendations. Also, they concluded that users' personality affects their susceptibility to different strategies.

The impact of the big five personality traits on the persuasion level of the six weapons of influence was also investigated by other researchers, such as Oyibo et al. [14], and Alkış and Temizel [15]. All of these studies agreed on a common conclusion that the level of persuasion of Cialdini's principles varies from one personality to another. However, the results of these studies were not completely consistent, even though they had the same study settings. To further highlight this issue, we compare the conclusions of three studies, which are summarized in Table 1.

Table 1. Summary of the compared studies

	Authors	Year	Participants
1	Oyibo et al. [14]	2017	People with Canadian origins
2	Sofia et al. [9]	2016	Greece, undergraduate and Ph.D. students
3	Alkış and Temizel [15]	2015	Turkey, Undergraduate Turkish students

Table 2 depicts a comparison between these three studies. Columns represent the six persuasive strategies of Cialdini, while rows represent the five personality traits [13]. Cells show the results of the three studies, as follows: "Y/N" is the answer (Yes/No) to the question "*does a persuasive strategy (X) influence persons who are high in personality (Z)?*". Empty brackets indicate that the relationship is not mentioned in the corresponding study. Curly brackets { }, round brackets (), and square brackets [] represent the results of the first, second, and third studies, respectively. For instance, the first cell (Openness X Authority) indicate that the first and the third study concluded that Authority does not persuade users who have high openness traits. For enhanced readability, we distinguished inconsistent answers with bold font.

Table 2. Comparison of the results of the three studies mentioned in Table 1

	Authority	Commitment	Social Proof	Liking	Reciprocity	Scarcity
Openness	{N} (Y) [N]	{} (Y) [Y]	{N} (Y) [Y]	{N} (Y) [Y]	{} (Y) [N]	{} (Y) []
Conscientiousness	{} (Y) [Y]	{Y} (Y) [Y]	{} (N) [N]	{N} (Y) [N]	{Y} (Y) [Y]	{} (Y) []
Extraversion	{} (N) [N]	{} (N) [Y]	{} (Y) [N]	{} (N) [Y]	{} (Y) [Y]	{} (N) [Y]
Agreeableness	{Y} (Y) [Y]	{Y} (Y) [Y]	{} (N) [Y]	{Y} (Y) [Y]	{} (Y) [Y]	{} (Y) []
Neuroticism	{} (Y) [N]	{} (Y) [N]	{Y} (Y) [N]	{} (Y) [N]	{} (Y) [Y]	{} (N) [Y]

As Table 2 shows, the three studies are not consistent in many cases (50% of the cases). This contradiction is because of neglecting other factors (e.g., the context), and not considering them along with the personality traits, although they influence users' decisions. That is, users' characteristics are not the sole determinant of the persuasion level of the six weapons of influence. This conclusion is in line with Oinas and Harjumaa [16] suggestion, who stated that: "*Without carefully analyzing the persuasion context, it will be hard or even impossible to recognize inconsistencies in a user's thinking, discern opportune and/or inopportune moments for delivering messages, and effectively persuade.*"

To this end, this paper investigates the effect of the context on users' persuadability to the six weapons of influence. To achieve this, we conducted a study to examine the role of the application domain as a vital aspect of the persuasion context. The next section discusses our study in detail.

3 The Study

We conducted a user study in the domain of RSs. The study considered two types of recommenders, namely E-commerce RSs (e.g., Amazon and eBay), and Movie RSs (e.g., YouTube and Netflix). This study aims to answer the following research questions:

– RQ1: *Do persuasive strategies have an impacting role in the decisions of RS users?*
– RQ2: *Does the application domain affects the susceptibility of RS's users to different persuasive strategies?*

- RQ3: *Does the persuasion level of the six weapons of influence in E-commerce RS differs from that in the movie RS domain?*

3.1 Study Design

Our study follows a within-subject design. It consists of a two-part questionnaire; each part reflects an application domain. In each part, we ask the participants to rate six persuasive sentences; each sentence represents one of Cialdini's principles. We adopted the persuasive statements described by Sofia et al. [9] for the movie RS, and then we followed the same convention to formulate persuasive statements for the e-commerce RS. Table 3 depicts the persuasive sentences that we used for both domains. The rationale behind adopting this methodology is because the authors conducted their study for the RS context, which is the same as our context. Also, the persuasive statements were expressed based on a well-designed methodology, which involved seventeen experts to choose the best matching sentence for each strategy.

In each part of our questionnaire, the participants were asked to rate the six sentences. Users give ratings according to the question: "*To what extent do you think that each of the following statements will influence your decision to buy an item (or to watch a movie) recommended to you?*"). Users were asked to give a rate in a 7-Likert scale from (-1) to (5), as follows: (-1) indicates a negative effect (i.e., the sentence may cause a resistance towards the recommendation), Zero (0) indicates no effect (i.e., zero is the neutral value), and 1 to 5 options are scaled from very low to very high positive effect.

Table 3. Persuasive statements as presented in the questionnaire. E-com = E-commerce

Principle	Corresponding statement
Authority	(E-com) The recommended item won 3 prizes as the best-manufactured product! (Movie) The recommended movie won 3 Oscars!
Commitment	(E-com) This item belongs to the kind of items you usually buy (Movie) This movie belongs to the kind of movies you enjoy watching
Social Proof	(E-com) 87% of users rated the recommended item with 4 or 5 stars! (Movie) 87% of users rated the recommended movie with 4 or 5 stars!
Liking	(E-com) Your Facebook friends bought this item! (Movie) Your Facebook friends like this movie!
Reciprocity	(E-com) A friend of you, who bought the item that you suggested to him/her in the past, recommends you this item! (Movie) A Facebook friend, who saw the movie that you suggested to him/her in the past, recommends this movie!
Scarcity	(E-commerce) The recommended item will be available for two months only! (Movie) The recommended movie will be available for two months only!

3.2 Participants Recruitment

We used two means to recruit participants, which are emails and posters distributed at the University of Ottawa. A total of 107 participants responded to the study. After excluding incomplete responses, we got 72 complete responses. To make sure that the results are representative, we filtered the data again, such that we exclude records that contain identical ratings for all sentences. After this step, we get a total of 70 responses.

4 Results

After collecting responses and filtering the data, we analyze them according to the research questions mentioned in Sect. 3. This section reports on results organized according to the research questions (RQ1–RQ3).

4.1 Impact of Persuasive Strategies

To answer the first research question (RQ1), we calculated the mean rate for each persuasive strategy in the e-commerce RS (Fig. 1a) and the movie RS (Fig. 1b). Also, the overall mean (i.e., the mean of all ratings in both domains) is illustrated in Fig. 2.

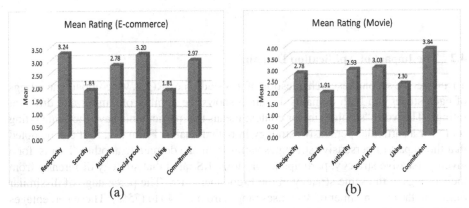

(a)   (b)

Fig. 1. Mean values for participants' ratings of each strategy in the e-commerce (a), and the Movie (b) domains

As illustrated in the figures, all mean values are greater than the neutral value (i.e., Zero), which indicates that all strategies are influential. This conclusion is true for both application domains. From Fig. 1a, it can be inferred that *Reciprocity* is the most influential strategy in the e-commerce RS, while *liking* is the least influential strategy. On the other hand, *Commitment* is the most influential strategy for users of movie RS (Fig. 1b), and *Scarcity* is the least influential strategy. The overall means (illustrated in Fig. 2) indicate that most of the participants believe that any of the six strategies can influence their decisions to some extent. *Scarcity* has the lowest mean value (1.87), which means that it is the least influential strategy. All other strategies have an overall mean greater than (2). The figure also shows that *Commitment* is the most powerful strategy, followed by *Social Proof*.

All the above observations answer the first research question; They show that the six strategies influence RS's users' decisions.

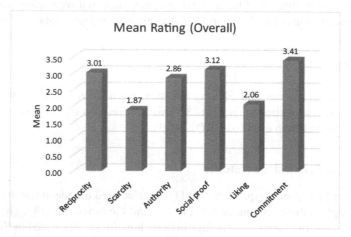

Fig. 2. Mean values for participants' ratings of each strategy in both domains (Overall)

4.2   The Impact of Application Domain

To answer the second research question of this study (i.e., RQ2), we compare the ratings of each strategy in both domains. Figure 3 shows the number of similar and different ratings. The word "similar" in our context means that participants gave the same rating score for a particular persuasive strategy in both domains. From Fig. 3, it can be noted that the impact of persuasive strategies varies from one domain to another. That is, for a given persuasive strategy, participants of movie RS rated that strategy differently from their ratings to the same strategy in the E-commerce RS. The percentage of dissimilar ratings to the total number of responses ranges from (57%) to (75%). These percentages indicate that persuasion levels vary from one domain to another.

Table 4 summarizes our results regarding the differences in users' ratings. The table is divided vertically into two parts, entitled All dissimilarity and Significant dissimilarity. All dissimilarity depicts statistics about all records that contain dissimilar ratings. The Significant dissimilarity focuses only on records with significant changes in the ratings. In this context, a rating difference is considered significant if the two given ratings belong to two different categories. The rating categories are defined as follows: we divided the 7-Likert scale into five categories: Negative (-1), No impact (0), Minor impact (1 and 2), Moderate impact (3), and Major impact (4 and 5). For instance, if a participant gives the Authority strategy rating -1 in the e-Commerce RS and 2 in the movie RS, it is considered as a significant dissimilarity. This is because, with the first rating (i.e., -1), the participant considered that Authority has a negative impact on her decision, while

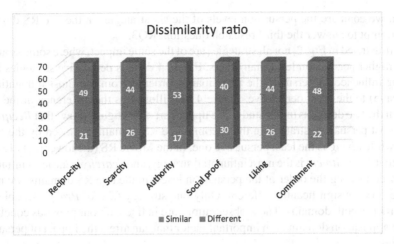

Fig. 3. Number of similar and different ratings between the two application domains

in the second rating (i.e., 2), she thinks that Authority has a positive influence on her decision.

The most important observation in this table is that most of the dissimilar records are significant; On average, 78% of all dissimilar ratings are "Significant dissimilar." This observation suggests that the persuasion level of a strategy varies significantly from one domain to another.

Table 4. Dissimilarity statistics

	All dissimilarity		Significant dissimilarity	
	# records	Mean	# records	Mean
Authority	49	1.76	44	1.75
Commitment	44	1.63	39	1.69
Social Proof	53	1.81	40	1.92
Liking	40	1.75	30	1.86
Reciprocity	44	1.82	33	1.878
Scarcity	48	1.85	31	2.06
Average	**46.33**	**1.77**	**36.16**	**1.86**

4.3 Persuasiveness Order

Section 4.1 showed that the six persuasive strategies are all effective to an extent. Section 4.2 demonstrated that the application domain affects the persuasion level of any strategy, such that the impact of a strategy varies from one domain to another. In this section, we compare the persuasion levels of the six strategies in the two RS domains, in an attempt to answer the third research question, RQ3.

As illustrated in Fig. 2, not all strategies are of the same impact, where some strategies have a higher persuasion level than others. Figure 4 depicts persuasive strategies based on their influence to persuade the participants, ordered from the most influential (or persuasive) to the least persuasive. Figure 4 also illustrates the difference in the order between the two domains under study. The upper part of the figure shows that *Reciprocity* is the most persuasive strategy in the E-commerce RS domain, followed by the *Social Proof*, while *Liking* is the least persuasive one. In the Movie RS (the lower part of Fig. 4) shows that *Commitment* is the most influential strategy, and *Scarcity* is the least influential one. By comparing the order of the persuasion levels in the two RS domains, we notice that the order is significantly different. Only one strategy (*Social Proof*) occupied the same order in both domains. These observations are in line with our previous conclusion that the application domain is an important factor that can affect the impact of persuasive strategies.

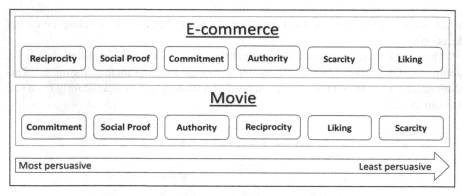

Fig. 4. The effectiveness of the six persuasive strategies in each domain

5 Discussion

The previous section discussed the results obtained from our study. The results demonstrate that persuasive strategies indeed affect the decisions of RS's users. In addition, the results show that the application domain is an important factor that affects the influential power of persuasive strategies.

According to the current results, persuasive strategies have more influential impacts on users of Movie RS than in E-commerce RS. In particular, our results show that the average of all ratings for all persuasive strategies in the Movie domain is (2.8), while in the E-commerce domain, the average is (2.6). The reason behind this is that buying an item means paying money. Normally, people do not pay for items if they do not need or like them. On the other side, people may watch a movie even if they are not sure that the movie will be interesting. For example, one of the participants has commented: *"I only buy when I need the item.*" The same participant has mentioned that she may watch an unknown movie if she had an idea about the story of the movie.

It is worthwhile to mention that our results still need to be compared to other studies to provide more precise conclusions. Oyibo et al. [11] have compared their study with Orji's study [17]. Specifically, they compared the results in terms of the persuasiveness order of the six weapons of influence. We extended this comparison by including our results. Figure 5 depicts this comparison. The order of our study in this figure is based on the whole population. That is, it reflects the ratings of all participants in the two domains.

The figure shows slight similarities between the three studies. For instance, it shows that all studies agree that *Commitment* is the most powerful strategy. However, it reveals a significant difference between our results and the results of the other two studies. The other two studies are similar in three cases; this is because these studies are very similar in term of the design; they have used the same instruments for ratings, and they have compared two similar populations [11]. Unlike ours, these studies did not consider context factors, such as the application domain.

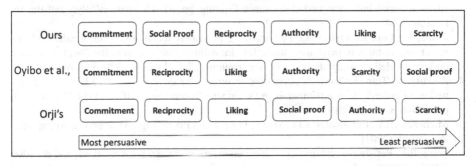

Fig. 5. Comparison between our results, the results of Oyibo et al. [11], and Orji's [17] results.

Having said that, we say that the persuasiveness of the six weapons of influence is affected by various factors, including users' characteristics and application domain. Thus, it is insufficient to consider one factor and ignore others. That is, the application domain should be studied in conjunction with other factors to advance the research in the persuasiveness of technologies, such as RSs.

6 Conclusion

This paper presents the results of a user study of 107 participants. The study discusses the impact of the application domain on the persuasiveness of the six principles of Cialdini. The recommender system is chosen as the context of persuasion; particularly, two areas of recommendations were considered, namely E-commerce recommendations and movie recommendations. To the best of our knowledge, this is the first study in the PT literature that discusses the relationship between the application domain and the persuasiveness of the six weapons of influence. Thus, this study helps in advancing the literature by providing insights on the best persuasive strategy for two application domains. Also, it opens the doors for future researches in this direction.

Our results show that: (1) the six principles are all influential to some extent, (2) the influence of each principle varies from one domain to another, and (3) based on the application domain, the principles have different orders in term of their persuasiveness effect. Despite these results, the application domain is not the only factor that affects the influential power of persuasive strategies. As described in Sect. 2.2, other researchers have studied some personality-related aspects, and they have found that these factors also have an impact on the persuadability of the users. So, as future work, we will first discover other aspects that have not been discovered yet. Then, we will study the relationships between these factors to come up with comprehensive guidelines for incorporating persuasive principles into technologies.

References

1. Perloff, R.M.: The Dynamics of Persuasion: Communication and Attitudes in the 21st Century, 2nd edn. Lawrence Erlbaum Associates Publishers, Mahwah (2003)
2. O'Keefe, D.J.: Trends and prospects in persuasion theory and research. In: Readings in Persuasion, Social Influence, and Compliance Gaining, pp. 31–43. Pearson/Allyn and Bacon, Boston (2004)
3. Aisha, M., Orji, R., Oyibo, K.: Personalizing persuasive technologies: do gender and age affect susceptibility to persuasive strategies? In: Adjunct Publication of the 26th Conference on User Modeling, Adaptation and Personalization, 2 July 2018, pp. 329–334. ACM (2018)
4. Alslaity, A., Tran, T.: Towards persuasive recommender systems. In: 2019 IEEE 2nd International Conference on Information and Computer Technologies (ICICT), 14 March 2019, pp. 143–148. IEEE (2019)
5. Michener, H.A., DeLamater, J.D., Myers, D.J.: Social Psychology. Thomson Learning, Inc., Wadsworth (2004)
6. Fogg, B.J.: Persuasive technology: using computers to change what we think and do **2000** (2002). Article no. 5
7. Kellermann, K., Cole, T.: Classifying compliance gaining messages: taxonomic disorder and strategic confusion. Commun. Theory **4**(1), 3–60 (1994)
8. Cialdini, R.B.: Harnessing the science of persuasion. Harvard Bus. Rev. **79**(9), 72–81 (2001)
9. Sofia, G., Marianna, S., George, L., Panos, K.: Investigating the role of personality traits and influence strategies on the persuasive effect of personalized recommendations. In: 4th Workshop on Emotions and Personality in Personalized Systems (EMPIRE), August 2016, p. 9 (2016)
10. Oyibo, K., Adaji, I., Orji, R., Vassileva, J.: The susceptibility of Africans to persuasive strategies: a case study of Nigeria. In: PPT@ PERSUASIVE 2018, pp. 8–21 (2018)
11. Oyibo, K., Adaji, I., Orji, R., Olabenjo, B., Vassileva, J.: Susceptibility to persuasive strategies: a comparative analysis of Nigerians vs. Canadians. In: Proceedings of the 26th Conference on User Modeling, Adaptation and Personalization, 3 July 2018, pp. 229–238. ACM (2018)
12. Gkika, S., Lekakos, G.: The persuasive role of explanations in recommender systems. In: The 2nd International Workshop on Behavior Change Support Systems (BCSS 2014), 22 May 2014, vol. 1153, pp. 59–68 (2014)
13. Tupes, E.C., Christal, R.E.: Recurrent personality factors based on trait ratings. J. Pers. **60**(2), 225–251 (1992)
14. Oyibo, K., Orji, R., Vassileva, J.: Investigation of the influence of personality traits on Cialdini's persuasive strategies. In: PPT@ PERSUASIVE 2017, pp. 8–20 (2017)
15. Alkış, N., Temizel, T.T.: The impact of individual differences on influence strategies. Personality Individ. Differ. **87**, 147–152 (2015)

16. Oinas-Kukkonen, H., Harjumaa, M.: Persuasive systems design: key issues, process model, and system features. Commun. Assoc. Inf. Syst. **24**(1), 28 (2009)

17. Orji, R.: Persuasion and culture: individualism-collectivism and susceptibility to influence strategies. In: PPT@ PERSUASIVE, 5 April 2016, pp. 30–39 (2016)

Exploring Susceptibility Measures to Persuasion

John Paul Vargheese[1]([⊠]), Matthew Collinson[1], and Judith Masthoff[1,2]

[1] University of Aberdeen, Aberdeen, UK
jpvargheese@acm.org, matthew.collinson@abdn.ac.uk
[2] Utrecht University, Utrecht, The Netherlands
j.f.m.masthoff@uu.nl

Abstract. There is increasing evidence that indicates how personalising persuasive strategies may increase the effectiveness of persuasive
technologies and behaviour change interventions. This has led to a wide
range of studies exploring self reported, perceived susceptibility to persuasion, which highlight the role of individual differences. Conducting
such studies, while accounting for individual differences can be challenging, particularly where persuasive strategies may be considered similar
due to their underlying components. In this paper, we present a study
exploring perceived susceptibility to Cialdini's principles of persuasion,
with a focus on how we can distinguish perceived susceptibility measures between the most recently identified Unity principle and Social
proof. This study was conducted using an online survey incorporating
perceived susceptibility measures to all seven Cialdini principles and a
measure of the actual effectiveness of seven corresponding persuasive
strategies. Our results indicate that while we are able to distinguish perceived susceptibility measures between Unity and Social proof, together
with Commitment, Scarcity and Reciprocity, we were unable to obtain
these measures for Liking and Authority.

Keywords: Susceptibility · Persuasion · Influence · Personalisation

1 Introduction

Persuasive technologies and behaviour change interventions are often designed to
apply personalised persuasive strategies to increase their effectiveness for encouraging individuals to change their behaviour [2,4,13,16,18,19,21,27]. This is
partly motivated by the results from recent studies that report how the effectiveness of persuasive strategies can vary based on individual differences such as age,
gender, culture, personality and other cognitive measures [6,12,25,29,30,37,41].
As such, personalising persuasive strategies is desirable as applying those which
are unsuitable or inappropriate may limit an intervention's effectiveness and
or result in demotivating individuals to perform a desired target behaviour
[1,17,22,24,36].

© Springer Nature Switzerland AG 2020
S. B. Gram-Hansen et al. (Eds.): PERSUASIVE 2020, LNCS 12064, pp. 16–29, 2020.
https://doi.org/10.1007/978-3-030-45712-9_2

Measuring individuals' perceived susceptibility to different persuasive strategies can help provide an insight into what strategies are most suitable and likely to be effective. However, this may be challenging particularly for scenarios where there may be underlying similarities between the persuasive strategies being considered for deployment.

Amongst the variety of persuasion and influence techniques available, persuasive technologies and behaviour change interventions are often designed to apply persuasive strategies based on Cialdini's [5] principles of persuasion. Recently, the original set of six principles was extended to incorporate a newly identified seventh principle, *Unity*. The principle of *Unity* suggests that an individual's behaviour may be influenced by reference to shared identities, the individual may consider themselves to be a member of, together with others. As such, persuasive strategies developed from the principle of *Unity*, can leverage the concepts of acting together and being together to influence behaviour [5]. This is comparable to the Granfalloon influence technique, which emphasises the individual's categorical and group membership association, to influence attitudes, beliefs and behaviour [33, 39].

Prior to the definition of *Unity*, the principle of *Social proof* suggests that an individual's behaviour may be influenced by the observation of others', whose actions and behaviour may be considered as correct, suitable and appropriate by the individual. While *Social proof* is distinguishable from *Unity*, both share a common underlying social component, namely the reference to the behaviour of others. The distinction between both lies in how *Unity* draws upon reference to the shared identities of the individual, which is absent from *Social proof* and may be considered to rely upon a broader and less specific social context. However, given the underlying similarities between both principles, assessing susceptibility for either simultaneously may be challenging, due to the potential overlap between strategies developed from these principles.

In this paper, we report our findings from an exploratory study of perceived susceptibility measures to Cialdini's [5] principles of persuasion. This study aims to validate the susceptibility to persuasion scale (STPS) [17], discover how to distinguish measures of perceived susceptibility to *Unity* and *Social proof* and whether this can be achieved together with the remaining five Cialdini principles.

In Sect. 2 we briefly review previous work concerning susceptibility measures for Cialdini principles and we outline the methodology of our study in Sect. 3. The results of the study are reported in Sect. 4 and finally we review these findings and outline our future work in Sect. 5.

2   Related Work

Table 1 lists all seven Cialdini [5] principles of persuasion, together with a summary on how these may be used to influence behaviour. The STPS [17] provides a means of measuring perceived susceptibility to the original six Cialdini [5] principles of persuasion, (excluding *Unity*). By measuring perceived susceptibility to different persuasive strategies, it is possible to personalise strategies by identifying which are most likely to be effective in addition to those which may be

Table 1. Cialdini's principles of persuasion with examples of behavioural influence [5].

Principle of persuasion	Summary
Reciprocity	We are likely to respond in kind as the receiving party in an exchange out of a sense of obligation to do so
Commitment and consistency	We aim to be consistent in our actions and decision to avoid complexity arising from inconsistencies in our behaviour
Social proof	Our actions beliefs and behaviours may be strongly influenced by what we observe in others as correct and/or appropriate
Liking	We may be significantly influenced by what is attractive and appealing to us
Authority	We will often accept the beliefs and attitudes of those we consider to be within a position of expertise
Scarcity	We are strongly influenced to avoid loss
Unity	Reference to shared identities we define ourselves as being a member of, together with others can strongly influence our behaviour

counterproductive and unsuitable for a given audience [17]. The effectiveness of the STPS has been demonstrated in a longitudinal study of actual effectiveness; where personalised persuasive strategies (developed using the STPS) were more effective for reducing eating between meals, compared to non-personalised persuasive strategies [17]. The STPS has been applied in studies investigating differences and similarities in perceived susceptibility to persuasion between nationalities [28], differences based on cultures [23], language [3] in addition to measuring susceptibility to persuasive strategies designed to increase physical activity for individuals with chronic obstructive pulmonary disease [40] and in predicting susceptibility to phishing emails [32]. In this paper, we build upon this existing work through an exploratory study designed to discover how we can distinguish perceived susceptibility measures between the most recently identified *Unity* principle and *Social proof* in addition to how these can be obtained together with perceived susceptibility measures for all other Cialdini [5] principles of persuasion.

3   Methodology

We measured perceived susceptibility to all seven Cialdini [5] principles using a survey that consisted of three sections and recruited participants from Amazon mechanical turk (MT). Prior to starting the survey, informed consent was acquired and a full summary of the research objectives was provided to participants. The first section captured participants' details including gender, age and location. The second section consisted of 46 question statements (Table 2), each with a seven item Likert scale ranging from strongly disagree to strongly agree. All 32 questions used to develop the original STPS scale as described in [17] were included, in addition to 10 questions designed to measure perceived susceptibility to the *Unity* principle. These were designed to assess whether participants' considered themselves to be influenced by membership of various potential social groups, through reference to shared identities of these groups within each *Unity* question. We also sought to provide scenarios that included potential overlap of behavioural determinants related to *Unity* and *Social proof* persuasive strategies. This was intended to assist us with discovering whether it was possible to distinguish perceived susceptibility measures between both principles as part of our research objectives. Four attention check questions were included, whereby participants were required to respond as instructed e.g. *Please select strongly disagree for this statement*. All 46 questions were displayed randomly, in 11 sets of four and one set of two. After responding to all questions, participants were provided with the opportunity to provide feedback on the study.

In the final section of the survey, participants were presented with a randomly selected persuasive message (based on one of the seven Cialdini [5] principles) which encouraged them to complete an optional ten item short personality inventory (TIPI) [10]. We included this section to provide a measure of actual effectiveness for all seven persuasive strategies. This also provided a means to investigate whether perceived susceptibility measures corresponded with participants' actual behaviour. This analysis was constrained to only those principles for which stable perceived susceptibility measures were acquired.

4   Results

To be eligible to participate in our study, participants were required to have a 95% acceptance rate (indication of previous work completed on MT considered to be of good quality) and be based in either the UK, USA or Canada. 320 participants completed the survey, 302 of which provided valid responses to the attention check questions. The final sample used in our analysis (rounded to the nearest whole number) consisted of 40% female, 59% male, 1% preferred not to indicate their gender, 1% aged 18–19, 24% aged 20–29, 42% aged 30–39, 16% aged 40–49, 12% aged 50–59 and 5% aged 60 or more. 98% of participants were based in the USA and 2% were based in Canada. 13% of participants received the Authority persuasive message, 12% Commitment, 15% Liking, 19% Reciprocity, 10% Scarcity, 17% Social proof and 13% Unity. 53% of participants completed the TIPI test, 47% did not.

4.1   Analysis of Perceived Susceptibility Measures

To discover whether our survey provided a means of distinguishing perceived susceptibility to *Unity* and *Social proof*, together with other Cialdini [5] principles,

Table 2. Survey questions including, STPS, Unity extension and attention checks.

Principle	Principle ID	Question statement
Unity	Unity1	Community is vital, we are all here for each other
	Unity2	When we are faced with a challenge my colleagues and I work together to find a solution
	Unity3	I am proud to be a member of the community and they are proud of me
	Unity4	My social network is close we try to help each other as much as we can
	Unity5	When faced with a decision I choose to do what is best for the team because this is also the best for me
	Unity6	I celebrate the achievements of others within my social network
	Unity7	I am more inclined towards suggestions from my community compared to those from others
	Unity8	Together my colleagues and I consider the outcomes of our actions for each other. before we agree what to do
	Unity9	I value recommendations from my social network
	Unity10	It is more important for me to be liked by my colleagues than my boss.
Reciprocity	Reciprocity11	When a family member does me a favour I am very inclined to return this favour
	Reciprocity12	I always pay back a favour
	Reciprocity13	If someone does something for me I try to do something of similar value to repay the favour
	Reciprocity14	When I receive a gift I feel obliged to return a gift
	Reciprocity15	When someone helps me with my work I try to pay them back
Scarcity	Scarcity16	I believe rare products (scarce) are more valuable than mass products
	Scarcity17	When my favourite shop is about to close I would visit it since it is my last chance
	Scarcity18	I would feel good if I was the last person to be able to buy something
	Scarcity19	When my favourite shampoo is almost out of stock I buy two bottles
	Scarcity20	Products that are hard to get represent a special value
Authority	Authority21	I always follow advice from my general practitioner
	Authority22	When a professor tells me something I tend to believe it is true
	Authority23	I am very inclined to listen to authority figures
	Authority24	I always obey directions from my superiors
	Authority25	I am more inclined to listen to an authority figure than a peer
	Authority26	I am more likely to do something if told than when asked
Commitment	Commitment27	Whenever I commit to an appointment I always follow through
	Commitment28	I try to do everything I have promised to do
	Commitment29	When I make plans I commit to them by writing them down
	Commitment30	Telling friends about my future plans helps me to carry them out
	Commitment31	Once I have committed to do something I will surely do it
	Commitment32	If I miss an appointment I always make it up
Social proof	Social proof33	If someone from my social network notifies me about a good book I tend to read it
	Social proof34	When I am in a new situation I look at others to see what I should do
	Social proof35	I will do something as long as I know there are others doing it too
	Social proof36	I often rely on other people to know what I should do
	Social proof37	It is important to me to fit in
Liking	Liking38	I accept advice from my social network
	Liking39	When I like someone I am more inclined to believe him or her
	Liking40	I will do a favour for people that I like
	Liking41	The opinions of friends are more important than the opinions of others
	Liking42	If I am unsure I will usually side with someone I like
Attention checks	Attention1	Please select Strongly agree for this statement
	Attention2	Please select Strongly disagree for this statement
	Attention3	Please select Strongly agree for this statement
	Attention4	Please select Strongly disagree for this statement

Table 3. Persuasive messages designed to encourage participants to complete the TIPI test.

Principle	Persuasive message
Unity	Please join your fellow participants by completing the following short personality test
Social proof	We would like to invite you to complete a short personality test. The majority of participants, have also completed this part of the study
Reciprocity	We will shortly process and approve your responses to this HIT. Meanwhile, please consider completing the following short personality test
Commitment	As part of your agreement to participate in this study, we would like to invite you to complete a short personality test
Liking	We hope you have enjoyed participating with our study and would like to invite you to complete a short personality test
Authority	We recommend completing the following short personality test to further support the research objectives of our study
Scarcity	We would like to invite you complete a short personality test. This is the last opportunity for you to contribute towards our research on social influence and persuasion

we conducted an exploratory factor analysis using principal component analysis (PCA). We used this approach to discover whether latent variables within the study data could be identified as Cialdini [5] principles and to discover whether participants' perceived susceptibility corresponded with measures of actual effectiveness.

As participant responses were captured using an ordinal scale, we created a polychoric correlation matrix from participant responses (to susceptibility questions) as suggested by [31]. Reviewing the correlation matrix revealed that all 42 susceptibility question responses correlated with others with at least $r = .3$. The Kaiser-Meyer-Olkin test measure of sampling adequacy was 0.93 and Bartlett's test of sphericity was significant ($\chi^2 = (861, N = 302) = 6560.346$, $p < .001$).

In order to determine the number of components to extract, we used parallel analysis (PA) [14] and Velcier's minimum average partial (MAP) test [38]. Results from these tests conflicted, with PA suggesting four components to retain and MAP suggesting five. Interpretation of the scree plot was inconclusive, given the potential for multiple inflexions. As suggested by [26], we investigated both four and five component solutions, which we deemed to be overly complex due to multiple high and low cross loadings of susceptibility questions across all components. We anticipated that this was likely due to the presence of redundant questions within both solutions resulting with increased complexity and consequently difficult to interpret. To resolve these issues, we used an iterative exploratory approach to identify which questions were most relevant to which component and which could be considered as redundant. To achieve this we used the following process.

We first set the number of components to extract based on the number of principles our survey was designed to measure. This is considered suitable given positive results reported in prior studies using questions included in our study [11]. Secondly, components would only be considered for extraction based on the latent root or Kaiser's criterion [15]. This is considered suitable provided the sample size is greater than 250, the average communality of the questions is greater than or equal to .6 [7] and when the number of variables included in the analysis is between 20 and 50 [11]. Thirdly, only stable components would be retained; that is components with a minimum of three strong loadings of at least .5 as these may be considered to be practically significant for developing a solution [11, 20, 26, 34]. Finally, a component solution would only be considered suitable provided all components were interpretable and demonstrated an optimal structure whereby responses for questions load highly on a single component only and may be considered conceptually related to that component. Solutions produced in our iterative exploratory analysis were required to meet all of these conditions.

A preliminary analysis revealed seven components within the data which match the number of principles our survey was designed to measure and each component met the latent root criteria of eigenvalues greater than one. Together these factors accounted for 59% of the variance. To improve interpretation of these components, we repeated the analysis using Oblimin rotation with seven components specified for extraction. To further improve interpretation and structural clarity of the seven components, questions with low primary loadings and or high cross loadings were removed individually and the component solution respecified (using a polychoric correlation matrix excluding values from questions removed). Questions removed from the initial seven component solutions included *Unity 10* and *Social proof 23* and this respecified solution accounted for 60% of the variance.

Upon removing *Social proof 23*, the seventh component was reduced below the latent root criteria and therefore was respecified to six components, which accounted for 59% of the variance. All five *Liking* related questions were removed from the six component solution due to high cross loading, none of which loaded onto a single component that could be considered as stable for the *Liking* principle. This resulted with increasing the cumulative variance the six component solution accounted for to 60%. We continued our exploratory process of removing questions individually from the six component solution considered as redundant. These included *Authority 12, Commitment 20, Scarcity 7, Authority 11, Unity 7, Unity 2, Reciprocity 2, Authority 16* and *Commitment 19*.

Upon removing *Commitment 19* from the six component solution, the sixth component was reduced below the latent root criteria and as such was removed, together with all *Authority* related questions, as these did not contribute to a stable component for this principle due to multiple high and low cross loading. The initial five component solution accounted for 64% of the variance, which

Table 4. Five component solution loadings with Oblimin rotation and Ordinal α for each component. Primary component loadings are shown in bold.

Question Id	Components labelled as Cialdini principles				
	Unity	Commitment	Social proof	Reciprocity	Scarcity
Unity1	**0.73**	0.06	−0.01	0.15	−0.08
Unity3	**0.73**	0.00	0.07	0.01	0.09
Unity4	**0.83**	−0.05	−0.01	0.02	0.07
Unity5	**0.60**	0.08	0.12	−0.03	0.06
Unity6	**0.88**	0.01	−0.12	−0.05	−0.07
Unity8	**0.56**	0.25	0.10	0.01	0.04
Unity9	**0.65**	−0.07	0.23	0.09	0.06
Reciprocity1	−0.05	0.07	−0.05	**0.82**	0.01
Reciprocity3	0.07	0.09	−0.05	**0.78**	−0.01
Reciprocity4	−0.02	−0.12	0.18	**0.77**	0.10
Reciprocity5	0.14	0.08	−0.04	**0.75**	0.01
Scarcity6	0.01	0.05	−0.13	0.08	**0.87**
Scarcity8	0.02	0.09	0.29	−0.15	**0.58**
Scarcity10	0.02	−0.07	0.05	0.02	**0.85**
Commitment17	0.00	**0.86**	0.02	0.00	0.02
Commitment18	−0.02	**0.74**	−0.07	0.12	−0.05
Commitment21	0.12	**0.79**	−0.07	−0.10	0.07
Commitment22	−0.04	**0.74**	0.16	0.14	−0.01
Social proof24	0.00	0.10	**0.73**	0.13	0.05
Social proof25	0.01	−0.02	**0.79**	0.02	0.00
Social proof26	0.03	−0.12	**0.81**	−0.07	−0.07
Social proof27	0.10	0.10	**0.71**	−0.02	0.09
Eigenvalues	4.0	2.85	2.75	2.79	2.04
% of variance	18	13	12	12	9
α	.89	.89	.8	.84	.73

after removing *Scarcity 7*, increased to 65%. The five components were labelled as *Unity, Commitment, Social proof, Reciprocity and Scarcity*.

A reliability analysis was performed to assess the consistency of the questions retained for measuring perceived susceptibility to the five Cialdini principles identified from our analysis. Following suggestions from [8,9,42] we calculated the ordinal α coefficient using a polychoric correlation matrix from the subset of retained questions for each component of the five component solution. The results indicate good reliability for *Unity, Commitment, Social proof* and *Reciprocity* and acceptable for *Scarcity*.

4.2   Analysis of Actual Effectiveness and Perceived Susceptibility

We used a χ^2 test to investigate the actual effectiveness of the seven strategies listed in Table 3 for encouraging participants to complete the TIPI test[1]. Results suggest that there is an overall significant difference in the distribution of actual effectiveness across all strategies: $\chi^2 = (302,6) = 16.811$, $p = .01, V = .236$. However, there was no significant difference in the distribution of actual effectiveness for any of the strategies based on participants' gender ($\chi^2 = (302,2) = 2.307$, $p = .31$, $V = .08$) or age ($\chi^2 = (302,5) = 3.14$, $p = .67, V = .1$). This suggests overall that the persuasive strategies differ in actual effectiveness, but these differences were not related to individual differences of age and gender between participants.

We further investigated the actual effectiveness of the strategies and participant responses to susceptibility to persuasion questions, to discover whether there was any significant difference in perceived susceptibility and the actual effectiveness of the strategies. To achieve this, we calculated composite perceived susceptibility scores using the median of participant responses for each set of perceived susceptibility questions, for only retained components of the PCA model (as listed in Table 4). We then compared the distribution of the susceptibility scores for each component of the PCA model, and the actual effectiveness of the corresponding strategy. This was measured in terms of whether participants were persuaded to complete the TIPI test or did not (for each of the five strategies listed in Table 4). To perform this analysis, we used a Mann-Whitney U test which is suitable for comparing the distribution between two independent groups (participants who were persuaded or not persuaded to complete the TIPI test) and a non-normally distributed dependent variable (composite perceived susceptibility scores for only the five stable retained components in Table 4) [35].

Table 5. Analysis of composite perceived susceptibility scores and participant behaviour.

Principle	Persuaded	Not persuaded	U	z	p	r
Unity	15	26	259	1.76	.086	.3
Commitment	20	16	172	0.388	.718	.1
Reciprocity	38	21	422	0.398	.69	.1
Scarcity	13	19	127.5	0.160	.88	0
Social proof	27	24	332.5	0.161	.872	0

Results from this analysis indicate that there is no significant difference in the distribution of participants' composite susceptibility scores for the

---

[1] This analysis was performed prior to investigating whether perceived susceptibility measures for each component of the PCA model in Table 4 corresponded with participants' actual behaviour.

Unity, Commitment, Reciprocity and *Scarcity* principles (see Table 5). However, an analysis of the distribution of susceptibility scores and whether participants were persuaded to complete the TIPI test or not (actual effectiveness irrespective of persuasive strategy received), indicates a significant difference in susceptibility scores amongst participants for *Unity* $(U(Persuaded = 160, Not\ Persuaded = 142) = 13109.5, z = 2.352, two-tailed, p = .019, r = .1)$, *Scarcity* $(U(Persuaded = 160, Not\ Persuaded = 142) = 12994.5, z = -2.219, two-tailed, p = .027, r = .1)$ and Social proof $(U(Persuaded = 160, Not\ Persuaded = 142) = 12898.5, z = 2.04, two-tailed, p = .04, r = .1)$ but not for *Reciprocity* $U(Persuaded = 160, Not\ Persuaded = 142) = 11730, z = 0.521, two-tailed, p = .602, r = 0)$ or *Commitment* $(U(Persuaded = 160, Not\ Persuaded = 142) = 12095, z = 0.995, two-tailed, p = .320, r = 1)$. This suggests that participants with greater composite susceptibility scores for *Unity, Scarcity* and *Social proof* were more likely to be persuaded to complete the TIPI test.

We investigated whether there was any significant difference in the distribution of composite susceptibility scores and participants' gender and age respectively. This was in order to discover whether participants' susceptibility to persuasion varied based on individual differences. Excluding participants who choose not to indicate their gender during our study, results from a Mann-Whitney U test indicate that there is a significant difference in the distribution of composite susceptibility scores for the *Social proof* principle and participants' gender $(U(Female = 123, Male = 178) = 12578, z = 2.212, two-tailed, p = .027, r = .1)$. This suggests that Male participants reported greater susceptibility to the *Social proof* strategy, compared to Female participants. There was no significant difference in the distribution of participants' composite susceptibility scores and participants' gender for the *Unity* principle $(U(Female = 123, Male = 178) = 10607.5, z = -0.466, two-tailed, p = .642, r = 0)$, *Reciprocity* $(U(Female = 123, Male = 178) = 11019, z = 0.103, two-tailed, p = .918, r = .1)$, *Scarcity* $(U(Female = 123, Male = 178) = 11936, z = 1.37, two-tailed, p = .171, r = .1)$ and *Commitment* principle $(U(Female = 123, Male = 178) = 9829, z = -1.544, two-tailed, p = .123, r = .1)$.

We investigated the impact of age on the distribution of composite susceptibility scores using a Kruskal-Wallis test, which is suitable for measuring a non-normally distributed dependent variable (composite susceptibility score) across multiple groups (age bands) [35]. Results indicate that there is no significant difference in the distribution of composite perceived susceptibility scores for the *Unity* principle, $(H(5) = 1.452, p = .919)$, *Reciprocity* $(H(5) = 5.514, p = .356)$, *Scarcity* $(H(5) = 1.872, p = .867)$, *Commitment* $(H(5) = 0.370, p = .996)$ and the *Social proof* principle $(H(5) = 8.401, p = .135)$.

4.3 Limitations

One of the limitations of this study centres on how there are a greater number of questions for *Unity*, compared to all other principles, including *Social proof*. We accepted this trade off as we sought to provide participants with scenarios that included potential overlapping of behavioural determinants related to *Unity* and *Social proof*; our objective was, in fact, to discover susceptibility measures to both, respectively.

With regards to measuring actual effectiveness during our study; while we assume participants who completed the TIPI were persuaded to do so, by stating that this section was optional and then applying a randomly selected persuasive strategy, we cannot rule out entirely that participants who completed the TIPI were motivated to do so for reasons outside our study design. Furthermore, our analysis of susceptibility and actual effectiveness is limited due to the sample being divided by those who completed the TIPI and based upon which of the seven persuasive strategies they received. This resulted in a low number of participants (who completed the TIPI) for each strategy, which limits our analysis and results for this part of the study.

5   Conclusion

In this paper, we investigated how we can distinguish perceived susceptibility measures to persuasive strategies based on *Unity* and *Social proof*, together with other Cialdini [5] principles. Results from our exploratory study indicate that while we are able to distinguish susceptibility measures for *Unity* and *Social proof*, together with *Commitment*, *Scarcity* and *Reciprocity*, with acceptable to good internal consistency, we are unable to measure these together with susceptibility to *Authority* and *Liking*. While the persuasive strategies for encouraging participants to complete the optional TIPI test differ in actual effectiveness, there appears to be no significant impact of individual differences amongst the participants, based on age and gender. There was also no significant difference in participants' susceptibility to persuasion and the actual effectiveness for each individual strategy, although it appears that participants with greater susceptibility to *Unity*, *Social proof* and *Scarcity* were more likely to complete the TIPI, irrespective of which strategy was received. We also discovered that male participants reported greater susceptibility to *Social proof*, compared to female participants. There was no significant impact of participants' age and susceptibility to persuasion.

In future work, we aim to build on our findings reported in this paper, by investigating how to extend our five component solution to incorporate measures of susceptibility to *Liking* and *Authority*. We also intend to investigate potential overlaps and similarities between other Cialdini [5] principles of persuasion, to discover how we can account for these and whether it is possible to develop susceptibility measures to persuasive strategies consisting of different combinations of Cialdini [5] principles. We believe this work can further help to design personalised persuasive strategies, taking into consideration overall perceived susceptibility to different strategies, different combinations of strategies together with individual differences.

Acknowledgements. This research is supported by the UKRI EPSRC award: EP/P011829/1.

References

1. Bell, M., et al.: Interweaving mobile games with everyday life. In: Proceedings of the SIGCHI Conference on Human Factors in Computing Systems, pp. 417–426. ACM (2006)
2. Beun, R.J.: Persuasive strategies in mobile insomnia therapy: alignment, adaptation, and motivational support. Pers. Ubiquitous Comput. **17**(6), 1187–1195 (2013). https://doi.org/10.1007/s00779-012-0586-2
3. Borges, S.S., Durelli, V.H., Reis, H.M., Bittencourt, I.I., Mizoguchi, R., Isotani, S.: Brazilian portuguese cross-cultural adaptation and validation of the susceptibility to persuasion scale (Br-STPS). In: 2017 IEEE 17th International Conference on Advanced Learning Technologies (ICALT), pp. 72–73. IEEE (2017)
4. Chittaro, L.: Tailoring web pages for persuasion on prevention topics: message framing, color priming, and gender. In: Meschtscherjakov, A., De Ruyter, B., Fuchsberger, V., Murer, M., Tscheligi, M. (eds.) PERSUASIVE 2016. LNCS, vol. 9638, pp. 3–14. Springer, Cham (2016). https://doi.org/10.1007/978-3-319-31510-2_1
5. Cialdini, R.: Pre-Suasion: A Revolutionary Way to Influence and Persuade. Simon and Schuster, New York (2016)
6. Ciocarlan, A., Masthoff, J., Oren, N.: Actual persuasiveness: impact of personality, age and gender on message type susceptibility. In: Oinas-Kukkonen, H., Win, K.T., Karapanos, E., Karppinen, P., Kyza, E. (eds.) PERSUASIVE 2019. LNCS, vol. 11433, pp. 283–294. Springer, Cham (2019). https://doi.org/10.1007/978-3-030-17287-9_23
7. Field, A., Miles, J., Field, Z.: Discovering Statistics Using R. SAGE Publications, London (2012)
8. Flora, D.B., Curran, P.J.: An empirical evaluation of alternative methods of estimation for confirmatory factor analysis with ordinal data. Psychol. Methods **9**(4), 466 (2004)
9. Gadermann, A.M., Guhn, M., Zumbo, B.D.: Estimating ordinal reliability for likert-type and ordinal item response data: a conceptual, empirical, and practical guide. Pract. Assess. Res. Eval. **17**(3), 1–13 (2012)
10. Gosling, S.D., Rentfrow, P.J., Swann Jr., W.B.: A very brief measure of the big-five personality domains. J. Res. Pers. **37**(6), 504–528 (2003)
11. Hair, J.F., Black, W.C., Babin, B.J., Anderson, R.E.: Multivariate Data Analysis: Pearson New International Edition. Pearson Higher Ed., Harlow (2013)
12. Hauser, J., Urban, G.L., Liberali, G., Braun, M.: Website morphing. Mark. Sci. **28**(2), 202–223 (2009)
13. Herrmanny, K., Ziegler, J., Dogangün, A.: Supporting users in setting effective goals in activity tracking. In: Meschtscherjakov, A., De Ruyter, B., Fuchsberger, V., Murer, M., Tscheligi, M. (eds.) PERSUASIVE 2016. LNCS, vol. 9638, pp. 15–26. Springer, Cham (2016). https://doi.org/10.1007/978-3-319-31510-2_2
14. Horn, J.L.: A rationale and test for the number of factors in factor analysis. Psychometrika **30**(2), 179–185 (1965)
15. Kaiser, H.F.: The application of electronic computers to factor analysis. Educ. Psychol. Meas. **20**(1), 141–151 (1960)
16. Kaptein, M.: Adaptive persuasive messages in an e-commerce setting: the use of persuasion profiles. In: European Conference on Information Systems (ECIS) (2011)

17. Kaptein, M., De Ruyter, B., Markopoulos, P., Aarts, E.: Adaptive persuasive systems: a study of tailored persuasive text messages to reduce snacking. ACM Trans. Interact. Intell. Syst. **2**(2), 10:1–10:25 (2012). https://doi.org/10.1145/2209310. 2209313. http://doi.acm.org/10.1145/2209310.2209313
18. Kaptein, M., Halteren, A.: Adaptive persuasive messaging to increase service retention: using persuasion profiles to increase the effectiveness of email reminders. Pers. Ubiquitous Comput. **17**(6), 1173–1185 (2013)
19. Kaptein, M., Markopoulos, P., De Ruyter, B., Aarts, E.: Personalizing persuasive technologies: explicit and implicit personalization using persuasion profiles. Int. J. Hum. Comput. Stud. **77**, 38–51 (2015)
20. MacCallum, R.C., Widaman, K.F., Zhang, S., Hong, S.: Sample size in factor analysis. Psychol. Methods **4**(1), 84 (1999)
21. Oinas-Kukkonen, H., Harjumaa, M.: Persuasive systems design: key issues, process model, and system features. Commun. Assoc. Inf. Syst. **24**(1), 28 (2009)
22. Orji, R.: Design for behaviour change: a model driven approach for tailoring persuasive technologies. Ph.D. thesis, University of Saskatchewan Saskatoon, SK, Canada (2014)
23. Orji, R.: Persuasion and culture: individualism-collectivism and susceptibility to influence strategies. In: PPT@ PERSUASIVE, pp. 30–39 (2016)
24. Orji, R.: Why are persuasive strategies effective? Exploring the strengths and weaknesses of socially-oriented persuasive strategies. In: de Vries, P.W., Oinas-Kukkonen, H., Siemons, L., Beerlage-de Jong, N., van Gemert-Pijnen, L. (eds.) PERSUASIVE 2017. LNCS, vol. 10171, pp. 253–266. Springer, Cham (2017). https://doi.org/10.1007/978-3-319-55134-0_20
25. Orji, R., Mandryk, R.L., Vassileva, J.: Gender, age, and responsiveness to Cialdini's persuasion strategies. In: MacTavish, T., Basapur, S. (eds.) PERSUASIVE 2015. LNCS, vol. 9072, pp. 147–159. Springer, Cham (2015). https://doi.org/10.1007/978-3-319-20306-5_14
26. Osborne, J.W., Costello, A.B., Kellow, J.T.: Best practices in exploratory factor analysis. In: Best Practices in Quantitative Methods, pp. 86–99 (2008)
27. Oyibo, K., Adaji, I., Orji, R., Olabenjo, B., Azizi, M., Vassileva, J.: Perceived persuasive effect of behavior model design in fitness apps. In: Proceedings of the 26th Conference on User Modeling, Adaptation and Personalization, pp. 219–228. ACM (2018)
28. Oyibo, K., Adaji, I., Orji, R., Olabenjo, B., Vassileva, J.: Susceptibility to persuasive strategies: a comparative analysis of Nigerians vs. Canadians. In: Proceedings of the 26th Conference on User Modeling, Adaptation and Personalization, pp. 229–238. ACM (2018)
29. Oyibo, K., Orji, R., Vassileva, J.: The influence of culture in the effect of age and gender on social influence in persuasive technology. In: Adjunct Publication of the 25th Conference on User Modeling, Adaptation and Personalization, pp. 47–52. ACM (2017)
30. Oyibo, K., Orji, R., Vassileva, J.: Investigation of the influence of personality traits on Cialdini's persuasive strategies. In: PPT@ PERSUASIVE, pp. 8–20 (2017)
31. Panter, A.T., Swygert, K.A., Grant Dahlstrom, W., Tanaka, J.S.: Factor analytic approaches to personality item-level data. J. Pers. Assess. **68**(3), 561–589 (1997)
32. Parsons, K., Butavicius, M., Delfabbro, P., Lillie, M.: Predicting susceptibility to social influence in phishing emails. Int. J. Hum. Comput. Stud. **128**, 17–26 (2019)
33. Pratkanis, A.R., Pratkanis, A., Aronson, E.: Age of Propaganda: The Everyday Use and Abuse of Persuasion. Macmillan, New York (2001)

34. Raubenheimer, J.: An item selection procedure to maximize scale reliability and validity. SA J. Ind. Psychol. **30**(4), 59–64 (2004)
35. Siegel, S.: Nonparametric Statistics for the Behavioural Sciences. McGraw, New York (1956)
36. Stibe, A., Cugelman, B.: Persuasive backfiring: when behavior change interventions trigger unintended negative outcomes. In: Meschtscherjakov, A., De Ruyter, B., Fuchsberger, V., Murer, M., Tscheligi, M. (eds.) PERSUASIVE 2016. LNCS, vol. 9638, pp. 65–77. Springer, Cham (2016). https://doi.org/10.1007/978-3-319-31510-2_6
37. Josekutty Thomas, R., Masthoff, J., Oren, N.: Adapting healthy eating messages to personality. In: de Vries, P.W., Oinas-Kukkonen, H., Siemons, L., Beerlage-de Jong, N., van Gemert-Pijnen, L. (eds.) PERSUASIVE 2017. LNCS, vol. 10171, pp. 119–132. Springer, Cham (2017). https://doi.org/10.1007/978-3-319-55134-0_10
38. Velicer, W.F.: Determining the number of components from the matrix of partial correlations. Psychometrika **41**(3), 321–327 (1976)
39. Vonnegut, K.: Cat's cradle. Penguin, London (1964)
40. Wais-Zechmann, B., Gattol, V., Neureiter, K., Orji, R., Tscheligi, M.: Persuasive technology to support chronic health conditions: investigating the optimal persuasive strategies for persons with COPD. In: Ham, J., Karapanos, E., Morita, P.P., Burns, C.M. (eds.) PERSUASIVE 2018. LNCS, vol. 10809, pp. 255–266. Springer, Cham (2018). https://doi.org/10.1007/978-3-319-78978-1_21
41. Wall, H.J., Campbell, C.C., Kaye, L.K., Levy, A., Bhullar, N.: Personality profiles and persuasion: an exploratory study investigating the role of the big-5, type D personality and the dark triad on susceptibility to persuasion. Pers. Individ. Differ. **139**, 69–76 (2019)
42. Zumbo, B.D., Gadermann, A.M., Zeisser, C.: Ordinal versions of coefficients alpha and theta for likert rating scales. J. Mod. Appl. Stat. Methods **6**(1), 4 (2007)

Integrating Persuasive Technology in Participatory Design Workshops: Prototypes for Participant Support

Max Jalowski$^{(\boxtimes)}$ (iD)

Chair of Information Systems – Innovation and Value Creation, Friedrich-Alexander-Universität Erlangen-Nürnberg (FAU), Lange Gasse 20, 90403 Nuremberg, Germany
max.jalowski@fau.de

Abstract. In participatory design, non-professional designers are also involved in the design process. Creativity and motivation play an important role, and non-professionals in particular can have problems of motivation or ability. Persuasive technologies can be used to positively influence participants' behavior. Applying a design science research approach, this study developed four persuasive technology artifacts to support workshop participants, based on existing work on participatory design, persuasive technologies, and creativity support tools. The following prototypes were implemented: (1) tablet-based support; (2) Bluetooth beacons for location-based triggers; (3) QR codes for additional information; and (4) a humanoid robot assistant. Each prototype incorporates persuasive strategies to exert a positive influence on workshop participants' behavior by enhancing motivation and ability and initiating triggers. In the absence of any previous concrete implementations of persuasive technologies for participatory design, the described artifacts extend the existing knowledge base by proposing in-person collaboration as a novel application field for persuasive technology.

Keywords: Persuasive technology · Participatory design · Tools for design workshops · Creativity support tools · Technologies for participatory design

1 Introduction

Digitization is now a ubiquitous feature of personal and working life. With increasing access to smartphones, wearables and other technical devices, integration of these technologies also opens new possibilities for collaborative processes. To date, this potential has been explored primarily in online communities [1, 2] but less so in offline settings such as design workshops. As one such application, *creativity support tools* can be used to increase users' creativity during the design process [3]. Research to date has focused primarily on user involvement, and the issue of how lead users' experiences and opinions can be integrated into the design process which is part of the discourse in innovation and design research [4, 5]. However, users need not be experts in a particular field to become involved in the development of products or services [6, 7]. Participatory design (PD) explores user participation in design processes [8]. In the past, mainly user-centered

© Springer Nature Switzerland AG 2020
S. B. Gram-Hansen et al. (Eds.): PERSUASIVE 2020, LNCS 12064, pp. 30–42, 2020.
https://doi.org/10.1007/978-3-030-45712-9_3

approaches were researched, today these approaches are shifting towards collective creativity [9]. In many cases, participants in these workshops are intrinsically motivated, which facilitates cooperation and overall user contribution to the design process [10, 11]. However, as PD seeks to include non-professional designers, it becomes important to find ways of integrating them into design activities [12]. While levels of motivation and distraction may vary [13, 14], participants can be engaged by introducing appropriate tools, techniques and methods [12]. The use of technical tools to support creativity has been the subject of extensive research [15, 16] as a central success factor for design, along with issues of distraction, motivation, and missing triggers. This opens up a new field of application for persuasive technologies that can change human behavior [17]. Three factors are important for a successful behavior change: motivation, ability, and triggers [18]. As PD often involves non-professional designers, these issues frequently become problematic, and persuasive technologies offer new possibilities for addressing them. Knowledge work and collaboration have already been identified as challenging fields for persuasive technology [19]. Previous studies have dealt mainly with user engagement in public events [20], feedback sharing [21], virtual collaborative environments [22], the influence of ubiquitous technology on PD [23], or conceptual research without the use of prototypes [24].

Focusing on the development of prototypes for applying persuasive technologies in PD workshops, the present study addresses the following research question: *How can persuasive technologies be implemented to support participants' knowledge, abilities and motivation in participatory design workshops?*

After outlining the relevant theoretical foundations of PD and associated technological support, the paper discusses the design science research (DSR) methodology. Four prototypes to support workshop participants are then described, and the paper concludes with a discussion of the study's contribution to existing research.

2 Theoretical Background

2.1 Participatory Design

PD is well established both as a field of research and as a widely used design method [8]. Among researchers, the rigor and accountability of PD are key concerns [25] while more practitioner-oriented studies focus on the implementation of design processes and the integration of various stakeholders, including potential users, developers, and contributors from other disciplines. Halskov and Hansen [26] identify politics, people, context, methods and product (in this case the result of such an activity) as fundamental aspects of PD, and special methods are required to integrate non-designers into design activities [12]. PD can facilitate activation of participants' tacit knowledge [5]; similar collaborative processes involving providers and customers [6, 7] include co-design and co-creation or customer co-creation [9, 27]. As the present study involves designing with users [27] rather than adopting a customer perspective, the PD approach was considered appropriate, falling somewhere between "community participation" and "design participation" [28].

We focus here on the workshop as a means of introducing novel procedures beyond the participants' habitual activities [29]. Our classification of PD activities is based on the framework of Sanders [30] and Sanders et al. [12], who identified three modes of participation: (1) making tangible things; (2) acting, enacting and playing; and (3) talking, telling and explaining. These three categories include various tools, techniques and methods that can be used in PD workshops. In Sect. 4 the artifacts are therefore assigned to the items *make*, *tell* and *enact*.

2.2 Technological Supports in Participatory Design

As discussed above, persuasive technologies can be used to support design processes. Previous studies have been less design-oriented [20, 21] or have focused on design and creativity without looking closely at participants' behavior. One research stream addresses the issue of creativity support tools [15, 16], which are thought to have considerable potential for supporting creative processes [31]. Research in this area focuses on user interfaces and software that help users to become more innovative and productive [32] at both individual and group levels [33]. To date, this research has focused primarily on collective creativity [34] and how creativity support tools can be applied in the ideation and evaluation phases to support collaboration between users [16]. These tools commonly employ a combination of physical and digital components [35]. Other approaches use mechanisms that include behavioral strategies [36]. In general, the timing of such interventions is important; intervening at the wrong time can have a negative influence on the creative process [37]. According to Frich et al. [15], a creativity support tool has at least one creativity-focused feature and can positively influence users' behavior. This applies to both experienced and inexperienced users at different phases of the creative process. Creativity also plays an important role in PD workshops [9], which typically involve participants with differing expertise and experience [12].

3   Research Design

To address the research question, the present study employs a Design Science Research (DSR) approach. The DSR paradigm is well established in information systems research as a means of developing problem solutions and innovative artifacts [38]. Among the different approaches to DSR, Hevner [39] described three distinct cycles: the *relevance* cycle (in which requirements are collected and field testing is performed); the *design* cycle (in which the artifact is built and evaluated); and the *rigor* cycle (which grounds the research and contributes to the existing knowledge base) [39]. Contribution to the knowledge base is an important element of DSR, and Gregor and Hevner [40] described different contribution types and example artifacts in terms of abstraction, completeness, and maturity. Based on their attempts to develop instances, constructs, and methods [40] for applying persuasive technologies in PD workshops, the present study adopts the problem-centered DSR methodology described by Peffers et al. [41]. The following paragraphs describe the different phases of the DSR process.

Problem and Motivation. PD is working with non-professional designers [12], we conducted observations of workshops with PD elements and identified problems in the behavior of the participants regarding motivation, ability and missing triggers. These components of the Fogg behavior model [18] can be addressed using persuasive technology. Our observations identified *pleasure/pain* and *social-acceptance/rejection* as particularly salient motivational issues (cf. [18]) while *physical effort* and *non-routine* activities were identified as ability issues (cf. [18]). Missing triggers (cf. [18]) were also identified as an issue during the workshop sessions. There is so far a lack of material on the use of technologies in design processes in literature (cf. Sect. 2.2). Therefore we address the implementation of persuasive technologies in PD workshops.

Objectives. Based on the observations and previous work on the identification and application of persuasive technologies in design workshops [24], and on the systematic integration of these into workshops with PD elements [42], the present study explores prototype solutions to enhance participants' motivation and ability and to provide appropriate triggers, based on the following objectives: (1) guide the workshop process; (2) support time management; (3) enhance ability; (4) enable location-based triggers; (5) introduce measures to provide in-depth explanations and assistance with tasks; and (6) develop a personal assistant to answer participants' questions about the process and tasks.

Design and Development. In this phase, particular emphasis was placed on the persuasiveness of the artifacts to be developed. Incorporating persuasive system features and design principles [43, 44], these were based on Fogg's eight-step design process [45]. As the specified objectives are diverse and cannot be represented in one artifact, several prototypes were developed. The development of the prototypes is detailed in Sect. 4. All prototypes were first developed conceptually before prototypes were implemented and iteratively refined.

Demonstration and Evaluation. The artifacts were first evaluated by the author with the developers at regular intervals with regard to the objectives. For this purpose, emphasis was placed on the artifacts' functionality, completeness, consistency, accuracy, and usability [38]. The artifacts were also discussed regularly with workshop moderators and further developed on the basis of their input. Up to this point, artificial evaluation strategies [46] were applied. After an adequate number of iterations, the artifacts are used and evaluated in PD workshops.

Communication. The communication of results through scientific publications and to practitioners plays an important role in DSR [40], and early work on the present project was presented and discussed at four scientific conferences. The results contribute to research on persuasive technology in design workshops and on the use of technologies in PD in general.

4   Artifact Description: Prototypes for Supporting Participants

This section provides a conceptual description of the four artifacts, along with their practical implementation. The conception of the artifacts is based on previous work by [24]. The development of the artifact follows parts of the eight-step design process [45] as well as persuasive systems design: the artifacts contain system features and persuasive design principles (cf. [43, 44]). The artifacts are designed to enhance the motivation and ability of workshop participants and to trigger desired behaviors [18].

For present purposes, a PD workshop is defined as a workshop containing elements of PD (cf. Sect. 2.1 and [30]), including e.g. Lego serious play, design thinking or business model development using paper-based tools or canvases. Workshops typically involve 10–20 participants including non-professional designers working in groups at different stations. Depending on the specific topic, participants might also switch tables or stations to work on different tasks. The artifacts are designed in a manner that they can be used separately or in combination in different types of workshops since they are easily configurable. The persuasion context mostly includes improving abilities and knowledge of the participants, design principles are described in the respective sections.

4.1   Artifact 1: Tablet-Based Participant Support

The first artifact is a tablet-based application to address especially objectives 1 to 3 (*guide the workshop process, support time management, and enhance ability*). The prototype is designed as a web-based application comprising a server and several clients and implemented in *angular.js* and *type script*. The clients are tablets placed on participants' tables; the workshop moderator also has a tablet to control progress, send messages, and start or stop a timer. The server holds the status and ensures that all clients receive the same information as provided by the moderator. Figure 1 shows a schematic of artifact 1 (left) and a screenshot of the prototype (right).

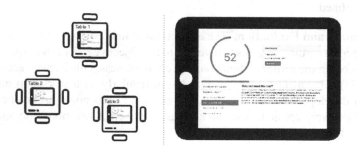

Fig. 1.   Artifact 1: tablet-based prototype

As this artifact mainly addresses general challenges that arise in design workshops, it can be used for making, telling, and enacting activities. The prototype primarily supports participants' time management by displaying the remaining time for the current task. This information is supplemented by details of the current task (e.g., *suggestions* on how to approach the task (*tunneling*) or division into sub-steps (*reduction*). The moderator can also send *triggers* and *reminders* to the participants in the form of messages. Depending on the current task, different examples of task completion can be displayed. In terms of the Fogg behavior model, the artifact contributes primarily to *ability* and *triggers*. In the future, functionalities such as feedback, questions, and tracking of participants' progress will also be implemented.

4.2 Artifact 2: Bluetooth Beacons for Location-Based Triggers

The second artifact addresses objectives 4 and 5 (*enable location-based triggers; introduce measures to provide in-depth explanations and assistance with tasks*) and consists of Bluetooth beacons and an associated app for smartphones and tables. A Bluetooth beacon is a small module that can be placed at or under tables or other work surfaces. On approach, a smartphone or tablet with the app installed can recognize and identify the Bluetooth module. The beacons are Arduino-based, with an attached HC-05 Bluetooth module. The app is running on Android devices. Figure 2 shows a schematic of artifact 2 (left) and a photo of the beacon as well as a mockup of the application (right).

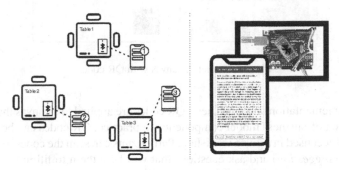

Fig. 2. Artifact 2: bluetooth beacons

To use artifact 2, each table is equipped with a Bluetooth beacon. Participants are either provided with tablets or can install a special app on their own smartphone. Artifact 2 is designed mainly for use in workshops that involve steps performed at different workstations. When a participant approaches the next station, they receive a push notification about the next step, which can be viewed in the app. This activates participants according to their location, helping to improve the atmosphere and participants' *motivation*. The push message also functions as a *trigger*, and *ability* can be enhanced by providing further information.

These application scenarios relate mainly to location-based triggers and the display of additional data and background information. Examples related to the current task can also be displayed on the smartphone or tablet. The location-dependent triggers facilitate making or enacting activities, and the triggers should enhance participants' motivation and ability. To integrate persuasiveness, *reminders*, *suggestions*, *reduction*, and *tunneling* can be implemented by sending messages and providing information.

4.3 Artifact 3: QR Codes for Additional Information

Objective 5 (*introduce measures to provide in-depth explanations and assistance with tasks*) is also addressed by artifact 3, which is simple and easy to use. Our workshop observations indicated that some participants find it difficult to ask the moderator for help when using Osterwalder and Pigneur's Business Model Canvas [47] or similar tools. These canvases are usually attached in poster form to movable walls to be filled with sticky notes. QR codes are easily integrated and can be scanned by participants' smartphones. Figure 3 shows an exemplary canvas with QR codes (left) and an example of a field including a QR code with additional information on the task (right).

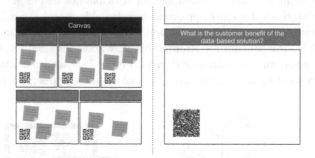

Fig. 3. Artifact 3: canvas with QR codes

In the implementation described here, QR codes are applied to a canvas that supports the elaboration of business model components; in practice, QR codes can be applied to almost any object used in a given workshop. Participants can scan the codes to get further information (*suggestion*) and ask questions that will help them to fill in the respective fields (*tunneling, reduction*). The QR codes support *praise*, encourage increased activity, and simplify tasks. They can be used in almost all PD activities and mainly promote enacting and making.

4.4 Artifact 4: Humanoid Robot Assistant

Objective 6 (*develop a personal assistant to answer participants' questions about the process and tasks*) is addressed in combination with objectives 1 to 3 by artifact 4. In general, this humanoid robot serves as an assistant, answering questions and providing information. The implementation described here is a NAO robot of the NAO V5 generation. The robot's humanoid construction enables it to move freely around the room from table to table. Although its features are similar to artifact 1, the robots' focus is on a verbal communication with participants and thus it introduces a social and more interactive component that the other artifacts do not serve. Figure 4 shows a schematic of artifact 4 (left) and a photo of NAO (right).

The robot is loaded with a configuration file before each workshop, including information on the process, tasks, and frequently asked questions. The NAO reacts to certain keywords and questions. By virtue of its social presence and humanoid appearance, it can play a persuasive role while leading work processes (*tunneling*) and even assisting. With further development, the NAO could also incorporate self-monitoring and cooperative elements such as recognizing and motivating inactive participants. In this way, the robot can contribute to improving participants' *motivation* and *ability*. In terms of PD elements, it has wide application in make, tell, and enact activities.

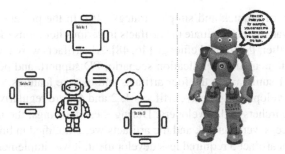

Fig. 4. Artifact 4: humanoid robot

4.5 Evaluation

According to Gregor and Hevner [40], artifacts should be evaluated for validity, utility, quality, and efficacy. To date, the described artifacts have been evaluated artificially

Table 1. Summary of artifacts in terms of application scenarios [24], PD activity [12, 30], behavior model elements [18], and persuasive design principles [43, 44]

	Application scenarios	PD	Behavior model	Persuasive design principles
A1	• Support decision making and explain or recommend actions • Show additional data or background information (e.g. task, examples) • Time management	Make, tell, enact	Ability, trigger	Reduction, tunneling, suggestions, reminders, self-monitoring, praise
A2	• Location-based triggers • Show additional data or background information (e.g. task, examples)	Make, enact	Trigger, motivation, ability	Reminders, suggestions, reduction, tunneling
A3	• Enhance activity by incorporating QR codes or RFID tags in the design process and displaying additional information	Enact, make	Ability, trigger	Praise, suggestions, tunneling, reduction
A4	• (Humanoid) robot persuading people to enact • (Humanoid) robot guiding processes or assisting	Make, tell, enact	Motivation, ability	Tunneling, social role, self-monitoring, cooperation

ex-ante by means of a quick and simple strategy [46]. In the present case, a criteria-based approach was used to evaluate the artifacts in various iterations (depending on the artifact) to assess their theoretical efficacy [46, 48]. All artifacts were evaluated in terms of objective, implementation, application scenario, PD support, and persuasive design principles. Table 1 summarizes the four artifacts and its core features.

During the development process, artifacts 1, 2 and 4 were regularly discussed with five different researchers and developers. During these meetings, the next steps in the development process were agreed, and the artifacts were modified in line with the feedback provided. As artifact 3 required less development, it was implemented for a workshop on a canvas for structuring the design thinking process. In initial observations, the tool was used by two of the three groups. Participants' responses indicated that the explanations and questions should be formulated more concisely, and that the ability to scan QR codes should be more clearly highlighted. All artifacts were developed continuously on the basis of discussions and feedback, and the discussions with the researchers and developers confirmed their theoretical efficacy. A further study will conduct an ex-post naturalistic evaluation [46, 48].

5 Discussion and Conclusion

This paper describes four artifacts to support PD workshop participants by providing detailed task explanations and assistance, guiding the process, enhancing time management, and providing location-based triggers. This kind of technological support for design processes has rarely been researched. Although some work on creativity support tools is broadly comparable, this often focuses on internet-based collaboration [15] rather than workshops, with the exception of such tools as large interactive displays that are also used in offline settings [35]. Relatively few studies in the persuasive technology literature relate to workshop support or creative processes, comparable works focus primarily on applications for sharing feedback [20, 49], gamified learning [50], or defining application scenarios [24]. In order to address this research gap, we developed four tangible artifacts based on technologies and devices that are widely used both in persuasive technology research [24, 51] and as creativity support tools [15].

In the workshop observations, we found that participants were often unfamiliar (*non-routine*) or uncomfortable (*pleasure/pain*) with the materials, tools, or methods used. Artifacts 1, 3, and 4 in particular serve to enhance participants' ability by providing task information, instructions, and examples. This encourages participants to ask questions and provides uncomplicated help with their own devices (*social-acceptance/rejection*). As we observed that missing triggers lead to incorrect task solution, artifacts 1, 2, and 4 were designed to serve as triggers if required. Along with ability and triggers, Fogg insisted that motivation is essential for behavior change [18], and this was supported here by interactivity and the novel use of new technologies. In particular, artifacts 2 and 4 introduced a playful component to the workshops, which can have a positive influence on motivation [14]. In some workshops, time management was also a problem. To address this issue, artifacts 1 and 4 can track the workshop's progress and inform participants through messaging. Furthermore, artifact 4 adds a gamified and social component that the previous artifacts do not incorporate. This paper opens a under-researched area for persuasive technology [19], i.e. the support of in-person collaboration utilizing the Fogg behavior model [18] and persuasive design principles [43].

The application of persuasive design principles to creativity support tools can have a positive influence on participants [15] – especially for inexperienced participants, who seem to benefit from better integration of these tools. As their use is independent of creative process phases, these artifacts align with basic features of creativity support tools [15]. In relation to PD, this work contributes primarily to the integration of technologies into the design process. While this issue has been referred to in some earlier studies [8, 52], it has not been explored in detail or by the use of concrete artifacts.

The present study demonstrates the use of persuasive technology to support PD through the systematic development of four artifacts, and the results contribute directly to the existing knowledge base [39]. As discussed earlier, the use of persuasive technologies in PD workshops remains relatively unexplored beyond the theoretical level. The work described here advances existing knowledge by implementing four prototypes: (1) a tablet-based support; (2) Bluetooth beacons for location-based triggers; (3) QR codes for additional information provision; and (4) a humanoid robot assistant. Each artifact incorporates persuasive strategies that can exert a positive influence on workshop participants' behavior by enhancing motivation and ability and initiating triggers. Artifacts 3 and 4 have already been tested in workshops; to date, the other two have only been used in artificial settings. Nevertheless, as concrete implementation scenarios including the prototypes for the application of persuasive technologies to PD workshops, all of these artifacts extend the existing knowledge base.

The development of these artifacts is based on previous work and workshop observations. Future work should place even greater emphasis on user acceptance of such technologies, and all artifacts should be extensively tested for further development in real-world settings. The present study represents a first step toward the more systematic use of persuasive technology in PD settings.

Acknowledgements. I would like to thank Prof. Dr. Kathrin M. Möslein and Martin Schymanietz for their support and comments on this work.

References

1. Piller, F.T., Schubert, P., Koch, M., Möslein, K.M.: Overcoming mass confusion: collaborative customer co-design in online communities. J. Comput. Commun. **10**(4) (2005)
2. Antikainen, M., Mäkipää, M., Ahonen, M.: Motivating and supporting collaboration in open innovation. Eur. J. Innov. Manag. **13**(1), 100–119 (2010)
3. Shneiderman, B.: Creativity support tools: a grand challenge for HCI researchers. In: Redondo, M., Bravo, C., Ortega, M. (eds.) Engineering the User Interface, pp. 1–9. Springer, London (2009). https://doi.org/10.1007/978-1-84800-136-7_1
4. Von Hippel, E.: Democratizing Innovation. The MIT Press, Cambridge (2005)
5. Björgvinsson, E., Ehn, P., Hillgren, P.-A.: Participatory design and "democratizing innovation". In: Proceedings of the 11th Biennial Participatory Design Conference PDC 2010, pp. 41–50 (2010)
6. Piller, F.T., Ihl, C., Vossen, A.: A typology of customer co-creation in the innovation process. SSRN Electron. J. **10** (2010)

7. Mustak, M., Jaakkola, E., Halinen, A.: Customer participation and value creation: a systematic review and research implications. Manag. Serv. Qual. **23**(4), 341–359 (2013)
8. Kensing, F., Blomberg, J.: Participatory design: issues and concerns. Comput. Support. Coop. Work **7**, 167–185 (1998)
9. Sanders, E.B.-N., Stappers, P.J.: Co-creation and the new landscapes of design. CoDesign **4**(1), 5–18 (2008)
10. Adler, P.S., Chen, C.X.: Combining creativity and control: understanding individual motivation in large-scale collaborative creativity. Acc. Organ. Soc. **36**(2), 63–85 (2011)
11. Battistella, C., Nonino, F.: Open innovation web-based platforms: the impact of different forms of motivation on collaboration. Innov. Manag. Policy Pract. **14**(4), 557–575 (2012)
12. Sanders, E.B.-N., Brandt, E., Binder, T.: A framework for organizing the tools and techniques of participatory design. In: Proceedings of the 11th Biennial Participatory Design Conference on PDC 2010, pp. 195–198. ACM Press, New York (2010)
13. Jarvela, S., Jarvenoja, H.: Socially constructed self-regulated learning and motivation regulation in collaborative learning groups. Teach. Coll. Rec. **113**(2), 350–374 (2011)
14. Algashami, A., Shahri, A., McAlaney, J., Taylor, J., Phalp, K., Ali, R.: Strategies and design principles to minimize negative side-effects of digital motivation on teamwork. In: de Vries, P.W., Oinas-Kukkonen, H., Siemons, L., Beerlage-de Jong, N., van Gemert-Pijnen, L. (eds.) PERSUASIVE 2017. LNCS, vol. 10171, pp. 267–278. Springer, Cham (2017). https://doi.org/10.1007/978-3-319-55134-0_21
15. Frich, J., MacDonald Vermeulen, L., Remy, C., Biskjaer, M.M., Dalsgaard, P.: Mapping the landscape of creativity support tools in HCI. In: Proceedings of the 2019 CHI Conference on Human Factors in Computing Systems - CHI 2019, Glasgow, pp. 1–18 (2019)
16. Gabriel, A., Monticolo, D., Camargo, M., Bourgault, M.: Creativity support systems: a systematic mapping study. Think. Ski. Creat. **21**, 109–122 (2016)
17. Fogg, B.: Persuasive computers. In: Proceedings of the SIGCHI Conference on Human Factors in Computing Systems - CHI 1998, pp. 225–232 (1998)
18. Fogg, B.: A behavior model for persuasive design. In: Proceedings of the 4th International Conference on Persuasive Technology - Persuasive 2009 (2009)
19. Torning, K., Oinas-Kukkonen, H.: Persuasive system design: state of the art and future directions. In: Proceedings 4th International Conference on Persuasive Technology - Persuasive 2009 (2009)
20. Stibe, A., Oinas-Kukkonen, H.: Designing persuasive systems for user engagement in collaborative interaction. In: Proceedings of the European Conference on Information Systems (ECIS) 2014, pp. 1–17 (2014)
21. Stibe, A., Oinas-Kukkonen, H., Lehto, T.: Exploring social influence on customer engagement: a pilot study on the effects of social learning, social comparison, and normative influence. In: 2013 46th Hawaii International Conference on System Sciences, pp. 2735–2744 (2013)
22. de Vreede, T., Nguyen, C., de Vreede, G.-J., Boughzala, I., Oh, O., Reiter-Palmon, R.: A theoretical model of user engagement in crowdsourcing. In: Antunes, P., Gerosa, M.A., Sylvester, A., Vassileva, J., de Vreede, G.-J. (eds.) CRIWG 2013. LNCS, vol. 8224, pp. 94–109. Springer, Heidelberg (2013). https://doi.org/10.1007/978-3-642-41347-6_8
23. Brereton, M., Buur, J.: New challenges for design participation in the era of ubiquitous computing. CoDesign **4**(2), 101–113 (2008)
24. Jalowski, M., Fritzsche, A., Möslein, K.M.: Applications for persuasive technologies in participatory design processes. In: Oinas-Kukkonen, H., Win, K.T., Karapanos, E., Karppinen, P., Kyza, E. (eds.) PERSUASIVE 2019. LNCS, vol. 11433, pp. 74–86. Springer, Cham (2019). https://doi.org/10.1007/978-3-030-17287-9_7
25. Frauenberger, C., Good, J., Fitzpatrick, G., Iversen, O.S.: In pursuit of rigour and accountability in participatory design. Int. J. Hum. Comput. Stud. **74**, 93–106 (2015)

26. Halskov, K., Hansen, N.B.: The diversity of participatory design research practice at PDC 2002–2012. Int. J. Hum. Comput. Stud. **74**, 81–92 (2015)
27. Sanders, E.B.-N.: From user-centered to participatory design approaches. In: Design and the Social Sciences, pp. 1–8. CRC Press, New York (2002)
28. Lee, Y.: Design participation tactics: the challenges and new roles for designers in the co-design process. CoDesign **4**(1), 31–50 (2008)
29. Muller, M.: Participatory design: the third space in HCI. In: Sears, A., Jacko, J.A. (eds.) The Human-Computer Interaction Handbook, pp. 1061–1081. Lawrence Erlbaum Associates, New York (2007)
30. Sanders, E.B.-N.: Perspectives on participation in design. In: Mareis, C., Held, M., Joost, G. (eds.) Wer Gestaltet die Gestaltung? Praxis, Theorie und Geschichte des Partizipatorischen Designs, pp. 65–78. Transcript Verlag, Bielefeld (2013)
31. Greene, S.L.: Characteristics of applications that support creativity. Commun. ACM **45**(10), 100–104 (2002)
32. Shneiderman, B., et al.: Creativity support tools: report from a U.S. national science foundation sponsored workshop. Int. J. Hum. Comput. Interact. **20**(2), 61–77 (2006)
33. Shneiderman, B.: Creativity support tools accelerating discovery and innovation. Commun. ACM **50**(12), 20–32 (2007)
34. Frich, J., Mose Biskjaer, M., Dalsgaard, P.: Twenty years of creativity research in human-computer interaction. In: Proceedings of the 2018 Designing Interactive Systems Conference 2018, DIS 2018, pp. 1235–1257 (2018)
35. Hartmann, B., Ringel Morris, M., Benko, H., Wilson, A.D.: Pictionaire - supporting collaborative design work by integrating physical and digital artifacts. In: Proceedings of the International Conference Computer Supported Cooperative Work, pp. 421–424 (2010)
36. De Rooij, A., Corr, P.J., Jones, S.: Creativity and emotion: enhancing creative thinking by the manipulation of computational feedback to determine emotional. In: Proceedings of the 2017 ACM SIGCHI Conference on Creativity and Cognition (2017)
37. Thomas, J.C., Lee, A., Danis, C.: Enhancing creative design via software tools. Commun. ACM **45**(10), 112–115 (2002)
38. Hevner, A.R., March, S.T., Park, J., Ram, S.: Design science in information systems research. MIS Q. **28**(1), 75–105 (2004)
39. Hevner, A.R.: A three cycle view of design science research. Scand. J. Inf. Syst. **19**(2), 87–92 (2007)
40. Gregor, S., Hevner, A.R.: Positioning and presenting design science research for maximum impact. MIS Q. **37**(2), 337–355 (2013)
41. Peffers, K., Tuunanen, T., Rothenberger, M.A., Chatterjee, S.: A design science research methodology for information systems research. J. Manag. Inf. Syst. **24**(3), 45–78 (2007)
42. Jalowski, M., Fritzsche, A., Möslein, K.M.: Facilitating collaborative design: a toolkit for integrating persuasive technologies in design activities. Procedia CIRP **84**, 61–67 (2019)
43. Oinas-Kukkonen, H., Harjumaa, M.: Persuasive systems design: key issues, process model, and system features. Commun. Assoc. Inf. Syst. **24**, 485–500 (2009)
44. Oinas-Kukkonen, H., Harjumaa, M.: A systematic framework for designing and evaluating persuasive systems. In: Oinas-Kukkonen, H., Hasle, P., Harjumaa, M., Segerståhl, K., Øhrstrøm, P. (eds.) PERSUASIVE 2008. LNCS, vol. 5033, pp. 164–176. Springer, Heidelberg (2008). https://doi.org/10.1007/978-3-540-68504-3_15
45. Fogg, B.: Creating persuasive technologies: an eight-step design process. In: Proceedings of the 4th International Conference on Persuasive Technology - Persuasive 2009 (2009)
46. Venable, J., Pries-Heje, J., Baskerville, R.: FEDS: a framework for evaluation in design science research. Eur. J. Inf. Syst. **25**(1), 77–89 (2016)
47. Osterwalder, A., Pigneur, Y.: Business Model Generation: A Handbook for Visionaries, Game Changers, and Challengers. Wiley, Hoboken (2010)

48. Sonnenberg, C., vom Brocke, J.: Evaluations in the science of the artificial – reconsidering the build-evaluate pattern in design science research. In: Peffers, K., Rothenberger, M., Kuechler, B. (eds.) DESRIST 2012. LNCS, vol. 7286, pp. 381–397. Springer, Heidelberg (2012). https://doi.org/10.1007/978-3-642-29863-9_28

49. Stibe, A., Oinas-Kukkonen, H.: Using social influence for motivating customers to generate and share feedback. In: Spagnolli, A., Chittaro, L., Gamberini, L. (eds.) PERSUASIVE 2014. LNCS, vol. 8462, pp. 224–235. Springer, Cham (2014). https://doi.org/10.1007/978-3-319-07127-5_19

50. Challco, G.C., Mizoguchi, R., Isotani, S.: An ontology framework to apply gamification in CSCL scenarios as persuasive technology. Rev. Bras. Informática na Educ. **24**(2), 67–76 (2016)

51. Orji, R., Moffatt, K.: Persuasive technology for health and wellness: state-of-the-art and emerging trends. Health Inform. J. **24**(1), 66–91 (2018)

52. Hagen, P., Robertson, T.: Dissolving boundaries: social technologies and participation in design. In: Proceedings of the 21st Annual Conference of the Australian Computer-Human Interaction Special Interest Group on Design: Open 24/7 - OZCHI 2009, pp. 129–136 (2009)

Persuasive in Practice, Digital Insights

Does Traffic Information Provided by Smartphones Increase Detour Behavior?

An Examination of Emotional Persuasive Strategy by Longitudinal Online Surveys and Location Information

Wenzhen Xu[1]([✉]) [iD], Yuichi Kuriki[1], Taiki Sato[2], Masato Taya[3], and Chihiro Ono[1]

[1] KDDI Research, Inc., Tokyo, Japan
{we-xu,yi-kuriki,ono}@kddi-research.jp
[2] EAST Nippon Expressway Company Limited Tohoku Office, Sendai, Japan
t.sato.br@e-nexco.co.jp
[3] KDDI Corporation, Tokyo, Japan
ma-taya@kddi.com

Abstract. To ease traffic congestion on the Tohoku expressway during the nationwide summer holiday, we conducted two sets of interventional experiments applying the emotional persuasive strategy to persuade potential Tohoku expressway users to switch to the Joban expressway over a four-week period. Specifically, we first conducted a longitudinal online survey with interventional content to examine the change of intention and behavior on route decisions. At the same time, we provided the same interventional content to another set of users by means of a smartphone application and tracked their location information during the experiment period (12 days within the four weeks) to validate the results of the survey study. The results indicate that: (1) Content with emotional priming significantly increases the detour intention, and has the potential to increase detour behavior. (2) The effects vary depending on additional factors, such as previous travel experience, and the presence of small children. Overall, the study shows that the emotional persuasive strategy is an effective way to change detour intention and behavior.

Keywords: Traffic congestion · Detour · Behavior change · Emotional persuasive strategy · Longitudinal survey · Location information

1 Introduction

According to the latest official statistics of East Nippon Expressway Co., Ltd. (NEXCO EAST, Japan), congestion on major express highways in Eastern Japan keeps on increasing, especially during the period of major national holidays, such as the New Year holiday, and summer holiday [1]. Experts claim that increasing congestion leads not only to delays and adverse economic consequences [2] but also an increase in the number of traffic accidents. These cause delays in evacuation and emergency response [3] and impose heavy physical and mental stresses on both drivers and passengers.

© Springer Nature Switzerland AG 2020
S. B. Gram-Hansen et al. (Eds.): PERSUASIVE 2020, LNCS 12064, pp. 45–57, 2020.
https://doi.org/10.1007/978-3-030-45712-9_4

To address congestion during holiday periods, planning agencies (i.e., governments and transportation companies), and researchers have been attempting to introduce behavior change strategies and systems that encourage travelers to shift their trips away from congested periods and corridors [4].

Most past empirical studies on behavior change in the congestion avoidance domain were conducted using a demand-based approach [5]. They mainly examined interventional effects adopting an extrinsic approach, which means using external stimuli such as *Charging* (e.g., increasing road tolls) [6] or *Rewarding* (e.g., providing credits or monetary incentives) [7, 8] to encourage people to change when they travel to off-peak times or switch their route. The results of these studies showed that *Rewarding* is an effective approach. However, other scholars have pointed out the limitations of the extrinsic motivation approach. They claimed that this approach is costly, and the effect cannot be stably maintained [9]. Moreover, as people easily become accustomed to incentives, the effect cannot be sustained over the long term [10]. In order to maintain the same effect, incentive providers have to keep on increasing the monetary reward.

On the other hand, the effectiveness of the intrinsic motivation approach to shape and reinforce a desirable behavior (e.g., environmental conservation) is supported by a large number of empirical studies. However, few of these studies were conducted in the context of travel or traffic behavior. The few previous studies that examined this approach focused on the effect of information presentation. For example, Okada et al. [9] created a smartphone game application to encourage users to take more breaks in service areas. In another example, Kuriki et al. [11] added visual impact to traffic information to motivate participants to avoid heavy congestion.

In addition to the ingenious ways of presenting information, we propose that the content of intervention information should play an important role in persuasive communication in the traffic context. In the present study, we focus on how an emotional persuasive strategy impacts route switching behavior.

In the present study, our goal is to encourage expressway users to switch their routes during national summer holiday periods. Specifically, as the field of our experiment, two major expressways were chosen, the Tohoku and Joban expressways. These connect the Tokyo (capital) region to the Tohoku (Northeastern) region (See Fig. 1). The Tohoku Expressway is routinely reported to exceed capacity during long holiday periods. According to traffic professionals from NEXCO East, one feasible solution is to encourage Tohoku expressway users to switch to the relatively empty Joban expressway. In this paper, we describe this route switching behavior as taking a *detour*.

The main aim of this paper is to examine the influence of an emotional persuasive strategy on changing detour intention and behavior. To examine this influence in more detail, we created three types of traffic congestion information with or without emotional priming content (landing page, LP). We randomly sent the LPs to three groups of participants through two different channels: a major online survey system and a smartphone portal application of one of Japan's main telecom providers (the participants in the two channels rarely overlapped). We then examined the effects of LPs by collecting both longitudinal survey data and location information data. (See Fig. 2: experiment flow)

The rest of the paper is organized as follows: Section 2 sets the theoretical framework, two theory-driven hypotheses, and one research question. Section 3 describes the experimental method and procedures in detail. Then, the main findings are presented in Sect. 4. This is followed in Sect. 5 by a general discussion that examines the empirical insights, theoretical implications, limitations, and future plans. Section 6 presents our conclusions.

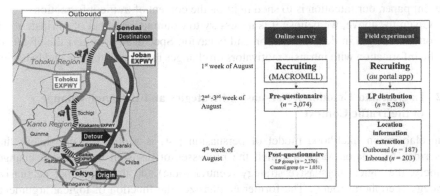

Fig. 1. Image of detour   **Fig. 2.** Experiment flow

2 Theoretical Framework, Hypotheses, and Research Questions

2.1 Extrinsic and Intrinsic Motivations and Behavior Change in the Traffic Context

Some psychologists have hypothesized that there are two basic types of motivation, namely, extrinsic motivation and intrinsic motivation. These motivations drive people to formulate one particular behavior or change one pattern of behavior to another [12]. One of the major differences between the two forms of motivation is the reasons or goals that lead to action. Extrinsic motivation refers to doing something because it leads to a separable outcome (e.g., money or grades), whereas intrinsic motivation refers to doing something because it is inherently desirable (e.g., an internal need).

In the context of traffic behavior change, the extrinsic motivation approach has been widely examined. For instance, Ben et al. [7] conducted a 13-week field study in the Netherlands to examine the effects of reward (i.e., money and credits) on rush-hour commute avoidance. The results appear to show that rewards do have a significant impact on switching commute time or changing commute mode. However, following a similar procedure, Kuriki et al. [11] conducted an 8-week longitudinal field study in Japan aiming to test the effects of digital credits on route switching. Their conclusion stands in contrast to the findings of Ben at al. The results of their study show that participants who were rewarded have even lower motivation in terms of detour intention and rates of behavioral change than those who only receive congestion information. These controversial results reflect the claim that the impact of extrinsic motivation will only work as long as the external stimulus is satisfying [10]. What is worse, unexpected extrinsic stimulus also tends to lead to a reduction in intrinsic motivation [13].

The few previous studies (e.g., [9, 11]) that have investigated the intrinsic motivation approach mainly focused on how information was presented (e.g., using gamification to encourage drivers to take a break in a service area, helping drivers avoid traffic jams by providing visual information). However, the impact of the actual content of traffic information on traffic behavior change has been rarely investigated. Therefore, in the present paper, our intention is to shed light on the content of traffic information.

Given the above, we believe it is necessary to examine the effect of intrinsic motivation on changes in detour intention and behavior. Specifically, we test the effects of traffic information with intrinsic motivators on changes in detour intention and behavior.

2.2 Logical and Emotional Persuasive Strategies and Behavior Change in the Traffic Context

The elaboration likelihood model of persuasion [14] is a dual process theory that describes two major ways in which the processes of decision making can change, namely, the logical persuasive strategy (central route) and the emotional persuasive strategy (peripheral route). The former emphasizes the function of logical arguments supported by facts, detailed pieces of evidence coupled with a logical reasoning process, whereas the latter emphasizes the function of emotional arousal (e.g., activation of empathy). Since the central route involves a high-level message elaboration in which a larger amount of cognition energy and time is needed, this would be effective only for people who have enough knowledge and have an interest in the content. Therefore, to persuade more of the audience within an extremely short time, most makers of TV or Internet commercials tend to choose the peripheral route. In the present study, we focus on the intrinsic motivation approach and aim to test the persuasive effect of peripheral route.

One of the main persuasive strategies of the peripheral route is emotional priming. This involves activating a particular emotion by exposing the audience to the same or related emotions. The effects of emotional priming have been widely examined in empirical psychological research. When primed by a helpless or cute figure (such as a cute infant's face), people tend to report higher intentions in regard to prosocial and sustainable behaviors (e.g., environmental conservation, cooperative behavior). A series of large-scale field experiments validated these findings [15]. One possible explanation is that cute figures activate instinctive nurturing behaviors in adults, motivating caregiving and protection. Scholars found that exposure to a cute infant face and eliciting prosocial behavioral intent can both activate the ventral striatum, which is the brain region associated with general altruistic behaviors [16]. That is to say, the response to cuteness and elicitation of prosocial behaviors may share a common neural basis.

In the present study, we regard detour behavior as prosocial behavior because avoiding a major traffic jam would not only reduce the physical and mental stress of drivers but also their fellow travelers'. Moreover, detour behaviors would also help to decrease the traffic accident rate and other forms of economic loss caused by congestion. To take a first step to examine the effects of emotional persuasive strategy in the context of traffic, we conducted both online questionnaire surveys and large-scale field experiments. Based on the review above, we formulated the following two hypotheses:

- H1: Traffic information created as part of an intrinsic motivation approach (without incentive) increases participants' detour intentions.
- H2a: Emotional priming (showing a picture of a crying child) increases participants' detour intentions.
- H2b: The same emotional priming would also promote participants' detour behaviors.

As the reactions to emotional priming [17] may vary depending on the person, we formulated an additional research question as follow:

- RQ: People with what user attributes would be easily influenced by intervention materials?

3 Method

3.1 Participants[1]

(1) Questionnaire Survey

Pre-questionnaire Survey: We recruited participants in Japan through a major online-survey company, MACROMILL, from July 27 to August 5. Respondents who met the following requirements were invited to answer the pre-questionnaire survey: (a) Android or iPhone user, (b) Residents living in the Kanto region except Ibaraki prefecture: Tokyo metropolitan area, Kanagawa prefecture, Saitama prefecture, Chiba prefecture, Tochigi prefecture, and Gunma prefecture, and (c) People who are planning to or for whom there is a high possibility that they will visit the Tohoku region from August 6 to August 17.

A total of 3,074 respondents ranging in age from their 20s to 60s participated in the pre-questionnaire survey (female: 927, male: 2147).

Post-questionnaire Survey: We sent a post-survey invitation to the participants of the pre-survey from August 23 to 31. We received 2,270 responses (female: 653, male: 1,617). The distribution of gender is similar to those of the pre-survey respondents. We also selected 1,031 participants who met the three screening requirements without answering the questionnaire as a control group (female: 431, male: 600).

(2) Field Experiment

We randomly sent traffic information with LPs to smartphone users of *au* (a major mobile carrier in Japan) who met the following requirements: (a) are active users of the *au* service top, a portal app of *au*, (b) agree to receive service information from the

---

[1] Conducting our experiments ethically was paramount to us. Specifically, we followed the key ethical principles outlined by Bryman and Bell [18] to make cautious effort to protect the dignity, autonomy and privacy of all the subjects during the entirety of data collection, data analyses and presentation of results.

app, and (c) are living in the Kanto region (Tokyo metropolitan area and the five other prefectures mentioned above) from August 6 to 17. We selected the users that signed the agreement allowing the use of location information for the subsequent statistical analyses. The sample sizes were 1,016 users for LP1, 1,063 users for LP2, and 1,035 users for LP3. We also randomly selected 5,095 smartphone users who met the same requirements but did not click the LPs as a control group. The total sample size for location information analysis comprised 8,208 users. The experiment flow is shown in Fig. 2.

3.2 Intervention Materials

We created three types of interventional materials (LPs) for the interventional experiments (the pre- and post-surveys and the field experiment). LP1 consisted of two parts, (A) the traffic congestion forecast for the Tohoku expressway from August 8 to 19, and (B) the suggestion on how to avoid congestion (map and estimated traffic conditions of the Joban expressway). In addition to A and B, we added part (C) a photograph of an upset driver with the catchphrase "You don't want a horrible traffic jam to ruin your trip" to LP2. LP3 contains the content of A, B, and an additional part (D) a photograph of a little girl crying in the car with the catchphrase "You don't want your little children to suffer that much in a horrible traffic jam" (See Fig. 3). The goal of the intervention was to persuade potential Tohoku expressway users to switch to the Joban expressway during the summer holiday period. We applied two types of emotional priming, a picture of upset co-travelers (C) and a picture of helpless small child (D), to activate the intrinsic motivation to initiate detour behavior. In the original experiment, the LPs are created in Japanese.

Fig. 3. Image of interventional materials

3.3 Measurements

In the pre-questionnaire, we first asked participants demographic information (i.e., residence, gender, age, marriage condition) and other user attributes (i.e., traveling experience to Tohoku region, driving experience, presence of co-visitors). We then asked them which expressway they prefer to use and who will make the decision. We then asked them if they have a willingness to change the route after checking the LPs.

In the post-questionnaire, we asked the participants which expressway they used and why they made the decision.

In the field experiments, we collected call detail records information of au smartphone users who signed the agreement allowing the use of location information (See more details in Sect. 3.3).

3.4 Analysis Plan of Location Information

We extracted and analyzed the call detail record (CDRs) location information of 8,208 *au* smartphone users according to the following rationale and procedures.

A CDRs is a data record produced by a telephone exchange or other telecommunications equipment. The record contains location information of the base station through which a user made a phone call or sent a message [19]. From a set of location information of base stations, we are able to estimate the location of our users.

We first extracted users who had log records in the Tohoku region by CDRs during the period from August 6 to 18. In this study, we defined the set of whole-day location data as the day that a user enters the Tohoku region as a *Trip*. We then processed the *Trip* data to estimate the user's origin and destination (OD) in accordance with the following procedures:

(1) We first calculated the distances among logs by longitude and latitude.
(2) We then compared the distances and chose the longest one as the estimated OD.
(3) We finally compared the record time of logs. We defined the earliest log as the origin and the latest log as the destination.

We only used the *trip* where O is in Kanto, and D is in Tohoku (outbound), or O is in Tohoku, and D is in Kanto (inbound). We also eliminated those users who used other modes of transport or where the user's log appeared in Tohoku before they accessed the LPs.

Since we could not access the information of users' original travel plans, we assumed that the original route would be the shortest one that connected O and D (original route). If a user's original route was estimated to be the Tohoku expressway and he/she actually used the Joban expressway after checking one of the LPs, we treat his or her action as a detour.

4　Results

In this section, the results of a series of Chi-square analyses and multiple comparison tests are reported.

Table 1. Intention to use Tohoku EXPWY

Tohoku EXPWY		Intervention	N	Intention (Tohoku EXPWY)	x^2	p
Outbound	LP1	Before	1021	69%	48	.000
		After	1021	54%		
	LP2	Before	1026	72%	57	.000
		After	1026	56%		
	LP3	Before	1027	69%	36	.000
		After	1027	56%		
Outbound	LP1	Before	1021	66%	57	.000
		After	1021	50%		
	LP2	Before	1026	68%	63	.000
		After	1026	51%		
	LP3	Before	1027	66%	46	.000
		After	1027	51%		

Table 2. Intention to use Joban EXPWY

Tohoku EXPWY		Intervention	N	Intention (Tohoku EXPWY)	x^2	p
Outbound	LP1	Before	1021	16%	32	.000
		After	1021	26%		
	LP2	Before	1026	12%	64	.000
		After	1026	26%		
	LP3	Before	1027	15%	31	.000
		After	1027	25%		
Inbound	LP1	Before	1021	16%	43	.000
		After	1021	28%		
	LP2	Before	1026	13%	63	.000
		After	1026	27%		
	LP3	Before	1027	17%	30	.000
		After	1027	28%		

4.1 Pre-questionnaire Survey

First, a Chi-square test of independence was conducted to examine the relation between detour intention and congestion information. The relation between these variables was significant. After checking the LPs, more people reported shifting from the Tohoku expressway to another highway (See Table 1). Similarly, the relation between the intention was also significant. After checking the LPs, more people reported their intention to use the Joban expressway (See Table 2).

Another set of Chi-square tests focused on people who reported using the Tohoku expressway before checking LPs. The objective was to test if intention changes were related to intervention content. The results were not found to be statistically significant, $X^2(2, N = 3074) = 2.1, p = .35$ (Outbound); $X^2(2, N = 3074) = 2.5, p = .29$ (Inbound). However, users who received LP2 reported a higher intention to make a detour (Outbound: LP1: 19%, LP2: 21%, LP3: 18%, Inbound: LP1: 22%, LP2: 24%, LP3: 20%).

To test the results in-depth, follow-up Chi-square tests were conducted to examine the impacts of LPs on detour intention by users' attributes.

The results show that for people who had a plan to travel with little children, LP3 had a significant impact on detour intention change, $X^2(1, N = 638) = 6.3, p < 0.01$) (see Fig. 4). For people who had experience in the Tohoku region, LP1 had a significant impact on detour intention change, $X^2(1, N = 666) = 3.7, p < 0.05$) (See Fig. 5). We also examined other user attributes, for example, residence, age, occupation, marriage situation, presence of other adult travelers, route decision maker or not, and drive by self or not. No significant results were confirmed.

4.2 Post-questionnaire Survey

We conducted a series of Chi-square tests and made multiple comparisons to examine the relation between self-reported detour behavior and intervention content. The results showed that for people who reported using the Tohoku expressway in the pre-questionnaire, LP3 had a significantly stronger impact on self-reported detour behavior

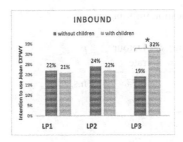

Fig. 4. Intention change (with children)

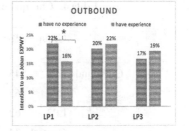

Fig. 5. Intention change (have experience)

Table 3. Chi square tests of self-report detour rate

	Total (N)	Detour (N)	Detour rate	p
Outbound	109	16	15%	n.s
	119	14	12%	
	87	10	11%	
	193	12	6%	
Inbound	106	16	15%	.01
	92	11	12%	
	90	21	23%	
	176	16	9%	

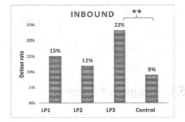

Fig. 6. Multiple comparison test

than the control condition (no intervention content), $X^2(3, N = 464) = 10.6, p < 0.01$) (See Table 3 and Fig. 6). The result of multiple comparison between LP3 and control group was significant, p < 0.01.

4.3 Field Experiment: Location Information

After excluding local residents of the Kanto and Tohoku regions, who traveled to Tohoku by other modes of transport, who arrived in the Tohoku region before they checked the LPs, and whose shortest route was estimated to be the Tohoku expressway, the data of 187 (outbound) and 203 (inbound) out of 8208 users were used in the final analyses. Chi-square tests were conducted to examine the relation between detour behavior and intervention contents. The results are shown in Table 4. The detailed explanation is presented in Sect. 5.1.

5 Discussion

In this section, we summarize the key empirical findings and their theoretical implications. We then discuss the limitations of the present study and disclose our future directions.

Table 4. Chi square tests of location information

	Group	Trip(N)	Detour(N)	Detour rate	p
Outbound	LP1	45	13	30%	n.s.
	LP2	62	15	27%	
	LP3	62	13	28%	
	Control	34	3	7%	
Inbound	LP1	45	15	33%	n.s.
	LP2	62	18	29%	
	LP3	62	25	40%	
	Control	34	9	26%	

5.1 Empirical Insights

Intrinsic Motivation and Detour Intention (H1)
The results of 4.1 demonstrated that congestion information has a motivating effect on detour intention. After being provided with congestion forecasting information, more participants reported that they were inclined to choose an alternative route to the Tohoku expressway. At the same time, more people showed a preference to use the Joban expressway as their first choice. Both these results are statistically significant. These results indicate that even without incentives, congestion forecasting information provided by reliable agencies (e.g., a major expressway company) also has a positive impact on people's detour intentions. One possibility is that after checking the information, people realized the severity of the congestion and consequently made an autonomous decision to switch to another route rather than being influenced by external factors. Therefore, H1a was supported.

Emotional Persuasive Strategy and Changes of Detour Intention (H2a)
The results of 4.1 also demonstrated that an emotional persuasive strategy might promote detour intention. However, the degree to which this has an influence may vary depending on the user's attributes, such as travel experience and the presence of little children. For people who have more experience driving to Tohoku, they may have a clearer understanding of the road situation and feel more confident than first-time travelers. They may be not easily affected by emotional issues but tend to focus more on real-time traffic information. On the other hand, LP3 with a crying girl may elicit empathy for people who travel with little children. This content may make them think more seriously about the congestion situation and come to a decision based on their concern for others. This could be one possible explanation as to why LP3 had a significant effect on the detour intention of certain users. The results also partially answered our research question that

travel experience and the presence of children could be potential moderators of the relation between emotional persuasive strategy and changes in detour intention.

Emotional Persuasive Strategy and Detour Behavior (H2b)
In Sects. 4.2 and 4.3, we examined the hypothesis of whether intervention materials with emotional priming promote detour behavior by self-reported survey and location information. While few of the results were statistically significant, interesting implications were examined. The only significant result was confirmed in 4.2. For people who reported using the Tohoku expressway in the pre-questionnaire survey, LP3 had a significant promotive effect on detour behavior. Although none of the remaining results were significant, they showed a tendency that people in emotional priming groups reported higher percentages of detour behavior. The results of 4.3 are consistent with those of 4.2. For example, during the outbound trip, the detour rates of LP2 and LP3 were 27% and 28%, respectively. The detour rate of the control group was only 7%.

In general, the results were also consistent with those for intention changes.

In addition, scholars in the field of persuasive communication claim that making changes in behavior takes more time and effort than changes of intention. A meta-analysis of the relation between intention and behavior showed that variables of intention could predict only 30% of behavior scores [20]. In sum, in order to make changes in behavior, efforts should be made to overcome other psychological and physical limitations.

5.2 Theoretical Implications

We highlight two significant theoretical contributions to the present study.

First, we expanded the emotional persuasive strategy of the elaboration likelihood model of persuasion in the context of traffic. Although this theoretical framework has been examined widely, such as in the domains of marketing, business negotiation, and advertising, very few empirical studies have examined it in the context of congestion avoidance. We took the first step in exploring the effects of emotional persuasive strategy on detour intention and behavior.

Second, we confirmed the effects of emotional priming by conducting large-scale field experiments. Although emotional priming has been used extensively in empirical studies in psychology, most of the experiments have been conducted purely in a laboratory environment. Besides, due to methodological limitations, most previous studies examined the immediate effects on intention rather than subsequent effects on behavior. In the present study, we filled in these two gaps by performing longitudinal online surveys and digital field surveys.

5.3 Limitations and Future Directions

First, we examined persuasive strategies in the context of an intrinsic motivation approach. Our results showed that in the case of typical intrinsic motivation, emotional persuasion has a significant impact on detour intention and behavior. It could serve as a potential substitute for the costly and unstable intervention of *Rewarding*. However, in the present study, we did not compare the intervention effects of emotional priming and rewarding directly. Besides, from a strict experimental point of view, an experimental manipulation should be conducted to test whether the emotional priming successfully activate feelings of empathy and altruistic motivation. Future investigations should be conducted to address these issues.

Second, the sample size for location information analysis is barely satisfactory. Although the results appear to validate the conclusions of survey studies, statistical significances were not examined. Furthermore, due to the sample sizes, we were not able to examine how variations in user attributes influenced detour behavior by location information. Further attempts should be made to enlarge the sample size and obtain more compelling conclusions.

6 Conclusion

In the present study, the objective was to ascertain if an emotional persuasive strategy would be effective in influencing detour intention and behavior. Two conclusions were reached based on the results of questionnaire surveys and the digital field experiment: (1) Intervention with emotional priming significantly increases detour intention, and has the potential to increase detour behavior. (2) The effects vary depending on user attributes. Overall, the results validated the theoretical framework of the elaboration likelihood model of persuasion in the context of traffic by multiple methodologies. Moreover, the results provided sound empirical evidence that an emotional persuasive strategy (peripheral route) should be not be ignored when creating persuasive systems and services.

References

1. https://www.e-nexco.co.jp/pressroom/press_release/tohoku/h25/0712/
2. Schrank, D., Eisele, B., Lomax, T.: TTI's 2012 urban mobility report. Texas A&M Transportation Institute. The Texas A&M University System, 4 (2012)
3. Litman, T.: Lessons from Katrina and Rita: what major disasters can teach transportation planners. J. Transp. Eng. 132(1), 11–18 (2006)
4. Litman, T.: The online TDM encyclopedia: mobility management information gateway. Transp. Policy 10(3), 245–249 (2003)
5. Shiftan, Y., Golani, A.: Effect of auto restraint policies on travel behavior. Transp. Res. Rec. 1932(1), 156–163 (2005)
6. Small, K.A., Verhoef, E.T., Lindsey, R.: The Economics of Urban Transportation. Routledge, London (2007)
7. Ben-Elia, E., Ettema, D.: Changing commuters' behavior using rewards: a study of rush-hour avoidance. Transp. Res. Part F: Traffic Psychol. Behav. 14(5), 354–368 (2007)
8. Tillema, T., Ben-Elia, E., Ettema, D., van Delden, J.: Charging versus rewarding: a comparison of road-pricing and rewarding peak avoidance in the Netherlands. Transp. Policy 26, 4–14 (2013)
9. Okada, N., Takeuchi, T., Tanikawa, T., Narumi, T., Hirose, M.: Influencing driver behavior based on intrinsic motivation. In: The 31st Annual Conference of the Japanese Society for Artificial Intelligence (2017). Originally in Japanese
10. Brickman, P.: Hedonic relativism and planning the good society. In: Adaptation Level Theory, pp. 287–301 (1971)

11. Kuriki, Y., Fukushima, A., Taya, M., Xu, W., Kameoka, H., Ono, C.: The effect of traffic information on detour behavior. In: The 60th Autumn Conference of Japan society of civil engineers (2019). Originally in Japanese
12. Ryan, R.M., Deci, E.L.: Intrinsic and extrinsic motivations: classic definitions and new directions. Contemp. Educ. Psychol. **25**(1), 54–67 (2000)
13. Lepper, M.R., Greene, D., Nisbet, R.: Undermining children's intrinsic interest with extrinsic reward; a test of 'Overjustification' hypothesis. J. Pers. Soc. Psychol. **28**, 129–137 (1973)
14. Petty, R.E., Cacioppo, J.T.: The elaboration likelihood model of Persuasion. In: Communication and persuasion, pp. 1–24. Springer, New York (1986). https://doi.org/10.1007/978-1-4612-4964-1_1
15. Wang, T., Mukhopadhyay, A., Patrick, V.M.: Getting consumers to recycle NOW! When and why cuteness appeals influence prosocial and sustainable behavior. J. Public Policy Mark. **36**(2), 269–283 (2017)
16. Glocker, M.L., Langleben, D.D., Ruparel, K., Loughead, J.W., Gur, R.C., Sachser, N.: Baby schema in infant's faces induces cuteness perception and motivation for caretaking in adults. Ethology **115**(3), 257–263 (2009)
17. Kollmuss, A., Agyeman, J.: Mind the gap: why do people act environmentally, and what are the barriers to pro-environmental behavior? Environ. Educ. Res. **8**(3), 239–260 (2002)
18. Bell, E., Alan, B.: The ethics of management research: an exploratory content analysis. Br. J. Manag. **18**(1), 63–77 (2007)
19. Horak, R.: Telecommunications and Data Communications Handbook. Wiley, Hoboken (2007)
20. Sheeran, P.: Intention—behavior relations: a conceptual and empirical review. Eur. Rev. Soc. Psychol. **12**(1), 1–36 (2002)

Evaluating the Susceptibility of E-commerce Shoppers to Persuasive Strategies. A Game-Based Approach

Ifeoma Adaji[(✉)] [iD], Nafisul Kiron [iD], and Julita Vassileva [iD]

University of Saskatchewan, Saskatoon, SK, Canada
{ifeoma.adaji,ni.kiron,julita.vassileva}@usask.ca

Abstract. Research suggests that persuasive strategies are more effective when tailored to individuals or groups of similar individuals. Demographic data such as gender, age, culture, and personality are being used in domains such as health to tailor persuasive strategies. However, in e-commerce, these factors are unknown to e-commerce companies making it impossible to use them to tailor persuasive strategies. Other factors such as shoppers' online motivation have been proposed as suitable factors to use in tailoring persuasive strategies in e-commerce. To contribute to research in this area, we investigated the susceptibility of e-commerce shoppers to persuasive strategies based on their online shopping motivation. To achieve this, we developed and evaluated a shopping game, *ShopRight* that simulates a retail store where players can shop for groceries. The healthiest product on each aisle is presented to the player along with a persuasive message. We recruited 187 participants to play *ShopRight* for at least three rounds. Players were classified into groups based on their online shopping motivation and their responses to the persuasive messages were recorded. Using pre- and post-game surveys, we also identified changes in attitude, intention, self-efficacy and perceived price of products.

1 Introduction

Research suggests that persuasive strategies are more effective when tailored to individuals or groups of similar individuals [10, 11]. Several factors have been used in tailoring persuasive strategies such as the personality traits of users [4, 8, 28] and their demographic data such as gender [5, 21, 29], culture [14, 20] and age [23]. However, in e-commerce, the use of these factors is not always possible because most e-commerce companies do not ask for the age, gender or culture of their clients at any time in the shopping process. In addition, most e-commerce companies allow shoppers to purchase items without having to register an account. Furthermore, the purchase history or shopping cart details of consumers do not always identify their gender, age or culture. Therefore, in order for persuasive strategies to be tailored to similar individuals in e-commerce (particularly for new companies) to make them more effective, other factors that can be used in tailoring persuasive strategies have to be explored.

Research in e-commerce suggests that consumers' online shopping motivation predicts high intention to purchase [22]. Consumers are motivated differently and thus

© Springer Nature Switzerland AG 2020
S. B. Gram-Hansen et al. (Eds.): PERSUASIVE 2020, LNCS 12064, pp. 58–72, 2020.
https://doi.org/10.1007/978-3-030-45712-9_5

behave differently when they shop online [7]. Therefore, knowing what motivates a consumer to shop is important in creating a personalized shopping experience for the consumer [22]. Pappas et al. [22] suggest that traditional techniques of personalization such as recommendations based on past purchases might not be enough to influence consumers when shopping online. This is because consumers have needs when they go online, and these needs are largely based on their shopping motivations which traditional techniques of personalization such as recommendations do not meet [22]. There is, therefore, a call to personalize shoppers' online experience using their shopping motivation.

Previous attempts at using shopping motivation to tailor persuasive strategies show that consumers are significantly influenced differently based on their online shopping motivation [1]. Adaji et al. [1] investigated the influence of persuasive strategies on shoppers based on the consumers' online motivation. Shoppers' motivation was determined using the typology of Rohm and Swaminathan [24]: *balanced buyers, variety seekers, store oriented shoppers,* and *convenience shoppers.*

To contribute to research in the area of tailoring persuasive strategies in e-commerce using shopping motivation, we investigate the susceptibility of e-commerce shoppers to persuasive strategies using a game-based approach. To achieve this, we developed a serious shopping game, *ShopRight* that simulates a consumer shopping for food items. We attempt to influence the players' shopping decisions by presenting them with food items along with persuasive messages that were developed using Cialdini's six persuasive strategies [6]. To evaluate *ShopRight,* we recruited 187 participants to play the game for at least three rounds and their responses to the various persuasive messages were recorded. Players were classified into groups based on their online shopping motivation using the typology of Rohm and Swaminathan [24]. In addition, we measured the change in players' self-efficacy, attitude, and intention before and after playing *ShopRight* to determine if the persuasive messages increased these determinants in the players.

The aim of this paper is to identify the susceptibility of shoppers to persuasive strategies based on their online shopping motivation using a game-based approach. In addition, this paper aims to identify any differences in the behavior of participants before and after playing the game.

This paper contributes to ongoing research in the area of tailoring persuasive strategies in e-commerce in three ways. First, we determine that persuasive strategies can be tailored to shoppers based on their online shopping motivation using a game-based approach. Second, we identify the persuasive strategies that people are most susceptible to based on their shopping motivation in the context of shopping for food items. Third, we determine that persuasive messages can bring about a change in self-efficacy, attitude, and intention.

2 Related Work

2.1 Shopping Motivation

Research suggests that classifying shoppers according to their shopping motivation and behavior can help businesses to effectively tailor products and services to the various segments of customers [24]. In addition, it helps businesses to better understand the attitude of their customers and what they look out for in their shopping decision-making process [13]. Rohm and Swaminathan [24] classified shopper types based on the shopping motivation of shoppers and proposed four categories: *convenience shoppers, variety seekers, balanced buyers,* and *store-oriented shoppers.* According to the authors, the *convenience shoppers* are motivated by online shopping convenience. Shoppers in this category do not typically seek immediate possession of their products. The *variety seekers* are more interested in seeking variety of products across various retailers and brands. The *balanced buyers* are motivated by the need to seek information online just like the *variety seeker.* However, the *balanced buyers* plan their shopping ahead unlike the *variety seekers.* The *store-oriented shopper* wants immediate possession of goods purchased and are more inclined to social interaction. Shoppers in this category prefer the feel of a physical store to an online marketplace.

We used the typology of Rohm and Swaminathan [24] in our study because it focuses on online shopping behavior and because the four categories identified by this typology are similar to that of other researchers such as [13] and [18].

The various categories of shoppers can be identified from their online click activities. For example, the *variety seekers* have a need for a variety of choices of stores, brands, and products, and they make comparisons while shopping [24]. This category of shoppers take time to compare promotions, prices, brands, and product features before making a purchase decision [13]. Therefore, by studying shoppers' clickstream while shopping, it is possible to identify if they are seeking a variety of products from several brands. *Store oriented shoppers,* on the other hand, seek social interaction [24], thus, will likely engage in interaction or dialogue with other consumers on the e-commerce platform before making a purchase. Interaction in e-commerce is usually by asking other customers questions about the products they have previously purchased [2] or by interacting with a site's chatbot if one exists. Thus, shoppers who typically interact with other consumers or with the site's chat agent before making purchases could be identified as *store-oriented* shoppers. In addition, *store oriented* shoppers are motivated by immediate possession of their goods [24]. It is likely that this category of shoppers will pay for express delivery of their products while other categories of shoppers will not. *Convenience shoppers* are motivated to shop online because of the convenience that online shopping provides them [24]. They shop online for specific products and services, they do not seek variety across several channels, and are motivated by the convenience of online shopping, effort and time saving [24]. Therefore, it is likely that *convenience shoppers* will not spend time and effort browsing different brands as *variety seekers* typically do. Their browsing patterns can be determined from their clickstream data. In addition, *convenience shoppers* are not motivated by social interaction and immediate possession [24]. Thus, it is likely that *convenience shoppers* will not interact on the social platform of the e-commerce site such as the review boards and the question and answer pages. In addition, it is likely that *convenience shoppers* will not pay for quick/express delivery but will settle for normal delivery since they are not motivated by immediate possession of their products.

2.2 Persuasive Strategies

Persuasive strategies change peoples' attitude or behavior without coercion or deception [6]. Several classifications of persuasive strategies exist such as Cialdini's six influence principles: *reciprocation, commitment, consensus, liking, authority* and *scarcity* [6]. The principle of *reciprocation* suggests that human societies subscribe to the rule of reciprocity, hence, humans feel obligated to return a favor they have received in the past. The principle of *commitment* suggests that humans tend to be consistent, therefore, it is likely that people will honor things they have committed to. *Consensus* principle proposes that people tend to manifest the same behavior and beliefs as others after observing several people behaving in a similar manner. *Authority* principle suggests that because humans are trained to believe in the obedience of authority figures, hence in deciding what action to take in any situation, information from people in authority could help humans make decisions. *Liking* principle posits that people are more persuaded by something/someone they like. *Scarcity* strategy suggests that humans seemingly have a desire for things that are scare, less readily available or limited in number.

These strategies have been used extensively in consumer studies and other domains, thus, we adopted them in this study.

3 *Shopright* Game Design

ShopRight is an interactive single-player educational game, designed to simulate a shopper walking along the aisle of a grocery store. The aim of the game is to influence the shopping decisions of players by presenting tailored persuasive messages that can change the players' shopping decision. In addition, *ShopRight* aims to educate shoppers on the healthiness of foods based on the food's nutritional value. Furthermore, *ShopRight* aims to make shoppers aware of the cost of foods they shop for; in particular, to show that they can shop for healthy foods on a budget. The player's objective is to shop for a healthy meal (breakfast, lunch or dinner) for one's self, a child, a friend or a significant other on a budget while trying to earn as many points as possible. Each food item is awarded points based on the healthiness of the food. The healthiness of each food is computed using the front-of-pack food labelling system of the United Kingdom[1]. We used this food labeling scheme to award points in *ShopRight* because of its ease of understanding and its influence on healthier shopping choices [25]. The healthier the items the player adds to their cart, the more points the player earns. Each round of the game consists of six aisles of groceries. For each round, the player has $20 in their virtual purse to shop for a meal. This amount is based on how much Canadians spend on average for a meal.

When the game starts, products are presented to players and they have the option to add the item to their cart or to skip to the next item. Each product, as shown in Fig. 1, is displayed with the name of the product, the nutritional value, and the price. The price and nutritional value of each item were obtained from the popular Canadian retail store Real Canadian Superstore's e-commerce website[2]. We selected 69 food items for *ShopRight* based on recipes we found on the popular food website allrecipes.com. Due to space constraints, we are unable to list the foods here.

Each round of the game consists of 6 aisles of different types of foods. Similar to what is obtainable in grocery stores, similar products are grouped together. A player can

---

[1] https://www.nutrition.org.uk/healthyliving/helpingyoueatwell/324-labels.html?start=3.

[2] https://www.realcanadiansuperstore.ca/.

Fig. 1. Game play of ShopRight

see the items that make up the aisle at the bottom of the screen as shown in Fig. 1. When the game starts, the player can view the nutritional information of the food on the screen and then decide whether to add the product to their cart.

While playing the game, persuasive messages pop up based on the persuasive strategies of Cialdini [6] asking players to add particular products to their carts. The responses of users to these persuasive messages are stored and used to measure the players' susceptibility to influence strategies.

As shown in Fig. 1, the right hand of the screen displays the number of points a player has earned, the money they have left and the total nutrients of the products they have added to their cart so far. While players can add items to their cart, they are unable to delete items. *ShopRight* was designed this way because shoppers have ample time to consider adding items to their cart since the game has no time constraints. In addition, because the player plays the game multiple times, it is expected that they get better at choosing products over time.

Persuasive Messages
One of the aims of the *ShopRight* is to investigate shoppers' susceptibility to persuasive strategies. Persuasive strategies were implemented as persuasive messages using Cialdini's persuasive strategies [6]. The messages presented to users were adapted from [12] and are shown in Table 1. The list of messages was reviewed by two experts in user interface design who are knowledgeable about persuasive strategies. The messages were also reviewed by two novices in persuasive strategies who were asked to explain their perceived meanings of the messages. The responses from the experts and novices showed that the messages were easy to understand and were unambiguous. We only investigated four of the six strategies of Cialdini [6] because these four are commonly used in e-commerce.

Each persuasive message was presented randomly to the player and was accompanied by the healthiest product on the aisle. For example, an implementation of *scarcity* is the message "*Last chance to buy strawberry*".

Table 1. Persuasive messages used in ShopRight. [this] was replaced with the product name

Persuasive strategy	Persuasive message
Scarcity	Only a few [this] are left in stock
Scarcity	Last chance to buy [this]
Scarcity	Rare [this] available today
Commitment	[this] will help you to achieve your daily nutritional goal
Commitment	Remember your set goal for total calories and consider if you want to buy [this]
Commitment	You've committed to shopping for a healthy meal. [this] will help you to achieve your set goal
Consensus	Someone in your social circle recommends [this]
Consensus	[this] is frequently bought together with an item in your cart
Consensus	[this] has been upvoted as a preferred item by many shoppers
Authority	Research suggests that foods such as [this] help you increase your muscle mass and strength
Authority	According to Health Canada, you should eat more foods rich in fiber. Add [this] to cart
Authority	According to Health Canada, your body uses energy from calories to do all of your daily activities. Add [this] to cart

4 Field Study

To determine the susceptibility of shoppers to persuasive strategies based on their online shopping motivation, we carried out a study of *ShopRight* using 187 participants. The design of the study and the methods used are presented in this section.

4.1 Study Design

We recruited participants to evaluate *ShopRight*. The participants were required to complete a pre-game survey, play the game at least three times and then complete a post-game survey. The pre-game survey included questions that measure consumers' online shopping motivation using the scale of Rohm and Swaminathan [24]. Participants were classified into the four categories of online shopping motivation *convenience shopper, variety seeker, store oriented shopper* and *balanced buyer* based on their response to the questions in the questionnaire. Participants were placed in the category that they scored highest in with a minimum score of 5 points (on a 7-point Likert scale). The pre- and post-game survey also included questions about (1) the consumers' self-efficacy using the scale of Sherer et al. [27], (2) attitude towards unhealthy foods using the scale of [17], (3) perceived cost of healthy foods using the scale of Zeithaml [30], and (4) intention to shop for healthy foods using the scale of [26]. We hypothesize that there will a significant increase in these factors after playing the game if the player is influenced by the tailored persuasive messages in the game. All questions were measured on a 7-point Likert scale.

In addition to the pre- and post-game survey, the game data from players was recorded. In particular, their responses to persuasive strategies presented to them, the amount of money they spent shopping, and the points they earned in the game.

4.2 Methodology

We measured the influence of persuasive strategies in two ways. First, we measured the response of shoppers to persuasive strategies using the game data. Second, we measured the players' attitude, self-efficacy, the perceived price of healthy foods, and intention to shop for healthy foods before and after playing the game.

Measuring Susceptibility to Persuasive Strategies Using Game Data
Each player is presented with 12 persuasive messages along with product suggestions and their responses to these messages are recorded. Their responses are either to add an item recommended to them to cart by clicking on the "add to cart" button on the pop-up message, or to reject the recommendation by clicking on the "cancel" button on the pop-up message. A positive response to a persuasive message is when a user adds a suggested item to their cart.

In analyzing the game data of participants for their susceptibility to persuasive strategies, we counted the number of persuasive messages that participants responded to at each round of the game. We then determined the average for each participant. We posit that a player will likely respond more to the strategies that they are susceptible to. In addition, we carried out a one-way repeated measure analysis of variance (ANOVA) with persuasive strategies as the within-subjects factor to determine if there were any significant differences in the susceptibility of strategies between the different persuasive strategies. Furthermore, we carried out a Bonferroni corrected post t-test between the experimental groups to determine what pairs of groups had the significant difference. All the assumptions for repeated measures ANOVA were met.

Measuring Behavior Change Using Attitude, Intention, and Self-efficacy
One of the aims of this paper is to measure the behavior change of users based on their susceptibility to persuasive strategies. We hypothesize that the persuasive messages that participants are influenced by will likely bring about a change in their behavior after playing *ShopRight*. Thus, in addition to measuring how susceptible players are to influence strategies, we measured their change in behavior after playing the game. Based on various behavioral studies and theories, research suggests that the main predictors of behavior are intention, attitude, and self-efficacy [3, 15, 19]. Participants were required to answer pre- and post-survey questions about intention, attitude, self-efficacy, and perceived price. We then computed the differences in their responses to identify any change in their behavior.

To determine if there were any statistical changes in these determinants pre- and post-game, we carried out a paired-samples t-test (also known as repeated measure t-test) of these determinants using the pre- and post-game data. All the assumptions for paired-samples t-test were met.

4.3 Data Collection and Filtering

We recruited participants to take part in the study through Amazon's Mechanical Turk (AMT). AMT allows one to recruit a diverse set of participants and is an accepted method of recruiting participants [8, 9]. To ensure the quality of the results that were collected from participants in the pre and post surveys, we included captcha questions on each page of the survey as suggested by [16] that require some level of reasoning and effort to answer. These captcha questions include basic multiple-choice addition and multiplication problems such as "What is 50 + 50?". Participants that failed the captcha questions were excluded from the survey. In addition, participants who recorded the same responses for all questions were excluded from the survey. Furthermore, we tracked participants using their AMT IDs and duplicate responses were excluded from the study. Participants were compensated with $3.00 USD for their time which is within the standard rates of tasks on AMT.

Participants were recruited for three categories: *convenience shoppers, variety seekers*, and a control group which consists of randomly selected participants from *balanced buyers* and *store-oriented shoppers*. This study was approved by the Behavioral Research Ethics Board of the University of Saskatchewan.

Participants
We recruited 203 participants to take part in this study out of which only 187 responses were useable based on the criteria described above. Table 2 shows the breakdown of our participants.

Table 2. Breakdown of study participants

Classification	Study group	N = 187
Shopping motivation	Convenience shoppers	74
	Variety seekers n = 66	66
	Control (randomly selected from convenience shoppers, variety seekers, store oriented shoppers, and balanced buyers)	47

5 Results

In evaluating *ShopRight*, we adopted two approaches: (1) we measured the susceptibility of participants to persuasive strategies using the game data they generated from playing *ShopRight* and (2) we measured the change in participants' self-efficacy towards healthy foods, attitude towards shopping for unhealthy foods, perceived price of healthy foods, and intention to purchase healthy foods before and after playing the game using the pre- and post-game survey responses. The results of analyzing these data are described in this section.

5.1 Susceptibility to Persuasive Strategies

Convenience Shoppers
The result of the one-way repeated measures ANOVA indicates that there was a statistically significant difference in the susceptibility of *convenience shoppers* to the four persuasive strategies *scarcity, consensus, commitment,* and *authority* $F(3, 216) = 9.851, p < .005$). This suggests that at least one group mean differs significantly from the other group means. To determine where this difference (or differences) lies, we carried out a Bonferroni corrected post-test t-test between the persuasive strategies. The result of this test indicates that there was a statistically significant difference in the mean susceptibility of *convenience shoppers* to the persuasive strategies *scarcity* and *consensus*, with *convenience shoppers* being more susceptible to *scarcity* compared to *consensus*, with a mean difference of 0.44 and $t(72) = 3.553, p < 0.0005$. Similarly, there was a statistically significant difference in the susceptibility of *convenience shoppers* to *scarcity* and *commitment*, with shoppers being more susceptible to *scarcity* compared to *commitment* with a mean difference of 0.37, and $t(72) = 3.227, p < 0.005$. Furthermore, there was a statistically significant difference between *scarcity* and *authority* with a mean difference of 0.550 and $t(72) = 4.745, p < 0.0005$. Figure 2a shows the means of the persuasive strategies.

 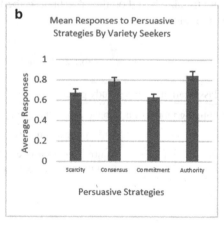

Fig. 2. (a) Mean responses of *convenience shoppers* to persuasive strategies. (b) Mean responses of *variety seekers* to persuasive strategies

There were, however, no significant differences between *consensus, commitment,* and *authority*. This result suggests that *scarcity* has the greatest influence on *convenience shoppers* compared to the other strategies and that the effect of *scarcity* on *convenience shoppers* significantly differs compared to the other strategies. However, it is not possible to tell which strategy has the least effect on *convenience shoppers*.

Variety Seekers

As shown in Fig. 2b, *variety seekers* had the highest mean susceptibility to *authority*, while this category of shoppers had the lowest mean susceptibility to *commitment*. To determine if the means of the persuasive strategies were significantly different, we carried out a one-way repeated measures ANOVA. The result suggests that there were no significant differences in the means of the persuasive strategies, $F(3, 192) = 1.241, p = .296)$. This result means that although *variety seekers* responded to more *authority* messages compared to the other persuasive strategies, we cannot conclusively state that the *variety seekers* were more susceptible to *authority* than the other strategies.

Control Group

We created a control group to determine the susceptibility of shoppers to persuasive strategies when their shopping motivation is unknown. We randomly selected 52 participants from the pool of participants who either did not score high enough to be part of the *convenience shoppers* and *variety seekers* described in the previous section or belong to *balanced buyers* and *store-oriented shoppers* categories. All four persuasive strategies had similar means ranging from 1.35 to 1.5. The result of a one-way ANOVA suggests that there are were no significant differences in the susceptibility of participants in this group to any of the persuasive strategies $F(3, 97) = 0.87, p = .46)$. This suggests that if people in a group are not similar, they are not significantly influenced by the same strategy compared to a group of similar people such as the *convenience shoppers* who are significantly influenced by *scarcity*.

5.2 Change in Self-efficacy, Attitude, Price, and Intention

Convenience Shoppers

Figure 3a shows the average means of *convenience shoppers'* self-efficacy towards healthy foods, attitude towards shopping for unhealthy foods, perceived price of healthy foods, and intention to purchase healthy foods before and after playing the game. There was a slight decrease in the mean self-efficacy of *convenience shoppers* after playing the game. Similarly, there was a decrease in the average attitude of *convenience shoppers* shopping for unhealthy foods. Furthermore, there was a slight decrease in the mean perceived price of healthy foods. On the other hand, there was an increase in the average intention of *convenience shoppers* to shop for healthy foods.

To determine if any of the difference in means was statistically significant, we carried out a paired sample t-test between the pre- and post-game data for each determinant. The result as shown in Fig. 3b indicates that the only significant difference in means is in the attitude of *convenience shoppers* towards shopping for unhealthy foods, $t(73) = -2.57, p < .05$, which decreased significantly.

Variety Seekers

Figure 4a shows the average means of *variety seekers'* self-efficacy towards healthy foods, attitude towards unhealthy foods, the perceived price of healthy foods, and intention to purchase healthy foods before and after playing the game. There was a slight increase in self-efficacy of participants before and after the game. Similarly, there was

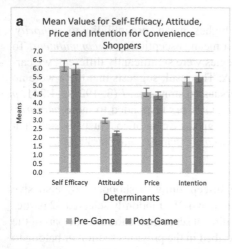
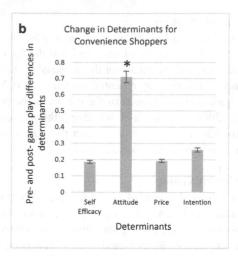

Fig. 3. (a) Pre- and Post-game mean values of determinants for *convenience shoppers*. (b) Difference in pre- and post- game questionnaire values for determinants. Asterisk indicates significant difference

an increase in intention to purchase healthy foods by *variety seekers*. On the other hand, there was a decrease in attitude towards purchase of unhealthy foods. Furthermore, there was a decrease in the perceived price of healthy food.

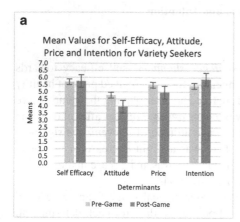
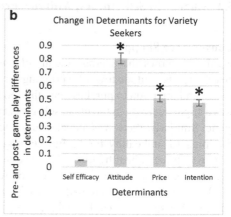

Fig. 4. (a) Pre- and Post-game mean values of determinants for variety seekers. (b) Difference in pre- and post- game questionnaire values for determinants. Asterisk indicates significant difference

To determine if there were any statistical significance in the differences of the means between the pre- and post-game results, we carried out a paired sample t-test between the pre- and post-game questionnaire values for each determinant. The mean attitude of *variety seekers* towards unhealthy foods decreased significantly after playing *ShopRight*, $t(65) = -2.052$, $p < .05$. Similarly, the mean perception of the price of healthy foods decreased significantly from a pre-game mean of 5.47 to 4.97, $t(65) = -2.192$, $p < .05$. Furthermore, the mean intention to shop for healthy foods increased significantly to an average of 5.89, $t(65) = 2.780$, $p < .05$. On the other hand, there was no significant difference in mean self-efficacy of *variety seekers* before and after playing *ShopRight*, $t(65) = 0.2825$, $p = .78$. Figure 4b shows the difference in determinants for *variety seekers* pre- and post-game.

5.3 Discussion

Susceptibility to Persuasive Strategies
As shown in Fig. 2a, *convenience shoppers* are more susceptible to *scarcity* compared to other persuasive strategies. *Convenience shoppers* are motivated by shopping convenience, effort and time-saving [24]. These categories of shoppers are neither motivated by the expectation of immediate possession of their goods nor are they motivated by social interaction. Furthermore, these shoppers do not seek variety across retail channels [24]. Since these shoppers do not seek variety, it is conceivable that they will be influenced to buy products that are scarce or limited. This result is in line with that of Adaji et al. [1] who, using a survey-based approach concluded that *convenience shoppers* have a higher susceptibility to *scarcity* compared to other strategies.

There was no significance between the response of *convenience shoppers* to *consensus, commitment,* and *authority*. While we can conclude from these findings that *convenience shoppers* will likely be influenced by *scarcity* compared to other strategies, we cannot conclude on which strategy they will likely not be influenced by. Therefore, if an e-business is implementing persuasive strategies based on shopping motivation, the recommended strategy for *convenience shoppers* is *scarcity*.

The game data results from Fig. 2b suggest that *variety seekers* responded more to *authority* strategy compared other strategies. In addition, they responded the least to *commitment* strategy. *Variety seekers* are motivated to seek for a variety of products across various stores, product types and brands [24]. They tend to browse several products and brands before making a purchase decision They are also known to comparison shop [24]. The result of a one-way repeated measures ANOVA suggests that the difference between *authority* and other strategies is not significant. Thus, we cannot conclusively state from the game data that *variety seekers* are more influenced by *authority* than other strategies. We expected significant differences between *authority* and other strategies in line with the results of Adaji et al. [1].

We plan to carry out this study on *variety seekers* using more participants; we believe that having more data could bring about significant differences.

Change in Self-efficacy, Attitude, Perceived Price and Intention
The attitude, perceived price, and intention to shop for healthy foods for *variety seekers* were significantly different after playing *ShopRight*. As shown in Fig. 4a and b there was a significant decrease in the attitude of *variety seekers* towards unhealthy foods and the price of unhealthy foods. There was however an increase in the intention of participants in this category to shop for healthy foods. A decrease in attitude towards unhealthy foods means that participants now see shopping for healthy foods as being

important, useful, worthwhile, enjoyable, pleasant and good. Therefore, a decrease is a positive outcome. Similarly, a decrease in the perceived price of healthy foods is a good thing because participants now see healthy foods as inexpensive, which they can buy on a budget. An increase in intention to shop for healthy foods is also a positive outcome. This result suggests that tailored persuasive strategies result in a positive change in attitude, self-efficacy, and intention.

The only change in *convenience shoppers* after playing *ShopRight* was in their attitude towards shopping for unhealthy foods which decreased significantly. A decrease in attitude towards unhealthy foods suggests that participants now see shopping for healthy foods as being important, useful, worthwhile, enjoyable, pleasant and good. Therefore, a decrease is a positive outcome.

6   Conclusion and Future Work

To contribute to ongoing research in tailoring persuasive strategies in e-commerce, we investigated the susceptibility of shoppers to persuasive strategies based on their online shopping motivation. To achieve this, we developed a shopping game, *ShopRight,* and recruited 187 participants to play the game. Participants were classified into groups based on their shopping motivation: *convenience shoppers, variety seekers, balanced buyers,* and *store-oriented shoppers.* While playing the game, players were presented with food items using various persuasive strategies. The responses of participants to these strategies were recorded. The participants also completed pre- and post-game surveys to determine if there were any differences in their self-efficacy towards healthy foods, attitude towards shopping for unhealthy foods, perceived price of healthy foods, and intention to purchase healthy foods before and after playing the game. Our results indicate that shoppers are influenced differently based on their online shopping motivation.

Our study has a few limitations. First, our sample size for each category of online shopping motivation is small. We are still in the process of collecting data; in the future, we will repeat this study with a larger sample size. Second, there are several other factors that could have influenced participants' choices of food items while playing the game such as dietary restrictions.

In the future, we plan to explore other data that were collected from participants while playing *ShopRight* such as the amount spent, the points earned and the time it took players to complete a session. We explored consumers' susceptibility to only four of Cialdini's six strategies. In the future, we plan to investigate participants' responses to the other two strategies that were not used in this study: *reciprocity* and *liking.*

References

1. Adaji, I., Oyibo, K., Vassileva, J.: Shopper types and the influence of persuasive strategies in e-commerce. In: International Workshop on Personalized Persuasive Technology, Waterloo 2018, pp. 58–65 (2018)
2. Adaji, I., Vassileva, J.: Perceived effectiveness, credibility and continuance intention in e-commerce. A study of Amazon. In: Proceedings of 12th International Conference on Persuasive Technology, Amsterdam 2017, pp. 293–306 (2017)

3. Ajzen, I., Fishbein, M.: The influence of attitudes on behavior. In: The Handbook of Attitudes, vol. 31, pp. 173–221 (2005)
4. Alkış, N., Taşkaya Temizel, T.: The impact of individual differences on influence strategies. Personality Individ. Differ. **87**, 147–152 (2015). https://doi.org/10.1016/J.PAID.2015.07.037
5. Busch, M., Mattheiss, E., Reisinger, M., Orji, R., Fröhlich, P., Tscheligi, M.: More than sex: the role of femininity and masculinity in the design of personalized persuasive games. In: Meschtscherjakov, A., De Ruyter, B., Fuchsberger, V., Murer, M., Tscheligi, M. (eds.) PERSUASIVE 2016. LNCS, vol. 9638, pp. 219–229. Springer, Cham (2016). https://doi.org/10.1007/978-3-319-31510-2_19
6. Cialdini, R.B.: Influence: Science and practice. Pearson Education, Boston (2009)
7. Ganesh, J., Reynolds, K., Luckett, M., Pomirleanu, N.: Online shopper motivations, and e-store attributes: an examination of online patronage behavior and shopper typologies. J. Retail. **86**(1), 106–115 (2010)
8. Hirsh, J.B., Kang, S.K., Bodenhausen, G.V.: Personalized persuasion: tailoring persuasive appeals to recipients' personality traits. Psychol. Sci. **23**(6), 578–581 (2012). https://doi.org/10.1177/0956797611436349
9. Jia, Y., Xu, B., Karanam, Y. and Voida, S. 2016. Personality-targeted gamification: a survey study on personality traits and motivational affordances. *Proceedings of the 2016 CHI Conference on Human Factors in Computing Systems* (2016), 2001–2013
10. Kaptein, M.: Adaptive persuasive messages in an e-commerce setting: the use of persuasion profiles. In: European Conference on Information Systems, p. 183 (2011)
11. Kaptein, M., Halteren, A.: Adaptive persuasive messaging to increase service retention: using persuasion profiles to increase the effectiveness of email reminders. Pers. Ubiquit. Comput. **17**(6), 1173–1185 (2013)
12. Kaptein, M., De Ruyter, B., Markopoulos, P.: Adaptive persuasive systems: a study of tailored persuasive text messages to reduce snacking. ACM Trans. Interact. Intell. Syst. **2**(2), 1–25 (2012)
13. Keng Kau, A., Tang, Y.E., Ghose, S.: Typology of online shoppers. J. Consum. Market. **20**(2), 139–156 (2003). https://doi.org/10.1108/07363760310464604
14. Kramer, T., Spolter-Weisfeld, S.: The effect of cultural orientation on consumer responses to personalization. Mark. Sci. **26**(2), 246–258 (2007)
15. Madden, T.J., Ellen, P.S., Ajzen, I.: A comparison of the theory of planned behavior and the theory of reasoned action. Pers. Soc. Psychol. Bull. **18**(1), 3–9 (1992). https://doi.org/10.1177/0146167292181001
16. Mason, W., Suri, S.: Conducting behavioral research on Amazon's Mechanical Turk. Behav. Res. Methods **44**(1), 1–23 (2012)
17. McGaghie, W.C., et al.: Development of a measure of attitude toward nutrition in patient care. Am. J. Prev. Med. **20**(1), 15–20 (2001). https://doi.org/10.1016/S0749-3797(00)00264-6
18. Moe, W.: Buying, searching, or browsing: Differentiating between online shoppers using in-store navigational clickstream. J. Consum. Psychol. **13**(1–2), 29–39 (2003)
19. Orji, R.: Design for behaviour change: a model-driven approach for tailoring persuasive technologies. University of Saskatchewan (2014)
20. Orji, R.: The impact of cultural differences on the persuasiveness of influence strategies. In: Proceedings of the 11th International Conference 2016 on Persuasive Technology, pp. 38–41 (2016)
21. Orji, R., Mandryk, R., Vassileva, J.: Gender and persuasive technology: examining the persuasiveness of persuasive strategies by gender groups. In: International Conference on Persuasive Technology, pp. 48–52 (2014)

22. Pappas, I., Kouurouthanassis, P., Giannakos, M., Lekakos, G.: The interplay of online shopping motivations and experiential factors on personalized e-commerce: a complexity theory approach. Telematics and Inform. **34**(5), 730–742 (2017). https://doi.org/10.1016/J.TELE.2016.08.021

23. Phillips, D.M., Stanton, J.L.: Age-related differences in advertising: recall and persuasion. J. Target. Meas. Anal. Market. **13**(1), 7–20 (2004). https://doi.org/10.1057/palgrave.jt.5740128

24. Rohm, A.J., Swaminathan, V.: A typology of online shoppers based on shopping motivations. J. Bus. Res. **57**(7), 748–757 (2004). https://doi.org/10.1016/S0148-2963(02)00351-X

25. Scarborough, P., Matthews, A.: Reds are more important than greens: how UK supermarket shoppers use the different information on a traffic light nutrition label in a choice experiment. Int. J. Behav. Nutr. Phys. Act. **12**(1), 151 (2015)

26. Schifter, D.E., Ajzen, I.: Intention, perceived control, and weight loss: an application of the theory of planned behavior. J. Pers. Soc. Psychol. **49**(3), 843–851 (1985). https://doi.org/10.1037/0022-3514.49.3.843

27. Sherer, M., Maddux, J.E., Mercandante, B., Prentice-Dunn, S., Jacobs, B., Rogers, R.W.: The self-efficacy scale: construction and validation. Psychol. Rep. **51**(2), 663–671 (1982). https://doi.org/10.2466/pr0.1982.51.2.663

28. Smith, K., Dennis, M., Masthoff, J.: Personalizing reminders to personality for melanoma self-checking. In: Proceedings of the 2016 Conference on User Modeling Adaptation and Personalization, pp. 85–93 (2016)

29. de Vries, R.A.J., Truong, K.P., Zaga, C., Li, J., Evers, V.: A word of advice: how to tailor motivational text messages based on behavior change theory to personality and gender. Pers. Ubiquit. Comput. **21**(4), 675–687 (2017). https://doi.org/10.1007/s00779-017-1025-1

30. Zeithaml, V.A.: Consumer perceptions of price, quality, and value: a means-end model and synthesis of evidence. J. Mark. **1988**, 2–22 (1988)

Learning and Teaching Experiences with a Persuasive Social Robot in Primary School – Findings and Implications from a 4-Month Field Study

Aino Ahtinen(✉) [iD] and Kirsikka Kaipainen [iD]

Tampere University, Korkeakoulunkatu 1, 33720 Tampere, Finland
{aino.ahtinen,kirsikka.kaipainen}@tuni.fi

Abstract. In the field of child-robot interaction (CRI), long-term field studies with users in authentic contexts are still rare. This paper reports the findings from a 4-month field study of robot-assisted language learning (RALL). We focus on the learning experiences of primary school pupils with a social, persuasive robot, and the experiences of the teachers of using the robot as a teaching tool. Our qualitative research approach includes interviews, observations, questionnaires and a diary as data collection methods, and affinity diagram as a data analysis method. The research involves three target groups: the pupils of a 3rd grade class (9–10 years old, n = 20), language teachers (n = 3) and the parents (n = 18). We report findings on user experience (UX), the robot's tasks and role in the school, and the experience of the multimodal interaction with the robot. Based on the findings, we discuss several aspects concerning the design of persuasive robotics on robot-assisted learning and CRI, for example the benefits of robot-specific ways of rewarding, the value of the physical embodiment and the opportunities of the social role adopted by the learning robot.

Keywords: Child-robot interaction · Robot-assisted learning · Persuasive design · User experience · Field study

1 Introduction

Social robot is an autonomous or semi-autonomous robot that communicates and inter-acts with human beings, and obeys the behavioral norms set by humans [1]. Social robots have many possible uses, including education [2, 24]. Social robots can be beneficial agents in children's *robot-assisted learning*. Their benefits may result from e.g. robots' motivational factors [22], ability to patiently repeat tasks [3], capability to adapt the learning tasks [18] and human-like interaction and presence [2, 16]. Motivation plays a strong role in learning, and due to social robots' characteristics, they have potential to act as motivators for learning [27]. *Persuasive Design* approach, e.g. [17], offers many tech-niques for designing technologies that can engage people and support motivation. In this article, we discuss Persuasive Design implications and considerations on robot-assisted learning and *child-robot interaction (CRI)*.

S. B. Gram-Hansen et al. (Eds.): PERSUASIVE 2020, LNCS 12064, pp. 73–84, 2020.
https://doi.org/10.1007/978-3-030-45712-9_6

Despite being popular research topics, robot-assisted learning and CRI have space for long-term studies conducted in natural settings. *Naturalistic studies* that utilize qualitative methods are still quite rare in the field of social robotics [9], and the studies that have been conducted in natural settings have actually often been restricted to a pre-defined space [4]. Social robots have a strong novelty effect that can soon wear off [10, 13], and long-term field studies are required to evaluate how long users' interest in a robot is maintained. In the research thus far, "long-term use" has usually meant "serial short-term interaction", and interaction with the robot has not taken place as a part of natural teaching and learning practice, but in a situation that has been defined and supported by the researchers [4].

In this paper, we report a 4-month user experience (UX) study that was carried out in *authentic context of use*, in a primary school setting, at the time when the school started to use a social robot for teaching languages. The use of the robot was defined entirely by the users, not by the researchers. Our research investigates the use of the robot from three perspectives: *pupils, teachers* and *parents*. We focus on *the robot's tasks, social role* and *interaction/behavior* as suggested in the design framework of socially interactive robots by Deng et al. [9]. This paper addresses the following research questions:

(1) **What are the teaching and learning experiences with the social robot focusing on the (A) tasks, (B) social role and (C) interaction/behavior of the robot?**
(2) **What are the considerations for the further design of social, persuasive robots for CRI?**

2 Related Work

2.1 Robot-Assisted Learning and Child-Robot Interaction

Research on social robots in education focusing on children is a popular topic [2, 16]. A recent meta-review reveals 101 articles in the area of educational robots, most of them focused on children [2]. On the field of robot-assisted language learning (RALL), the **typical tasks** of a robot in learning include teaching vocabulary [13, 25], reading and speaking skills, grammar and sign language [24]. Usually the robot's tasks are defined by the researchers. Thus, there is a need to explore the tasks that a robot is used for when it acts as a natural part of the learning environment. This relates to our *RQ1A*.

In general, children have a positive attitude towards robots [26], and studies have shown some evidence of better learning outcomes when studying with the robots, e.g. [12, 24]. A robot can adopt **different roles** in teaching: teacher or tutor, peer or learning companion, and novice [2]. The role of the teacher/tutor has been the most popular role so far (ibid.). However, research has shown that children perform better and are more focused when the robot behaves like a peer rather than a tutor [27]. Presenting the robot in the role of peer may also increase the acceptance towards unexpected behavior of a robot, e.g. if its speech recognition fails [3]. In their study, Tanaka et al. [22] found out that children started to treat the QRIO robot as a peer rather than a toy, and they expressed plenty of care-taking behaviors towards the robot, also discussed by Turkle [23]. Kanda et al. [14] found that children wanted to become "friends" with Robovie robot. Thus, it seems that children tend to develop social bonds with educational robots. Our *RQ1B* focuses on the roles that the robot adopts in a naturalistic school setting.

Social robots utilize **multimodal interaction** to aim for more natural communication. It seems that any social behavior and cues built on an educational robot improves learning outcomes and experience [3]. The most obvious form of social behavior is the use of speech as an interaction modality, e.g. [13, 15, 25]. However, technical challenges still limit the proper use of natural dialogue in robot-assisted learning [15]. In addition to verbal interaction, social robots are capable of non-verbal communication, e.g. using gestures, movements and proximity. For example, De Wit et al. [8] found higher level of engagement during learning activities when gestures were used. Also, Leite et al. [16] present an empathic model for CRI by utilizing, e.g. facial expressions on the robot. They found that it had a positive impact on long-term interaction with the robot. As Serholt et al. [20, p. 7] note, it is *"important for the future of CRI to consider what modes of communication come naturally to children."* This relates to our *RQ1C*.

2.2 Persuasive Design in Robot-Assisted Learning

Motivation plays a strong role in learning. The field of *Persuasive Design*, e.g. [17] utilizes many techniques to design technologies that can persuade and support motivation, e.g. by *goal setting, tracking performance, showing progress, adoption of a social role, supporting rehearsal, giving feedback* and *providing virtual rewards*. In addition, they can give *information and advice, remind,* and *utilize social support and competition* as motivational factors. According to research, robots can act as motivators in learning [7, 27]. *Persuasive Robots* mean social robots that are designed to change people's attitudes and/or behavior [4, 21]. Persuasive robotics is still mostly unexplored ground although some research has been conducted [4, 11, 19, 21]. Bertel [4] summarizes the possibilities of the social robots as persuaders through *alignment of appearance, behavior and tasks (personalization), emotional expressions, distinctive features of speech, gestures, positioning and posture (multimodal interaction)* and through *the perceived social role*. Leite et al. [16] present a list of guidelines for the design of social robots for long-term interaction. Their work suggests that the robot's *appearance* needs to fit its *purpose* – attention needs to be paid when selecting appropriate physical embodiment for the robot to be used with the children. The robot should be able to show *incremental novel behaviors* over time, also stated by Kanda et al. [14]; information about the user and their *affective state* needs to be used for the *adaptation* of the robot's behavior and expressing empathy, and the robot would need to remember the past actions with the user [16].

Robotic persuasion is multi-modal and thus, it might provide stronger persuasive effect than persuasion that uses less modalities. Physical embodiment provides benefits in tasks that require a relationship-oriented approach: physical embodiment increases the feeling of social presence and thus improves multimodal communication, perceived trust, pleasurable experiences, attractiveness and perception of how helpful the robot is [9]. Our *RQ2* extends the discussion around the Persuasive Design on the robot-assisted learning and CRI by addressing persuasion on social robots in the long-term naturalistic setup.

3   Methodology and Study Procedure

3.1   Participants

Three user groups participated in the study: the pupils of a 3rd grade class (9–10 years old, n = 20), language teachers (n = 3) and the parents (n = 18) of the participating pupils. The language teachers were between 41–50 years old, female, had at least ten years of teaching experience, and had no prior experience with robots. The parents were 70% female and half of the parents were 36–45 years old. Research ethics and data security were strictly considered in the study. Identification information was not collected of the children, all data were anonymized and observations were not linked to a specific child in any phase. The participation to the study was voluntary and the participants were able to end participation at any time. The permission to conduct the study at the school was obtained from the city's education and learning services and the school's rector. The consent for pupils' participation was obtained from their parents. The interaction and tasks between the pupils and the robot was defined by the teachers.

3.2   Data Collection

The 4-month user experience study was carried out in a Finnish primary school in September-December 2018. The data was collected with a multi-method approach including observations, online diary, online questionnaires and semi-structured interviews.

Observations. Four observation sessions, one each month, were conducted in the classroom context during 3rd grade English language classes. Each session lasted for two hours and was conducted with the same class. Two observers were present in the sessions and used a semi-structured observation sheet. The observations focused on interaction with the robot, tasks conducted with the robot, children's emotional reactions, atmosphere in the class, challenges in use, and the teacher's role in robot-assisted learning. Classroom observations took place under the supervision of a teacher.

Online Diaries. The teachers were instructed to fill in an online diary after each time they used the robot in teaching. The diary included nine questions. Six of them were close-ended and concerned the teaching context: taught language, teaching situation (classroom or small groups), grade of pupils, number of pupils using the robot, how many times the pupils had used the robot before, and duration of use. The rest of the questions were open-ended and dealt with the task(s) conducted, feelings and experiences, and challenges. In total, 49 diary responses were received from three teachers.

Online Questionnaires for Teachers. The teachers filled in two online questionnaires: the first one before the study began (in April 2018), focusing on their expectations towards using the robot in teaching. The second questionnaire was conducted in October 2018 with the focus on teachers' experiences of robot-assisted teaching related to e.g. children's motivation, ways to utilize the robot, and the challenges in use.

Online Questionnaire for Parents. Parents were invited to complete an online questionnaire during the latter half of the study period. The questions focused on e.g. things that children had said about the robot at home and how did they describe the learning with the robot. It also included questions that parents were instructed to ask from their children, such as their experiences with the robot.

Interviews with Teachers. Interviews were conducted for three teachers in the end of the usage period. The interviews lasted for 30–45 min and followed a semi-structured discussion guide that dealt with e.g. the teaching experiences with the robot, the perceived role of the robot in class and the challenges teachers had encountered with it.

3.3 Data Analysis

The Affinity Diagram technique [6] was used for the thematic analysis of the qualitative data collected from observations, interviews, and open-ended answers from online questionnaires and diaries. Observation notes were written by hand, and they were transcribed and coded after the session. The data were transferred as affinity notes including a single observation and the session code on each note. Open-ended answers from questionnaires and diaries were formulated into affinity notes with user codes. Interviews were audio recorded and transcribed verbatim, and affinity notes were formulated from the transcripts. The affinity diagram was built by two researchers. We focused on specific topics related to the research questions of this study, excluding themes that were out of scope. The final Affinity Diagram focusing on our research questions consisted of 7 main categories and 37 sub-categories. The quotes from participants have been translated from Finnish for this article. The name of the robot has been removed.

3.4 The Language Learning Robot and App

We used the language learning robot Elias (eliasrobot.com) on our research. It is a mobile app that, in our case, worked together with a 60-cm tall Nao (softbankrobotics.com), social humanoid robot (see Fig. 1). The Nao robot is capable of e.g. walking, talking, gesturing, playing audio files and face recognition. The learning content for the app has

Fig. 1. The language learning robot and the mobile app (eliasrobot.com).

been developed by an educational technology company and co-designed together with the language teachers.

At the time of the study, the robot was able to teach English, French and German, and it had two difficulty levels for English and one level for German and French. It included several learning themes, e.g. greetings, colors, foods and emotions. The basic structure of the robot-assisted lesson was the following. First task was to repeat vocabulary of the selected theme. The mobile app showed images about the selected theme, e.g. emotions, foods, numbers, or colors; the robot said the word aloud, and the child repeated it. This was done three times per each word. After that, the child was expected to remember the learned words. The mobile app showed the images and the child said the words aloud for the robot. The next step was the dialogue: the mobile app's images guided the dialogue between the child and the robot. The final phase was the free dialogue with the robot about the selected topic. During the learning session, the robot provided various rewarding gestures and movements, such as cheering, nodding, dancing and clapping, as well as verbal feedback for the performance.

4 Findings

4.1 Overall Learning and Teaching Experience

During the study, the robot was used in teaching in two primary settings: (1) with the whole class, or (2) with groups of 2–4 pupils who completed 5–15 min lessons with the robot in corridor while the rest of the class worked on other tasks in the classroom.

Positive Feelings and Motivation to Learn. The robot appeared to evoke positive feelings such as happiness and curiosity in pupils: *"It's nice, I like it, it's funny."* When learning with the robot, they laughed and smiled, encouraged each other and even the robot: *"Everything that the robot does, [the pupils] laugh and giggle. It's amazing."* (Teacher1). When the robot was used in a corridor outside the classroom, other pupils passing by looked at it and sometimes shouted its name eagerly or clapped their hands. The teacher who taught the observed class was excited and eager to use the robot in teaching: *"For me this has been really inspirational. After each lesson, I have the feeling that this is so great."* (Teacher1). Most pupils appeared enthusiastic and motivated to learn English with the robot and did the tasks that it asked them to do. Teachers appreciated the robot's ability to create **a relaxed and focused atmosphere** in the class: *"Pupils were able to concentrate surprisingly well, even the rascals."* (Teacher2). While most pupils appeared eager to interact with the robot when it was in the class, they patiently waited their turn. Over-excitement was only seldom observed: a few times the pupils in a small group started making fun of the robot's utterances after they had completed the lesson. However, while just the presence of the robot was enough to evoke enthusiasm in the initial use, over time the novelty wore off and the teacher had to plan more carefully how to use the robot in the actual teaching: *"If I haven't planned myself something to do with the robot, it's no longer a surprise element that it's here. Then it's my responsibility to have a lesson plan which utilizes the robot."* (Teacher1). Also the role of the relevant and varying learning content on the robot became much stronger after the initial excitement towards the robot itself slightly decreased. Although the strong excitement towards the robot mildly decreased, **the motivation to learn** with the robot remained high on the pupils throughout the study period – they were willing and motivated to study with it even in the end of the 4-month research period.

Negative Experiences. While negative experiences were rarely observed or reported, they are important to point out. Situations in which the robot did not work as expected occurred during the study, causing frustration in teachers because they felt that time was wasted, although technical problems did not bother pupils as much: *"Pupils still wait unusually patiently, even though the robot doesn't do what it's asked to do, and are delighted about the things it does."* (Teacher2). Still, frustration related to the robot's imperfect speech recognition was expressed also by some pupils: *"Sometimes it gets confused and you cannot talk to it or it doesn't listen"*. Two of the teachers felt their enthusiasm to use the robot in their own teaching was dampened by technical problems, although they were generally positive towards the robot. Disappointment, possible feeling of failure and loss of motivation were mentioned by two teachers when they described a situation in which pupils in the class spoke with the robot and got a response from it, except for one pupil who the robot ignored, i.e. its speech recognition did not work: *"One pupil was not understood and didn't want to come [to speak with the robot] after that. The child was crushed when [the robot] didn't understand."* (Teacher3). A couple of pupils also expressed wariness and hesitation when the robot was first introduced, and occasionally the robot's sudden movements frightened a child for a moment.

4.2 Tasks of the Robot and Teacher-Robot Collaboration

While the robot was originally intended primarily for language learning, **various other uses for it were invented at the school**. One of the teachers was especially active in engaging in various projects with the robot and pupils, e.g. writing and filming the story of the robot: *"There was writing, mother tongue, and television/media skills and coding. Well, there was also language when the writers also translated [the story] into English, so that it became bilingual."* (Teacher1). The robot also had a role in a school festival. Moreover, another teacher saw that the positive side of technical problems was that pupils got a learning experience of turn taking and that things do not always go according to plan. We observed that **teachers had a strong role in integrating the robot into teaching.** The robot was a new tool to the teachers and thus there were no ready-made practices or guidelines in how to integrate it into teaching. Creativity and flexibility were needed from the teachers to integrate the robot into lessons. Planning of a robot-assisted lesson required extra effort compared to a traditional lesson.

The robot was likewise new to the pupils and especially first uses of the robot required a lot of help from the teacher, who had to go back and forth between the classroom and the small group who was interacting with the robot. *"During the first lesson I was busy to be in the classroom and in the corridor. Differentiation [of teaching] was challenging. For the second lesson I got an instructor and it helped."* (Teacher1). Furthermore, help was not always available when the robot had technical problems such as stopping responding to commands. The teachers felt they lacked time to get deeply familiar with the robot and develop their own ways of using it in teaching. *"I think the school should have a tutor [to help with the robot]."* (Teacher1). During the study, we noticed that the best way to support the formation of robot-assisted teaching practices and manage the possible technical challenges is the **peer-support inside the school** – the most enthusiastic teachers could act as instructors. It would also be important to have some guidelines and scenarios about how to use the robot in teaching.

4.3 Roles of the Robot

The robot became a popular **"dude" or mascot of the school** with whom children liked to act in many ways and projects. Throughout the study period, the children were curious and interested about it and they considered it as motivational for learning. Children seemed to express **empathy and tenderness towards the robot**. They were petting, hugging and tickling it, and asked empathic questions from it. Even the oldest boys expressed caring behavior towards the robot and played with it. The robot seemed to have become everybody's friend and a positive character. We recognized two specific roles for the robot: encourager and learning companion.

Encourager. Two teachers pointed out that some shy and quiet children were encouraged by the robot to speak aloud: *"It's been great to see that the quietest pupil in the class can be the most proactive and enthusiastic when working with the robot."* (Teacher2). Some pupils also referred to this characteristic of a robot as something that motivates them to learn: *"The robot is kind-hearted and encouraging."* While the robot was generally perceived as a peer, even a friend, its encouraging and friendly characteristics appeared to give it a sense of authority so that pupils obeyed its suggestions and followed instructions most of the time.

Learning Companion. Many pupils experienced that the robot inspired them to learn because it was a fun learning companion and provided variety in teaching methods: *"[The robot] inspires because learning with it is different than with a teacher."* One pupil also stated that the robot is nice because it is cute and helps in studying. While learning outcomes were not assessed in this study, there were signs that at least some pupils felt they learned better with the robot: *"I remember words much better with the robot."*

4.4 Multimodal Interaction and Behavior of the Robot

Verbal Communication. Most pupils were approaching the robot and interacting with it naturally and bravely. Speech seemed to be the most natural interaction modality: *"Kids are very excited about the robot and brave to talk, and they want to talk to it."* (Teacher2). Children talked to it spontaneously. There were challenges in speech recognition, and the robot did not always understand what children were speaking. The pupils usually remained patient and tried to talk louder or closer to it, or raise its attention by shouting it by name. Speech recognition was more successful with older children.

Nonverbal Communication. Physical embodiment with gestures and movements seemed to make the robot to appear as a lively creature for the pupils. Pupils often greeted the robot, tried to take contact with it, looked it into eyes, liked to be close to it and touch it. The robot had several different kinds of gestures and movements, which made the interaction pervasive and interesting, and made learning a rewarding experience. Pupils imitated the gestures and movements of the robot, e.g. clap of hands, cheers and nods, and they were happy to receive a gestural reward after the learning task. For example, when the robot was nodding, one child commented *"It showed that I did it right."* Gaze contact with the robot was very important for children, and they were constantly seeking for it, e.g. by moving their face into very close distance to the face of the robot: *"Don't look up, look at me!"* They also made comments about whom the robot was looking at.

The robot had some **robotic ways of interaction**, too. Based on our observations, "the candy eyes", i.e. colorfully lighted eyes with a sound effect, acted as the robot's strongest rewarding element. Collecting "candy eyes" motivated pupils to repeat the words all over again and they started to compete about how many candy eyes each group got: *"Let's try to collect 25 candy eyes!"* We observed that the rewarding elements of the robot worked best when they were not presented too often. In this way, pupils waited for them to appear, and did not get bored on them. Entertaining movements, like dancing, cheering and dabbing, also acted as good rewarding elements as well as active breaks for the pupils. Some movements were designed to support learning directly, e.g. a song "head, shoulders, knees and toes" and movements while learning verbs. The movements of the robot were well noticed and remembered by the pupils.

We observed that the **robot's appearance and embodiment** were suitable for schoolchildren. Most children approached the robot without hesitance and seated themselves at a very close distance. When they talked to the robot, they set their face next to the face of it. They often wanted to touch and pet the robot, especially its head and hands, hold its hand and tickle it. One characteristic that made the robot seem more lively was its "own life" – due to occasional bugs and technical faults, the robot sometimes seemed to live its own life by making sudden, funny comments and reactions. For example, it could suddenly tell a joke in between the lesson: *"I like the unexpectedness of the robot, otherwise it would be boring."* (Teacher1).

5 Discussion and Conclusion

During our 4-month user experience study of the social and persuasive robot for learning, we observed that it became a well-known and **popular mascot in the school**. It adopted a positive role as **an encourager and learning companion** for the pupils. It was able to create positive **atmosphere** for learning in class, and pupils considered it as a **motivational** "dude". Pupils were willing to learn with the robot throughout the research period and did what it asked them to do. We consider the learning robot as an assistant for the teacher with its own strengths, with a lot of potential to be used in various ways at school and for **multiple projects**. It has power to motivate pupils, as other studies have also found [7, 27]. From the teachers' perspective, there is a need for support and models for taking the robot into classroom as a routine part of teaching. Scenarios and guidelines about the robot-assisted learning would be needed, as well as the models about how frequently and for what tasks the robot would be taken into. The most enthusiastic teachers, the forerunners, could act as peer-supporters.

Related to the interaction between the children and the robot, we observed many **persuasive and motivational principles** presented on the persuasive design models, e.g. on [17]. Next, we discuss the most striking aspects. **The physical embodiment and appearance** of the robot seemed to be well accepted and suitable for the children. It is no wonder that Nao is the most popular platform for robot-assisted learning [2]. The physical and lively robot itself acted as a very strong source of initial excitement and motivation. In general, children approached the robot very naturally. They stated it looked cute and they were willing to interact and learn with it by using several modalities (speech, gestures, gaze, movements and touch). Being close to it, seeking for its eye contact, talking to it and touching it happened spontaneously. Thus, **the physical presence** of the robot seemed to be an important factor in interaction and learning. As Deng et al. [9] discuss, physical embodiment is best suited for robots that act in social tasks. Due to its physical embodiment and liveliness, the robot adopted a clear **social role** in the school as a popular and friendly encourager and learning companion. The robot's ability to **"live its own life"** partly due to some bugs and technical flaws increased the perception of it having its own interesting personality and will. The role of the learning content inside the robot seemed to increase dramatically after the initial excitement about the robot itself slightly decreased. The relevancy of the learning tasks given by the robot and how the teacher integrated the robot to the teaching started to play a strong role then. There needs to be a lot of variation on the robot's learning content, and it needs to **evolve**. It would also be important to develop it to be able to adapt to pupils' levels and states, as also noted by e.g. Leite et al. [16]. In any case, the physical robot and its learning content together, when integrated efficiently to the teaching, seemed to support and motivate **rehearsal** and repetition, which are the main keys in language learning.

Robots have special "robot-like" ways for non-verbal communication, such as lights and sounds. **The robot-like rewarding** was one of the most striking persuasive element on the robot of our study. The "candy eyes" and special movements gained a lot of interest and excitement from the pupils and made the robot appear as a different kind of a character than the teacher – the robot had some different and special elements when compared to the human teacher. It appears possible to design strong rewarding elements on social robots to boost pupils' motivation to accomplish learning tasks. Especially candy eyes raised **competition** among pupils, which made them repeat the vocabulary endlessly. In future designs, we would like to emphasize the role of robot-like ways to persuade. This may also relate to ethics. Especially small children tend to perceive social robots as friends rather than tools, and create social bonds with them [14, 22]. It would be important for the children to understand that robots are just technological devices and not human-like creatures. That is why we would prefer to design more robot-like persuasive behaviors, rather than too human-like, for robots that interact with children.

We noticed also social persuasive principles on the interaction between children and the robot. The robot initiated **collaboration** – we noticed that the children were encouraging each other and even the robot itself when working in small teams. They were behaving well with the robot, and showed characteristics of empathy during the interaction. Even for the oldest boys it was socially acceptable to show empathy and play with the robot. Bertel [5] and Turkle [23] have made similar observations about the caring behavior towards the social robots. This potential to support learning of social skills could be further explored in future research.

Naturalistic long-term studies can reveal users' experiences that would remain unnoticed in one-time or short studies, and provide insight into contextual factors that cannot be investigated in the lab. Naturalistic studies are still quite rare in the field of human-robot interaction [9], giving much novelty value for our research. Our qualitative approach aims at understanding the phenomena on CRI that lasts for several months, and the user experiences of robot-assisted learning both from the pupils' and teachers' perspectives. Learning outcome was not in the focus of our study, but it is an important topic that is being studied by several other research projects. Our future work will focus on robot-specific ways of persuasion in CRI and the ethical aspects of robot-assisted learning and persuasion. We are also interested in exploring more about the possibilities of haptics as an interaction modality on CRI, as touching and being close to the robot was very natural for the children.

Acknowledgments. We express our warmest gratitude to all of our study participants, city of Tampere, Utelias Technologies Oy and Elias the robot.

References

1. Bartneck, C., Forlizzi, J.: A design-centred framework for social human-robot interaction. In: 13th IEEE International Workshop on Robot and Human Interactive Communication 2004, pp. 591–594. IEEE (2004)
2. Belpaeme, T., Kennedy, J., Ramachandran, A., Scassellati, B., Tanaka, F.: Social robots for education: a review. Sci. Robot. **3**(21), eaat5954 (2018)
3. Belpaeme, T., et al.: Guidelines for designing social robots as second language tutors. Int. J. Soc. Robot. **10**(3), 325–341 (2018)
4. Bertel, L.B.: PEERS: Persuasive Educational and Entertainment Robotics: a design-based research approach to social robots in teaching and learning. Doctoral dissertation, Aalborg Universitetsforlag (2016)
5. Bertel, L.B., Hannibal, G.: Tema 2: the NAO robot as a Persuasive Educational and Entertainment Robot (PEER)–a case study on children's articulation, categorization and interaction with a social robot for learning. Tidsskriftet Læring og Medier (LOM) **8**(14), 1–22 (2016)
6. Beyer, H., Holtzblatt, K.: Contextual Design: Defining Customer-Centered Systems. Elsevier, Amsterdam (1997)
7. Conti, D., Carla, C., Di Nuovo, S.: "Robot, tell me a tale!": a social robot as tool for teachers in kindergarten. Interact. Stud. **20**(2), 1–16 (2019)
8. de Wit, J., et al.: The effect of a robot's gestures and adaptive tutoring on children's acquisition of second language vocabularies. In: Proceedings of the 2018 International Conference on Human-Robot Interaction, pp. 50–58. ACM (2018)
9. Deng, E., Mutlu, B., Matarić, M.J.: Embodiment in socially interactive robots. Found. Trends® Robot. **7**(4), 251–356 (2019)
10. Gockley, R., et al.: Designing robots for long-term social interaction. In: 2005 IEEE/RSJ International Conference on Intelligent Robots and Systems, pp. 1338–1343 (2005)

11. Ham, J., Bokhorst, R., Cuijpers, R., van der Pol, D., Cabibihan, J.-J.: Making robots persuasive: the influence of combining persuasive strategies (gazing and gestures) by a storytelling robot on its persuasive power. In: Mutlu, B., Bartneck, C., Ham, J., Evers, V., Kanda, T. (eds.) ICSR 2011. LNCS (LNAI), vol. 7072, pp. 71–83. Springer, Heidelberg (2011). https://doi.org/10. 1007/978-3-642-25504-5_8

12. Han, J.: Robot-aided learning and r-learning services. In: Chugo, D. (ed.) Human-Robot Interaction. IntechOpen, London (2010)

13. Kanda, T., Hirano, T., Eaton, D., Ishiguro, H.: Interactive robots as social partners and peer tutors for children: a field trial. Hum. Comput. Interact. **19**(1–2), 61–84 (2004)

14. Kanda, T., Sato, R., Saiwaki, N., Ishiguro, H.: A two-month field trial in an elementary school for long-term human–robot interaction. IEEE Trans. Robot. **23**(5), 962–971 (2007)

15. Kennedy, J., et al.: Child speech recognition in human-robot interaction: evaluations and recommendations. In: Proceedings of the 2017 ACM/IEEE International Conference on Human-Robot Interaction, pp. 82–90 (2017)

16. Leite, I., Castellano, G., Pereira, A., Martinho, C., Paiva, A.: Empathic robots for long-term interaction. Int. J. Soc. Robot. **6**(3), 329–341 (2014)

17. Oinas-Kukkonen, H., Harjumaa, M.: Persuasive systems design: key issues, process model, and system features. Commun. Assoc. Inf. Syst. **24**(1), 28 (2009)

18. Ramachandran, A., Huang, C.M., Scassellati, B.: Toward effective robot–child tutoring: internal motivation, behavioral intervention, and learning outcomes. ACM Trans. Interact. Intell. Syst. (TiiS) **9**(1), 2 (2019)

19. Saunderson, S., Nejat, G.: It would make me happy if you used my guess: comparing robot persuasive strategies in social human-robot interaction. IEEE Robot. Autom. Lett. **4**(2), 1707–1714 (2019)

20. Serholt, S., Barendregt, W.: Robots tutoring children: longitudinal evaluation of social engagement in child-robot interaction. In: Proceedings of the 9th Nordic Conference on Human-Computer Interaction, p. 64. ACM (2016)

21. Siegel, M., Breazeal, C., Norton, M.I.: Persuasive robotics: the influence of robot gender on human behavior. In: 2009 IEEE/RSJ International Conference on Intelligent Robots and Systems, pp. 2563–2568. IEEE (2009)

22. Tanaka, F., Isshiki, K., Takahashi, F., Uekusa, M., Sei, R., Hayashi, K.: Pepper learns together with children: development of an educational application. In 2015 IEEE-RAS 15th International Conference on Humanoid Robots (Humanoids), pp. 270–275 (2015)

23. Turkle, S.: A nascent robotics culture: new complicities for companionship. American Association for Artificial Intelligence Technical Report Series AAAI (2006)

24. van den Berghe, R., Verhagen, J., Oudgenoeg-Paz, O., van der Ven, S., Leseman, P.: Social robots for language learning: a review. Rev. Educ. Res. **89**(2), 259–295 (2019)

25. Vogt, P., et al.: Second language tutoring using social robots: a large-scale study. In 14th ACM/IEEE International Conference on Human-Robot Interaction (HRI), pp. 497–505. IEEE (2019)

26. Westlund, J.K., Breazeal, C.: The interplay of robot language level with children's language learning during storytelling. In: Tenth annual ACM/IEEE International Conference on Human-Robot Interaction Extended Abstracts, pp. 65–66. ACM (2015)

27. Zaga, C., Lohse, M., Truong, Khiet P., Evers, V.: The effect of a robot's social character on children's task engagement: peer versus tutor. ICSR 2015. LNCS (LNAI), vol. 9388, pp. 704–713. Springer, Cham (2015). https://doi.org/10.1007/978-3-319-25554-5_70

(Expressive) Social Robot or Tablet? – On the Benefits of Embodiment and Non-verbal Expressivity of the Interface for a Smart Environment

Andrea Deublein$^{(\boxtimes)}$ and Birgit Lugrin$^{(\boxtimes)}$

Human-Computer Interaction, University of Würzburg, Würzburg, Germany
andrea.deublein@gmail.com, birgit.lugrin@uni-wuerzburg.de

Abstract. Smart home systems increasingly find their way into private households and efforts are being made to integrate lifelike user interfaces (e.g. social robots) to facilitate the interaction with the smart environment. Considering this, the question arises which benefits such embodied user interfaces offer compared to conventional devices. We are presenting a user study within a smart office setting in which 84 participants were either interrupted by a tablet, a non-expressive social robot, or an expressive social robot by being asked to perform tasks regarding their physical well-being. Results show that each type of user interface bears different advantages. While the tablet comes with a significantly higher usability and a lower level of perceived workload, both versions of the social robot outperform the tablet in terms of social perception and the overall evaluation of the interaction. Overall, the results provide valuable insights informing designers of smart environments which device to choose to enhance certain aspects of the quality of interaction.

Keywords: Human-robot interaction · Smart environment · Smart home · User interface · Embodiment · Expressivity · Well-being

1 Introduction

In today's society, many technical developments are about to become part of our everyday life. Not only should such systems be integrated into our homes and support us in accomplishing tasks (e.g. by mowing the garden), but also actively contribute to our well-being (e.g. by suggesting useful activities for us). Particularly embodied, expressive devices seem suitable to support and persuade us in a natural manner. However, to date, it is not clear to what extend the embodiment and non-verbal expressivity of such life-like systems impact user perception when they are actually implemented as the interface within a smart home.

In this contribution, we investigate how the choice of interaction device in a smart environment affects the overall interaction quality. Thereby, we look into

© Springer Nature Switzerland AG 2020
S. B. Gram-Hansen et al. (Eds.): PERSUASIVE 2020, LNCS 12064, pp. 85–97, 2020.
https://doi.org/10.1007/978-3-030-45712-9_7

different dimensions of user perception: on the one hand, we examine possible negative effects of the interruptions prompted by the respective smart environment's interface, on the other hand, we aim to gain insights into the potential benefits of an (expressive) social robot in that domain.

In the following subsections, we introduce the key concepts necessary for our endeavour.

1.1 (Embodied) User Interfaces in Smart Environments

Smart environments are getting more and more popular. Currently, interaction with and control of the smart environment is mainly done via interfaces on smartphones or tablet computers, e.g. [13].

The application of social robots in smart environments has gained increasing attention recently. In general, social robots are designed to provide a natural and intuitive interface that facilitates communication by verbal and non-verbal channels. Research in the field of social robotics postulates that the physical embodiment of devices bears great advantages such as enhancing social presence or engaging in physical tasks [5].

To investigate which channels are actually used to communicate in smart environments, Holthaus et al. [19] provided a multi-modal corpus that was recorded in a smart environment (including a social robot), in which participants had to solve certain tasks to explore intuitive forms of interaction. Work that has investigated social robots in smart offices addresses how the acceptance of such robots can be increased [26] or highlights the importance of integrating the user into the process of designing the robot [31].

A task frequently reported on for social robots in the home environment (mainly in the domain of elderly care) is to provide reminders, to deliver messages, or to give suggestions for personal well-being, e.g. [2,10,15,17,28].

1.2 Emotional and Social Expressivity

Emotional display seems to be a key factor for social robots - especially the importance of communicating the affective state of a social robot through facial expressions, gaze, and affective speech has been highlighted [6]. An expressive robot has been shown to outperform the same robot which does not provide emotional display, e.g. in the domains of storytelling [32] or gaming [22].

Examining the persuasive power of a social robot in a home setting in relation to its level of agency, Midden and Ham [25] found that the social behaviour of a robot had a positive impact on people's own behaviour compared to an energy meter. However, different levels of agency did not have an effect.

Only few studies have directly compared the interaction with a social robot to more traditional devices. So far, it has been shown that people interacting with a social robot experience more joy and build a closer relationship to the user interface than during the interaction with a desktop computer [21]. This is supported by another study, in which a social robot was evaluated to be more pleasureable and significantly more usable (less complex and easier to learn) than a tablet [16]. However, these findings are contradicted by Luria et al. [23] according to whom traditional user interfaces (e.g. smartphones) are classified as significantly more usable than a social robot.

1.3 Interruptions for Behaviour Change

It is considered a social norm not to interrupt a person while they are concentrating on something, unless sufficiently important arguments would justify it [3]. One reason behind this is that, especially in today's performance-oriented society, an interruption also means distraction, which consequently might lead to reduced productivity [24,29]. Given this, however, it seems even more desirable to have systems that interrupt our busy everyday life and help us stay healthy, e.g. by suggesting well-being tasks.

Research has mainly focused on the timing when a system should interrupt a person. Bailey et al. [3] showed that particularly the cognitive workload at the moment of the potential interruption is decisive [1]. In a smart office environment, these indicators for a reasonable time of user interruption have been shown: the activity of the user, the number and activity of other persons present, as well as environmental information such as the current time, or whether the office door is closed [20].

The authors [3] also summarized negative consequences of interruptions by an interface: (1) An interrupted task is executed more slowly than a uninterrupted one; (2) an interrupted task is subjectively perceived as more difficult; (3) a person experiences more distress if their primary task is disturbed by a peripheral one.

We are not aware of work that investigated whether the type of device that triggers the interruption has an effect on the perceived workload of the task or on the person's overall experience.

1.4 Contribution

Considering that social robots are increasingly emerging as smart home interfaces and are expected to positively impact the interaction with [5] and the persuasive power of [14] the system, the question arises to what extend their embodiment and non-verbal expressivity actually add value compared to conventional devices.

The present contribution gives first indications on how the choice of interaction device in a smart environment as well as differences in its emotional display affect various dimensions such as usability, social perception, perceived workload, overall suitability, and quality of interaction.

2   Experimental Setup of the Smart Office Environment

To investigate the benefits of the embodiment and expressivity of a user interface for a smart environment, we created a realistic setup of a smart office within one of our offices at the University of Würzburg. It contained i.a. two desks separated by a wall - one dedicated to the experimenter, the other to the participant.

2.1 Implementation of the User Interfaces' Behaviour

We used three interfaces for our study, which differed in the following modalities:

1. **Tablet**: No anthropomorphic embodiment, no emotional expressivity.
2. **Neutral Social Robot**: Anthropomorphic embodiment, no emotional expressivity.
3. **Emotional Social Robot**: Anthropomorphic embodiment and emotional expressivity.

The tablet condition was meant to reflect the current situation of controlling a smart home. For the present study, we chose an Apple iPad mini (7.9 in. display) and its integrated iMessage service. Incoming text messages were indicated by a preset tone. For the two social robot conditions, we chose the expressive social robot Reeti[1]. The Reeti robot is 44 cm tall and has 14 degrees of freedom in its head and neck area. For speech output, the text-to-speech function was used. The robot's behaviour was modeled by using the Visual SceneMaker [12].

Exactly the same wording was used across all three conditions, but was communicated differently: While the tablet simply displayed textual messages on its screen, the neutral social robot spoke the respective words via the integrated text-to-speech system while moving its lips. The expressive social robot additionally showed several non-verbal expressions (e.g. smile, wink, head tilt) accompanying its verbal behaviour.

Fig. 1. Recreated scene of a participant interacting with the social robot.

Figure 1 shows an exemplary interaction with the Reeti robot. For the participants, it seemed as if they were interacting directly with an autonomous smart home system. However, the clues were initiated by the experimenter in a *Wizard of Oz* setting.

2.2 Office Work and Physical Well-Being Tasks

In smart environments, hints are usually given while users are doing other activities. Therefore, we kept participants busy during the session with a repetitive task we stated to be important for our research. This so-called "Emotional Tagging" consisted of five fairy tales, which should be prepared using a coding template for a voice actor. Printed on paper, participants should mark which feelings they connected to the respective text passage (e.g., "anxious," "interested," "scared"). It was explained that the goal of the emotional tagging was not to complete all of the fairy tales, but a conscientious approach within the time available.

---

[1] Reeti robot: http://www.robopec.com/en/products/reeti-robopec/.

To improve the physical well-being in such routines, the smart home system asked participants to perform tasks during their work. These tasks were based on findings of the German Federal Institute for Occupational Safety and Health [33]. In particular, the system asked to improve their posture and relax their muscles (task 1), to drink some water (task 2), and to walk a few steps (task 3). A side table with a glass of water on top was added to the office environment and sufficient space for movements was assured. An overview of the test room is shown in Fig. 2.

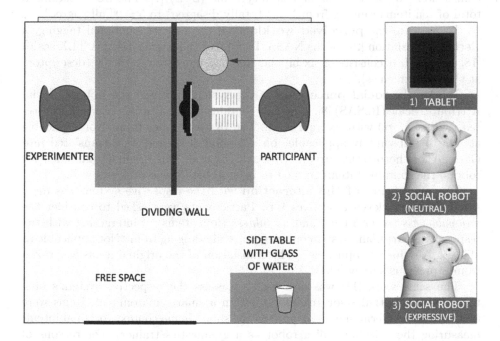

Fig. 2. Experimental setup

3 User Study

A user study with a 1×3 between-subjects design was carried out to compare the three conditions. Our key question was whether the embodiment and non-verbal expressivity of the central smart home user interface does add value. As shown in Sect. 1, science is still divided over the examined interfaces' benefits. Though we expect differences in one direction or another, it is impossible to make concrete hypotheses. We therefore pose the following research questions:

RQ1: Do the three user interfaces differ in terms of usability?
RQ2: Do the three user interfaces differ in terms of perceived workload?
RQ3: Do the three user interfaces differ in terms of their social perception?

RQ4: Do the three user interfaces differ in terms of the evaluation of the interaction with the respective system?

RQ5: Do the three user interfaces differ in terms of assessed suitability as central user interface within a smart environment?

3.1 Questionnaires

The **usability** of the respective user interface was measured with a German translation [30] of the System Usability Scale (SUS) [7]. The SUS contains a total of ten items ranging from 1 = "Totally disagree" to 5 = "Fully agree".

To measure the **perceived workload** of the task of emotional tagging, a German translation [27] of the NASA Task Load Index scale (NASA TLX scale) [18] was used. It consists of six bipolar items ranging from 0 to 100 (descriptors at the two extremes).

To rate the **social perception** of the system, we used the Robotic Social Attributes Scale (RoSAS) [8]. The scale contains three subscales (*warmth, competence, discomfort*) with six items each. The 18 items range from "Not applicable at all" to "Absolutely applicable" on a 5-point scale and were translated into German for the present survey. Although the scale was originally intended for robots, the contained items seemed to be suitable for the tablet as well.

The **evaluation of the interaction** with the respective system was measured by using eleven adjectives [11]. Participants were asked to consider the *enjoyableness* (seven items) and *usefulness* (four items) of interacting with the respective smart home system on a 5-point scale ranging from "Not applicable at all" to "Absolutely applicable". The translation of the original items was taken from a previous survey [9].

The same work [11] was also used to assess the respective system's **suitability as central user interface** within a smart environment. Items were translated into German and adapted to the smart home context (original intent: measuring the suitability of a robot as a gymnastics trainer). For reasons of consistency, a 5-point scale was used ("Completely disagree" to "Fully agree").

In the end, the participants had to give an indication of their technical affinity and the regularity of their usage of smart home systems. Depending on the condition, the regularity of using tablet computers (condition 1) respectively social robots in general and Reeti in particular (conditions 2 and 3) was queried as well. In a final socio-demographic questionnaire, participants were asked about their gender, age, highest education, and their major subject of study.

3.2 Procedure

The Participants were greeted by the experimenter, randomly assigned to one of the three conditions, and introduced to the task of emotional tagging. They were also informed that a smart home system was installed in the room, which would guide them through the experiment as well as pay attention to their physical well-being. Participants were asked to follow the system's instructions, which ensured that all of them went through the same tasks. Each session lasted approximately 30 min and consisted of the following steps:

Part 1 (about 15 min): Interaction with the smart office (performing the well-being tasks) while working on the task of emotional tagging.
Part 2 (10–15 min): Questionnaires (usability, perceived workload, social perception, evaluation of the interaction, suitability as central user interface, socio-demographics).

3.3 Participants

A total of $N = 84$ participants took part in the study. All of them were students in their Bachelor studies in the fields of Media Communication ($n = 68$; 81.0%) and Human Computer Interaction ($n = 16$; 19.0%) and recruited via an internal pool of participants. However, the experimenter did not know them in advance. Participants were $M = 21.25$ years old ($SD = 1.93$), $n = 20$ (23.8%) were male and $n = 64$ (76.2%) female. The majority stated to feel above average in dealing with computer technology ($n(\text{"pretty save"}) = 41$; 48.8% and $n(\text{"very save"}) = 17$; 20.2%). Despite this high level of technological affinity, hardly anyone had experience with smart home systems: 88.1% ($n = 74$) of the participants interacted with a smart home system for the first time in the present study. The participants distributed evenly over the three experimental conditions ($n = 28$ per condition) and the experimental groups did not differ statistically in terms of the demographic variables collected.

4 Results

All mean values and standard deviations of the experimental groups are illustrated in Fig. 3.

We used one-factorial variance analyses (ANOVAs) for independent samples to explore our research questions. For all analyses the Type I error rate was set to .05. A level of $p < .01$ is seen as highly significant, $p < .001$ as most significant, and a level of $p < .1$ as marginally significant (c.f. [4] for fields of studies that are hitherto little researched).

Regarding the systems' **usability** (RQ1), significant differences were found between the conditions ($F(2, 47.51) = 4.78$, $p < .05$, $\eta^2 = .08$). In detail, a significant difference was found between the tablet and the neutral social robot ($p < .05$ (.25, 95%-CI[.01, .49])) as well as a marginally significant difference between the tablet and the expressive social robot ($p < .1$ (.18, 95%-CI[−.02, .18])). This indicates the tablet having the highest usability, followed by the expressive social robot.

In terms of **perceived workload** (RQ2), results can be regarded as marginally significant ($F(2, 81) = 3.09$, $p < .1$, $\eta^2 = .07$). In particular, the difference was found between the tablet and the expressive social robot ($p < .1$ (−6.33, 95%-CI[−12.81, .14])). Thus, participants felt more stressed by the task when interacting with the expressive social robot than when interacting with the tablet.

With regard to the systems' attributed **social perception** (RQ3), we found most significant differences between the conditions ($F(2,\ 81) = 9.66$, $p < .001$, $\eta^2 = .19$). In detail, the tablet differs from both social robot conditions: While the difference between tablet and expressive social robot is highly significant ($p < .01(-.36,\ 95\%\text{-CI}[-.60,\ -.12])$), the difference between tablet and neutral social robot is considered as most significant ($p < .001\ (-.40,\ 95\%\text{-CI}[-.64,\ -.16])$). Thus, the neutral social robot was attributed the highest social characteristics, the tablet the lowest ones. The subscales give additional insights: On the subscale *warmth*, we found a most significant difference ($F(2,\ 81) = 23.07$, $p < .001$, $\eta^2 = .36$) between the conditions tablet and neutral social robot ($p < .001$ [4] $(-1.06,\ 95\%\text{-CI}[-1.52,\ .60])$) as well as between tablet and expressive social robot ($p < .001\ (-1.18,\ 95\%\text{-CI}[-1.64,\ .73])$). The subscale *discomfort* reveals a highly significant difference ($F(2,\ 81) = 4.65$, $p < .05$, $\eta^2 = .10$) between the

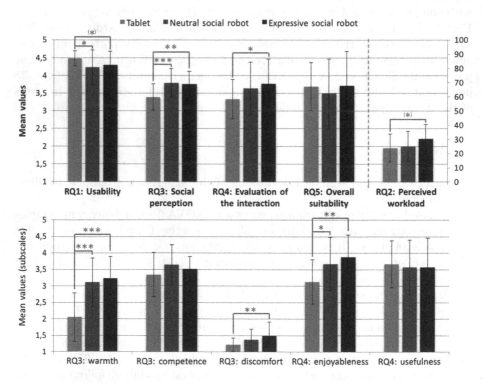

Fig. 3. Mean values and standard deviations for RQ1–5. Significance levels: * = p < .05; ** = p < .01; *** = p < .001; (*) = p < .10.

Note: Main results are illustrated in the upper diagram, subscales' results in the bottom one. The scale of RQ2 (0–100) differs from the others (1–5) and is thus to be read on the right hand side secondary axis.

tablet and the expressive social robot ($p < .01$ (.27, 95%-CI[.06, .48])). In terms of the subscale *competence*, however, no significant differences could be found between the conditions ($F(2, 50.85) = 1.55$, $p = .22$).

The participants' **evaluation of the interaction** (RQ4) revealed a significant difference between the conditions ($F(2, 81) = 3.18$, $p < .05$, $\eta^2 = .07$). In particular, significant differences were found between the tablet and expressive social robot ($p < .05$ ($-.44$, 95%-CI[$-.86$, $-.01$])). Participants interacting with the latter found the interaction to be significantly more positive than those who had been assigned the tablet condition. A closer look at the subscales provides further details: The subscale *enjoyableness of interaction* shows highly significant differences between the conditions ($F(2, 81) = 8.03$, $p < .01$, $\eta^2 = .17$). Again, the tablet differs from both social robot conditions. In this case, however, the tablet was rated significantly worse than the neutral social robot ($p < .05$ ($-.54$, 95%-CI[-1.00, $-.08$]), the difference to the expressive social robot is even highly significant ($p < .01$ ($-.74$, 955%-CI[-1.20, $-.29$])). Regarding the subscale *usefulness of interaction*, we could not observe significant differences between the conditions ($F(2, 81) = .14$, $p = .87$).

In terms of the systems' overall **suitability as central user interface** (RQ5), no significant differences between the conditions were observed either ($F(2, 81) = .53$, $p = .59$). Accordingly, it must be assumed that the embodiment and non-verbal expressivity of the user interface had no effect on the systems' perceived suitability as the central smart home user interface.

5 Discussion

With regard to RQ1, it first should be noted that all groups' mean values are in the upper 20% of the scale. This implies that the **usability** of all conditions was classified as overall positive. The fact that the tablet shows a higher usability than both social robot conditions is in line with the results of Luria et al. [23], according to which accustomed devices are classified as more usable than those with which users have had little contact. Interestingly, the usability of the tablet differs significantly from that of the neutral social robot, but only marginally from that of the expressive social robot. Therefore, although no explicit benefit of expressive behaviour could be proven, the implemented expressivity of the social robot seems to have had a positive effect on the perceived usability.

The results of RQ2 show that the interruptions by the expressive social robot caused a higher **perceived workload** than those by the tablet. The workload in the neutral social robot condition does not differ significantly from any of the other two groups, but is closer to the values of the tablet condition. This suggests that the higher perceived workload was not provoked by the social robot itself, but by the additional movements of the expressive version. However, the average perceived workload was very low across all conditions.

According to our findings regarding RQ3, the **social perception** of the social robot in the two respective conditions is rated significantly higher than that of the tablet. In detail, the tablet differs highly significantly from the expressive social robot and, surprisingly, even most significantly from the neutral one.

This contradicts earlier findings (c.f. Sect. 1.3), according to which the expressive social robot should outperform the neutral one in this regard. A possible explanation can be found in the subscale *discomfort*: While the tablet reaches the best value here, the expressive social robot is classified as highly significantly more uncomfortable, while the neutral one does not differ significantly. Presumably, the additional movements of the robot were perceived as distracting.

With regard to the **evaluation of the interaction** (RQ4), the expressive social robot performs significantly better than the tablet, while the neutral social robot does not differ significantly from the other two conditions. In particular, the subscale *enjoyableness of interaction* shows that the interaction with the tablet was perceived as less joyful than the ones with the neutral (significant difference) and the expressive social robot (highly significant difference). This result supports previous findings [21,23]. On the subscale *usefulness of interaction*, none of the interfaces differs significantly from the others. However, it must be noted that for all devices the perceived usefulness of interaction is very low. This could be due to the artificial setting and the quite frequent interruptions necessary for the study.

The results of RQ5 show no significant differences in the three interfaces' **suitability as central user interface**. This can be explained by the findings from RQ 1–4, where each condition proved individual advantages. Accordingly, most of the aspects queried in RQ5 are relatively identical across the experimental groups. Nevertheless, it should be noted that all mean values of the ascribed suitability are in the upper half of the scale, indicating that every system examined was rated as suitable overall. Given the proven benefits of the expressive social robot, it is desirable to further improve its expressive behaviour in order to reach its full potential as central user interface. By doing so, current weaknesses could be transformed into future strengths.

6 Conclusion

In this contribution, we explored whether a social robot (with or without nonverbal expressivity) as the interface of a smart office is beneficial compared to the more common interface of a tablet computer. During a laboratory user study, we measured user ratings of the systems' usability, social perception, suitability as central user interface, as well as participants' perceived workload and evaluation of the interaction with the system. Our results indicate that none of the experimental conditions was generally perceived superior to the others. Rather, each interface revealed advantages on different dimensions. In terms of usability and perceived workload, the tablet performed best. With regard to social perception and overall evaluation of the interaction, both robot version (neutral and expressive) outperformed the tablet. Although the expressive social robot performed slightly better than the neutral one, hardly any significant differences were found between the two robot conditions.

While much more research is needed to define clear guidelines for interface designers of smart environments, the present study is, nevertheless, a first step to highlight the potential benefits of different devices by directly comparing them on several dimensions. As a next step, the persuasive power of different implementations needs to be investigated.

References

1. Adamczyk, P.D., Iqbal, S.T., Bailey, B.P.: A method, system, and tools for intelligent interruption management. In: Proceedings of the 4th International Workshop on Task Models and Diagrams, pp. 123–126 (2005)
2. Ahn, B.K., Ahn, H.S., Sutherland, C., Lim, J., MacDonald, B.: Development and evaluation for human-care scenario using social robots. In: Proceedings of HRI 2018 Workshop on Social Human-Robot Interaction of Human-Care Service Robots (2018)
3. Bailey, B.P., Konstan, J.A., Carlis, J.V.: The effects of interruptions on task performance, annoyance, and anxiety in the user interface. Interact 1, 593–601 (2001)
4. Bortz, J.: Statistik für Human- und Sozialwissenschaftler, 6th edn. Springer, Heidelberg (2005). https://doi.org/10.1007/b137571
5. Breazeal, C., Dautenhahn, K., Kanda, T.: Social robotics. In: Siciliano, B., Khatib, O. (eds.) Springer Handbook of Robotics, pp. 1935–1972. Springer, Cham (2016). https://doi.org/10.1007/978-3-319-32552-1_72
6. Breazeal, C.: Emotion and sociable humanoid robots. Int. J. Hum. Comput. Stud. 59(1-2), 119–155 (2003)
7. Brooke, J.: SUS - a quick and dirty usability scale. Usability Eval. Ind. 189(194), 4–7 (1996)
8. Carpinella, C.M., Wyman, A.B., Perez, M.A., Stroessner, S.J.: The robotic social attributes scale (RoSAS) development and validation. In: Proceedings of the 2017 ACM/IEEE International Conference on Human-Robot Interaction, pp. 254–262 (2017)
9. Deublein, A., Pfeifer, A., Merbach, K., Bruckner, K., Mengelkamp, C., Lugrin, B.: Scaffolding of motivation in learning using a social robot. Comput. Educ. 125, 182–190 (2018)
10. Elinas, P., Hoey, J., Little, J.J.: HOMER: human oriented messenger robot. In: AAAI Spring Symposium on Human Interaction with Autonomous Systems in Complex Environments, pp. 45–51 (2003)
11. Fasola, J., Matarić, M.J.: Using socially assistive human-robot interaction to motivate physical exercise for older adults. Proc. IEEE 100, 2512–2526 (2012)
12. Gebhard, P., Mehlmann, G., Kipp, M.: Visual SceneMaker - a tool for authoring interactive virtual characters. J. Multimodal Interfaces 6(1), 3–11 (2012)
13. Gentner, A., Wagner, G.: Licht ins Dunkel - Erfolgsfaktoren für das Smart Home. Deloitte & Touche GmbH (2013)
14. Ghazali, A.S., Ham, J., Barakova, E., Markopoulos, P.: Persuasive Robots Acceptance Model (PRAM): roles of social responses within the acceptance model of persuasive robots. Int. J. Soc. Robot., 1–18 (2020). https://doi.org/10.1007/s12369-019-00611-1
15. Gross, H.M., et al.: Progress in developing a socially assistive mobile home robot companion for the elderly with mild cognitive impairment. In: 2011 IEEE/RSJ International Conference on Intelligent Robots and Systems, pp. 2430–2437. IEEE (2011)

16. Hammer, S., Kirchner, K., André, E., Lugrin, B.: Touch or talk?: comparing social robots and tablet pcs for an elderly assistant recommender system. In: Proceedings of the Companion of the 2017 ACM/IEEE International Conference on Human-Robot Interaction, pp. 129–130 (2017)
17. Hammer, S., Lugrin, B., Bogomolov, S., Janowski, K., André, E.: Investigating politeness strategies and their persuasiveness for a robotic elderly assistant. In: Meschtscherjakov, A., De Ruyter, B., Fuchsberger, V., Murer, M., Tscheligi, M. (eds.) PERSUASIVE 2016. LNCS, vol. 9638, pp. 315–326. Springer, Cham (2016). https://doi.org/10.1007/978-3-319-31510-2_27
18. Hart, S.G., Staveland, L.E.: Development of NASA-TLX (Task Load Index): results of empirical and theoretical research. Adv. Psychol. **52**, 139–183 (1988)
19. Holthaus, P., et al.: How to address smart homes with a social robot? A multi-modal corpus of user interactions with an intelligent environment. In: Proceedings of the 10th International Conference on Language Resources and Evaluation (LREC 2016), pp. 3440–3446 (2016)
20. Hudson, S., et al.: Predicting human interruptibility with sensors: a Wizard of Oz feasibility study. In: Proceedings of the SIGCHI Conference on Human Factors in Computing Systems, pp. 257–264 (2003)
21. Kidd, C.D., Breazeal, C.: Robots at home: understanding long-term human-robot interaction. In: 2008 IEEE/RSJ International Conference on Intelligent Robots and Systems, pp. 3230–3235. IEEE (2008)
22. Leite, I., Pereira, A., Martinho, C., Paiva, A.: Are emotional robots more fun to play with? In: RO-MAN 2008 - The 17th IEEE International Symposium on Robot and Human Interactive Communication, pp. 77–82. IEEE (2008)
23. Luria, M., Hoffman, G., Zuckerman, O.: Comparing social robot, screen and voice interfaces for smart-home control. In: Proceedings of the 2017 CHI Conference on Human Factors in Computing Systems, pp. 580–628 (2017)
24. Mark, G., Gonzalez, V.M., Harris, J.: No task left behind? Examining the nature of fragmented work. In: Proceedings of the SIGCHI Conference on Human Factors in Computing Systems, pp. 321–330 (2005)
25. Midden, C., Ham, J.: The illusion of agency: the influence of the agency of an artificial agent on its persuasive power. In: Bang, M., Ragnemalm, E.L. (eds.) PERSUASIVE 2012. LNCS, vol. 7284, pp. 90–99. Springer, Heidelberg (2012). https://doi.org/10.1007/978-3-642-31037-9_8
26. Mitsunaga, N., Miyashita, Z., Shinozawa, K., Miyashita, T., Ishiguro, H., Hagita, N.: What makes people accept a robot in a social environment? Discussion from six-week study in an office. In: 2008 IEEE/RSJ International Conference on Intelligent Robots and Systems, pp. 3336–3343. IEEE (2008)
27. Pfendler, C., Widdel, H.: Gedächtnisleistung und Beanspruchung beim Wiedererkennen von farbigen und schwarzen Reizmustern auf elektronischen Anzeigen. FAT Bericht **81** (1988)
28. Pollack, M.E., et al.: Pearl: A mobile robotic assistant for the elderly (2002)
29. Renaud, K., Ramsay, J., Hair, M.: "You've got e-mail!" ... shall i deal with it now? Electronic mail from the recipient's perspective. Int. J. Hum. Comput. Interact. **21**(3), 313–332 (2006)
30. Ruegenhagen, E., Rummel, B.: Fragebogen zur System-Gebrauchstauglichkeit (2013)
31. Severinson-Eklundh, K., Green, A., Hüttenrauch, H., Oestreicher, L., Norman, M.: Involving users in the design of a mobile office robot. IEEE Trans. Syst. Man Cybern. Part C (Appl. Rev.) **34**, 113–124 (2004)

32. Striepe, H., Lugrin, B.: There once was a robot storyteller: measuring the effects of emotion and non-verbal behaviour. In: Kheddar, A., et al. (eds.) ICSR 2017. LNCS, vol. 10652, pp. 126–136. Springer, Cham (2017). https://doi.org/10.1007/978-3-319-70022-9_13

33. Windel, A.: Auf und nieder - immer wieder! Mehr Gesundheit im Büro durch Sitz-Steh-Dynamik. Technical report, Bundesanstalt für Arbeitsschutz und Arbeitsmedizin (BAuA) (2013)

Persuasive Technologies for Health and Wellbeing

Persuasive Feedback for Fitness Apps: Effects of Construal Level and Communication Style

Jasmin Niess[1]([✉]) [iD], Sarah Diefenbach[2] [iD], and Paweł W. Woźniak[3] [iD]

[1] University of Luxembourg, Esch-sur-Alzette, Luxembourg
jasmin.niess@uni.lu
[2] LMU Munich, Munich, Germany
[3] Utrecht University, Utrecht, The Netherlands

Abstract. Persuasive technologies to support behaviour change (e.g., fitness trackers) have become increasingly popular among consumers and healthcare providers. However, studies show that such technologies often fail to offer long-term engagement and tangible health benefits. In this regards, the specific design of persuasive messages provided by the device and users' reactions to it may play a critical role. Our research explores the potential of applying theories of construal level and communication style to formulating feedback messages in self-improvement technologies. Two experiments (N = 190, N = 177) examine the influence of these two factors on goal commitment and affect-based evaluation for situations of fitness goal attainment and failure. Overall, construal level and communication style were relevant factors with independent influence. In the positive situation of goal attainment, high construal level and a friendly communication style resulted in significantly more goal commitment and positive affect than low construal level and a dominant communication style. In the negative situation of failure, results were overall less unambiguous and need to be consolidated by further research. Implications for the design of persuasive feedback are discussed.

Keywords: Persuasive feedback · Physical activity · Self-improvement

1 Introduction

An ever increasing number of people are starting to use mobile applications to improve their fitness level and well-being [22]. One essential aspect to make mobile fitness applications more meaningful and support behavioural change is appropriate feedback [2]. However, results focusing on the benefits of self-improvement technologies are inconclusive, with some presenting promising results [5], whereas others point to issues research in persuasive technology still needs to address. For instance, many fitness apps still struggle to deliver long-term health benefits [16]. Most users stop using their apps after a short usage period [13], partly due to frustration with feedback and goal setting modalities [4].

© Springer Nature Switzerland AG 2020
S. B. Gram-Hansen et al. (Eds.): PERSUASIVE 2020, LNCS 12064, pp. 101–112, 2020.
https://doi.org/10.1007/978-3-030-45712-9_8

The critical influence of the particular way the app provides feedback also becomes comprehensible when considering the role of technology as a social agent [2]. Humans have a tendency to interact with media in a social way [18]. Thus, one might conclude that technologies for self-improvement may slip into the role of an interactive coach [21,25]. In parallel to a human coach, where communication is an essential part to support behaviour change (e.g., in coaching [12]), interactive coaches may be more or less successful depending on the way they 'speak' to the user [3].

In this paper, we explore the degree of influence of the tone in which persuasive feedback is given (the communication style: friendly versus dominant) and the cognitive strategy of interpretation suggested by the formulation of the message (construal level, low/concrete versus high/abstract) impact the affective response and goal commitment of participants in a physical activity context. In short, the construal level describes how concretely or abstractly something is represented in a person's mind, which is naturally affected by the words to describe it with; e.g. walking 1000 steps each day (concrete) versus becoming a fitter person (abstract). In addition, we explore these effects for two types of feedback content; success versus failure (here: fitness goal attainment or lack thereof).

The present paper is structured as follows: The next section discusses relevant theoretical background connected to our research endeavour, including construal level theory [26] and research on communication styles of interactive tools for self-improvement [21]. The subsequent sections present two empirical studies, followed by a general discussion of our study findings and future research.

2   Background

We first introduce construal level theory [26]. Then we report on past work on communication styles of interactive technologies for self-improvement.

2.1   Construal Level Theory

Construal level theory (CLT) originates from work by Trope et al. [26]. CLT differentiates between high level construals, which are relatively abstract, and low-level construals, which are relatively concrete. The construal level has been identified as relevant for the further cognitive processing of information and a number of additional psychological variables. For instance, when a horse is construed more abstractly, i.e. as a mammal, the information regarding the species of the mammal, i.e. the horse, is omitted. Activities can also be construed in more abstract or more concrete terms. High construal level can be induced by providing the reasons for an activity; low construal by the information on how an activity is performed. This in turn means that superordinate goals should be more salient when construed more abstractly. Thus, depending on whether an object or activity is represented in a more abstract or more concrete way, we are considering or omitting certain attributes of it. Fujita et al. [10] conducted a sequence of experiments using different manipulations to investigate the influence of construal level on self-control, showing that higher construal levels led to higher self-control. In conclusion, the authors claimed that any factor that influences the level of construal could potentially influence self-control and actions of individuals. One of such influencing factors could be a person's mood, given that a positive mood has been associated with processing visual information on a more global level than a neutral mood [11]. Along these lines, Labroo and Patrick demonstrated that being in a positive mood led to more abstract thinking and a focus on superordinate goals, whereas a negative mood shifted the focus more on subordinate goals [17]. In consequence, a positive mood may activate a more abstract construal level and subsequently support self-control. Our research may provide another step in this direction, investigating how a shift in construal level is influencing the affective and motivational experience of mobile fitness app feedback. In addition, given the central relevance of emotions for achievement and motivation [24], we also consider the so-called communication style of interactive products [21] as another potential influencing factor of peoples' affective and motivational experience in the context of goal achievement.

2.2 Conceptualising Communication Style of Interactive Technologies

As already argued in the 90s by Nass et al. [20], society is heading towards a time where more and more technologies turn into interactive partners or coaches [14]. Scholars found that humans act towards computers based on behavioural scripts of human-human interaction, as for example, applying social norms such as courtesy or screaming at their computer if it doesn't behave the way they wished [8,20]. Given this natural tendency of humans to engage in social interaction with technology, the deliberate design of the communication and dialogue in Human-Computer Interaction (HCI) seems of vital importance for the resulting user experience, particularly for the context of technology supporting behaviour change such as the design of fitness apps. Recent work on the border of Psychology and HCI found that users are able to perceive the communication style of interactive technologies for self-improvement and to differentiate between different styles [21]. Further, they found that different communication styles seem to be connected to different affective and emotional reactions [4,21]. Based on recent research on communication styles of self-improvement technologies [4,21], we chose two communication styles to focus and operationalise in our experiments, namely, the so-called friendly/cooperative communication style and the critical/dominant communication style. The friendly/cooperative communication style can be described as friendly, helpful and resilient. When implemented in a self-improvement technology, the feedback messages of the medium would be friendly, understanding and supportive. For example, if a user failed to reach their fitness goal, the technology might comment on this with 'Keep pushing and don't give up'. In contrast, the critical/dominant style of communication focuses on the mistakes and weaknesses of the user. Hence, the feedback would reprimand the user and focus on their imperfections, e.g. 'You failed. You have to get a move on now'.

3   Research Goals and Contributions

The design of persuasive systems to support behavioural change is a complex endeavour. Affective and cognitive factors should be considered when designing persuasive feedback. Affective experiences have a bidirectional connection to construal level and are of relevance for achievement [24]. Previous research showcased the impact of communication style of self-improvement technologies on the behaviour change process and pointed towards a more positive reaction towards the friendly communication style. Thus, the present study investigates the effect of level of construal and communication style on affective response and goal commitment in a mobile fitness application context. The present paper is, to the best of our knowledge, the first study exploring communication style in a controlled environment and applying construal level theory in persuasive feedback.

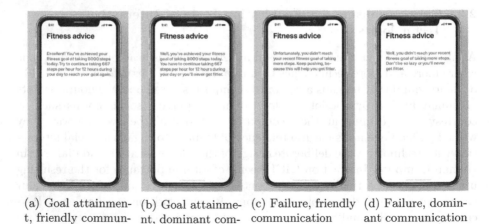

(a) Goal attainment, friendly communication style, low construal level.

(b) Goal attainment, dominant communication style, low construal level.

(c) Failure, friendly communication style, high construal level.

(d) Failure, dominant communication style, high construal level.

Fig. 1. Examples of mockup mobile application screens presented in the survey.

4   Study 1 (Goal Attainment)

Based on previous research showing that abstract construal prompts a focus on the positive reasons underlying experiences [7,27], we hypothesise that abstract construal should lead to a more positive affective response and higher goal commitment. Furthermore, we predict that a friendly communication style should lead to a more positive affective response and higher goal commitment in a positive situation (goal attainment). Specifically, we hypothesise:

- **H1a**: High level of construal results in a significantly more positive affective response than low level of construal.
- **H1b**: Friendly communication style results in significantly more positive affective response than dominant communication style.
- **H1c**: At high level of construal, the positive effect of a friendly communication style on affective response is more pronounced than at low level of construal.
- **H2a**: High level of construal results in significantly more goal commitment than low level of construal.
- **H2b**: Friendly communication style results in significantly more goal commitment than dominant communication style.
- **H2c**: At high level of construal, the positive effect of a friendly communication style on goal commitment is more pronounced than at low level of construal.

4.1   Design and Method

Our study used a 2 (construal level: abstract vs. concrete) × 2 (communication style: friendly vs. dominant) between subjects design with four different vignettes. In vignette studies, participants are asked to see the world through the eyes of a hypothetical person in a specific scenario. As shown in previous applications, vignette studies balance the benefits of experimental research with high internal validity and the advantages of applied research with high external validity [1]. The vignette study was conducted online and the participants were randomly assigned to one of four conditions.

Participants. We recruited 190 participants (111 male, 79 female), aged 19–69, $M = 35.97$, $SD = 11.56$ using Amazon Mechanical Turk (MTurk). Given that replications studies in different areas of research using MTurk led to comparable results as the original studies [23], MTurk has become a popular means of recruitment for research in Psychology [27] and Human-Computer Interaction [6]. The recruited participants resided in the United States or the European Union. We required participants to have completed at least 1,000 HITs with a 95% acceptance rate, in line with past work in Psychology and HCI [6]. The survey took an average of 3 min 14 s to complete and the participants received $0.80 as compensation.

Procedure. In the online vignette study, users were presented with a neutral description of the situational context. They were asked to imagine that they have recently downloaded a fitness app, in order to become more active. Furthermore, they have been informed that they have used it all week and that they have recently increased their step goal to 8000 steps per day. The participants have been told that they wake up in the morning and the fitness app presents them with the following feedback, which they study carefully. Afterwards, we showed a prototype phone screen with fitness advice in one of the randomly assigned conditions, informing them that they had achieved their goal. Figure 1 shows examples of the screens.

Measures. After the survey introduction, we presented the participants with questions regarding their demographic data. We then inquired about their affective response and their goal commitment. The order of the scales has been randomised. We administered the Goal Commitment Scale [15], where the participants indicated their agreement on a Likert scale from very strongly disagree to very strongly agree. We queried the affective response of the participants based on the items used by Williams et al. [27]. The participants evaluated the extent to which the feedback of the fitness app felt 'pleasant', 'desirable', 'painful', and 'unpleasant' (latter two reverse-coded). These responses were made on 7-point scales anchored by 'not at all' and 'very'.

4.2   Results — Study 1

How do level of construal and communication style of fitness app feedback influence users' affect-based evaluations of the feedback when they achieved their goal? To answer this question, a two-way ANOVA was conducted. This analysis revealed a significant main effect of the construal level manipulation ($F(1, 186) = 4,709$, $p = .031$). Participants who were presented with the feedback in a concrete manner reported lower evaluations ($M = 16.85$, $SD = 7.26$) compared to those who were presented with the feedback in an abstract manner ($M = 19.52$, $SD = 7.12$). Thus, H1a is confirmed. There was also a statistically significant main effect of the communication style manipulation ($F(1, 186) = 55,411$, $p < .001$). Participants who were presented with the dominant communication style reported lower evaluations ($M = 14.90$, $SD = 7.03$) compared to those who were presented with the friendly communication style ($M = 21.80$, $SD = 5.75$). Thus, H1b is confirmed. There was no interaction between the construal level and the communication style factors ($p > .05$). Thus, H1c is not confirmed.

How do level of construal and communication style of fitness app feedback influence users' goal commitment when they achieved their goal? To answer this question, a two-way ANOVA was conducted. This analysis revealed a significant main effect of the construal level manipulation ($F(1, 186) = 7,589$, $p = .006$). Participants who were presented with the feedback in a concrete manner reported lower goal commitment ($M = 29.91$, $SD = 6.12$ compared to those who were presented with the feedback in an abstract manner ($M = 32.41$, $SD = 5.54$). Thus, H2a is confirmed. There was also a statistically significant main effect of the communication style manipulation ($F(1, 186) = 5,564$, $p = .019$). Participants who were presented with the dominant communication style reported lower goal commitment (M = 30.27, SD = 5.93) compared to those who were presented with the friendly communication style ($M = 32.25$, $SD = 5.82$). Thus, H2b is confirmed. There was no interaction between the construal level and the communication style factors ($p > .05$). Thus, H2c is not confirmed. Figure 2 presents the results.

5   Study 2 (Failure)

Study 2 replicates study 1 in negative situations (failure; i.e. where users failed to reach a goal and the fitness app is confronting them with an according message), in order to test the generalisability to both positive and negative situations. We expected the same effects as for study 1. Hence, the present study also investigates the effect of level of construal on affective response and goal commitment in a mobile fitness application context. Similar to study 1, we are combining this approach with an inquiry regarding the communication style of self-improvement technologies.

In line with our previously described assumptions, we hypothesise that abstract construal would lead to a more positive affective response and higher goal commitment. Furthermore, we predict that a friendly communication style would lead to a more positive affective response and higher goal commitment. In the present study we are exploring these assumptions in a negative situational context (failure). Specifically, we hypothesise:

- **H3a**: High level of construal results in a significantly more positive affective response than low level of construal.
- **H3b**: Friendly communication style results in significantly more positive affective response than dominant communication style.
- **H3c**: At high level of construal, the positive effect of a friendly communication style on affective response is more pronounced than at low level of construal.
- **H4a**: High level of construal results in significantly more goal commitment than low level of construal.
- **H4b**: Friendly communication style results in significantly more goal commitment than dominant communication style.
- **H4c**: At high level of construal, the positive effect of a friendly communication style on goal commitment is more pronounced than at low level of construal.

5.1   Design and Method

Again our study used a 2 (construal level: abstract vs. concrete) × 2 (communication style: friendly vs. dominant) between subjects design with four different vignettes. Similar to study one, the vignette study was conducted online and the participants were randomly assigned to one of four conditions. The procedure was similar to study 1, apart from one detail. Users were informed that they had failed to achieve their goal. Figure 1 shows examples of the screens. The measures used were similar to the measures applied in study 1.

Participants. We recruited 177 participants (104 male, 73 female), aged 20–69, $M = 33.45$, $SD = 9.35$ using Amazon Mechanical Turk (MTurk). The recruited participants resided in the United States or the European Union. We required participants to have completed at least 1,000 HITs with a 95% acceptance rate, in line with past work in Psychology and HCI [6] The survey took an average of 3 min 04s to complete and the participants received $0.80 as compensation.

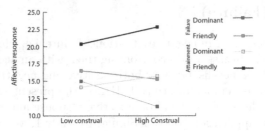

(a) Average total affective response in the two experimental conditions (construal level, communication style) in both situations, i.e. goal attainment (Study 1) and failure (Study 2).

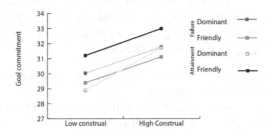

(b) Average total goal commitment in the two experimental conditions (construal level, communication style) in both situations, i.e. goal attainment (Study 1) and failure (Study 2).

Fig. 2. A visual summary of the results of the two studies.

5.2   Results — Study 2

How do level of construal and communication style of fitness app feedback influence users' affect-based evaluations of the feedback when they did not achieve their goal? To answer this question, a two-way ANOVA was conducted. This analysis revealed a significant main effect of the construal level manipulation ($F(1,173) = 7,069$, $p = .008$). Participants who were presented with the feedback in a concrete manner reported higher evaluations ($M = 15.62$, $SD = 5.64$) compared to those who were presented with the feedback in an abstract manner ($M = 13.77$, $SD = 6.16$). Thus, H3a is not confirmed. There was also a statistically significant main effect of the communication style manipulation ($F(1,173) = 6,401$, $p = .012$. Participants who were presented with the dominant communication style reported lower evaluations ($M = 13.63$, $SD = 6.12$) compared to those who were presented with the friendly communication style ($M = 15.81$, $SD = 5.60$). Thus, H3b is confirmed. There was no interaction between the construal level and the communication style factors ($p > .05$). Thus, H3c is not confirmed. Figure 2 presents the results. How do level of construal and communication style of fitness app feedback influence users' goal commitment when they did not achieve their goal? To answer this question, a two-way ANOVA was conducted. This analysis revealed a significant main effect of the construal level manipulation ($F(1, 173) = 4,031, p = .046$). Participants who were presented with the feedback in a concrete manner reported lower goal commitment ($M = 29.77, SD = 5.70$) compared to those who were presented with the feedback in an abstract manner ($M = 31.37, SD = 5.48$). Thus, H4a is confirmed. There was no statistically significant main effect of the communication style manipulation ($F(1, 173) = 0.146, p > .05$. Thus, H4b is not confirmed. There was no interaction between the construal level and the communication style factors ($p > .05$). Thus, H4c is not confirmed. Figure 2 presents the results.

6   Discussion

In brief, our results show that abstract compared to concrete construal leads to a more positive affective response in the event of goal attainment, as assumed in **H1a**. A more abstract construal might shifted the focus to higher level goals (seeing the forest instead of focusing on the trees). We hypothesise that this shift in focus might enhance the positive experience of achieving a fitness goal through adding meaning to the achieved step goal. The participants perhaps perceive the situation as positive because they have not only achieved their step goal but also come a step closer to their overall goal of becoming fitter. Additionally we found that affective responses varied significantly between the two different communication styles, as assumed in **H1b**. Depending on how the message of goal attainment was communicated, participants showed different affective reactions, with the friendly communication leading to more positive affect.

Other than assumed (**H1c**), the interaction between level of construal and communication style regarding affective response was not significant. Construal level and communication style thus seem to have separable influences on affect-based evaluations Furthermore we found that there was a significant difference between the message framed on different levels of construal regarding goal commitment in the positive situation of goal attainment. In line with **H2a**, the more abstract construal level led to higher goal commitment than the more concrete construal level. This finding may be explained through the relationship between construal level and self-control, with high construal level having a positive impact on perceived self-control [10]. In light of previous findings, linking higher self-control to higher goal commitment [19]. It thus seems plausible that high levels of construal go along with higher goal commitment. However, future research is needed to get insights into the exact relations between the three variables (construal level, self-control, goal commitment) and possible mediating effects. Furthermore, in line with **H2b**, goal commitment was affected by the used communication style in the message on goal attainment, with the friendly communication resulting in higher commitment than the dominant communication style. We assume that the friendly, supportive communication style might increase participants' perceived self-efficacy, which in turn, in line with the results from

Locke et al. [19], could have led to higher goal commitment. As also for affective response, the interaction effect between level of construal and communication style on goal commitment was not significant. Thus, other than assumed in **H2c**, the effects of construal level and communication style are merely additive.

In the negative situation of failure, our results showed a significant effect of the level of construal on the affective response. However, other than assumed in **H3a**, a lower construal level resulted in a more positive affective response. This result contradicts previous findings regarding construal level and evaluations of experiences [27]. A possible explanation can be construed in light of the studies by Eyal et al. [7]. They found that participants in a higher construal level mindset judged moral transgressions more harshly than participants in the low construal level condition, arguing that the abstract mindset might have promoted a focus on the higher level moral principles that have been violated, rather than the concrete deed. The level of construal thus affects the basis of evaluation, and negative events appear even more serious when considered on a high compared to a low level of construal, given that superordinate, moral principles have been violated. Our findings in the failure condition might be interpreted in a similar way: The superordinate goal of our participants was to become fitter, however, they failed in achieving their goal, i.e. a negative event. This failure might have appeared even more severe in the high construal level condition, which promoted a stronger focus on the superordinate goal than the low construal level condition. This might explain the less positive affective response in the high compared to the low construal level condition. As assumed in **H3b**, we found a significant effect of communication style on affective response, with the message of failure being communicated by a friendly communication style leading to a more positive affective response than the dominant communication style. Our results in the failure condition also showed a significant effect of the construal level on goal commitment.

In line with **H4a**, more abstract construal resulted in higher goal commitment. In parallel to study 1 and the positive situation of goal attainment, we hypothesise that a high construal level has a positive impact on self-control [9], which may also facilitate goal commitment. Furthermore, high level of construal may support participants to see the forest (getting fitter) instead of the trees (failure regarding the step goal today). In consequence, the high level of construal might activated a defensive orientation in action, thus showing the participant that they can still push to reach their superordinate goal and therefore leading to less negative impact on goal commitment.

This line of reasoning, however, contradicts to some extent the interpretation of the (unexpected) finding on affective response, where we speculated that failure might have appeared more severe in the high construal level condition, due to the activation of a superordinate goal and leading to a more negative affective reaction. In sum, it still requires further research to understand the exact mechanisms behind the effects of construal level and their impact on participants' experience and goal commitment in the condition of failure. Future research could utilise longitudinal, qualitative studies to further explore and validate our findings. Other than in study 1 and the positive event of goal attainment, in the event of failure, communication style had no effect on goal commitment, leading to the rejection of **H4b**. In parallel to study 1 and the positive situation of goal attainment, in study 2 and the negative situation of failure no significant interactions between level of construal and communication style were found, either on affective response or on goal commitment.

Altogether, the differences between the findings for situations of goal attainment and failure highlight the importance of distinct studies on the effects of construal level and communication style in light of the context, namely, the self-improvement message being communicated. Depending on the message content and its valence, how the persuasive message is communicated has varying consequences for peoples' experience and commitment to a goal.

7 Conclusion

This paper investigated the effects of construal level and communication style to communicate mobile fitness application feedback to participants who have either met or not met their fitness goal. We conducted two between-subject online studies with four conditions each–four different mobile fitness app messages. It is, to the best of our knowledge, the first empirical investigation of the application of construal level theory and the communication styles of interactive technologies for self-improvement in a controlled, experimental setting. The present research broadens our understanding of the psychological effects of communication style and construal level of persuasive feedback. We have outlined the first steps of how the design of future persuasive technology feedback could apply psychological theory in meaningful ways to design for a positive, long-term experience.

References

1. Aguinis, H., Bradley, K.J.: Best practice recommendations for designing and implementing experimental vignette methodology studies. Organ. Res. Methods **17**(4), 351–371 (2014)
2. Ansems, E.L., Hanci, E., Ruijten, P.A.M., IJsselsteijn, W.A.: I focus on improvement: effects of type of mastery feedback on motivational experiences. In: Oinas-Kukkonen, H., Win, K.T., Karapanos, E., Karppinen, P., Kyza, E. (eds.) PERSUASIVE 2019. LNCS, vol. 11433, pp. 213–224. Springer, Cham (2019). https://doi.org/10.1007/978-3-030-17287-9_18
3. Beun, R.J., et al.: Talk and tools: the best of both worlds in mobile user interfaces for e-coaching. Pers. Ubiquit. Comput. **21**(4), 661–674 (2017). https://doi.org/10.1007/s00779-017-1021-5
4. Diefenbach, S., Niess, J., Mehner, M.: Technologies for self-improvement: the right communication between product and user. In: Persuasive Technology 2016 Adjunct Proceedings, pp. 10–13 (2016)
5. Kersten-van Dijk, E.T., Westerink, J.H., Beute, F., IJsselsteijn, W.A.: Personal informatics, self-insight, and behavior change: a critical review of current literature. Hum. Comput. Interact. **32**(5–6), 268–296 (2017)

6. Epstein, D.A., Ping, A., Fogarty, J., Munson, S.A.: A lived informatics model of personal informatics. In: UbiComp 2015, pp. 731–742. ACM, New York, NY, USA (2015). https://doi.org/10.1145/2750858.2804250
7. Eyal, T., Liberman, N., Trope, Y.: Judging near and distant virtue and vice. J. Exp. Soc. Psychol. **44**(4), 1204–1209 (2008)
8. Fogg, B.J.: Persuasive technology: using computers to change what we think and do. Ubiquity **2002**, 5 (2002)
9. Fujita, K., Roberts, J.C.: Promoting prospective self-control through abstraction. J. Exp. Soc. Psychol. **46**(6), 1049–1054 (2010)
10. Fujita, K., Trope, Y., Liberman, N., Levin-Sagi, M.: Construal levels and self-control. J. Pers. Soc. Psychol. **90**(3), 351 (2006)
11. Gasper, K., Clore, G.L.: Attending to the big picture: mood and global versus local processing of visual information. Psychol. Sci. **13**(1), 34–40 (2002)
12. Gerrig, R.J., Zimbardo, P.G., Zimbardo, P.G., Psychologue, E.U., Zimbardo, P.G.: Psychology and Life. Pearson, Boston (2010)
13. Gouveia, R., Karapanos, E., Hassenzahl, M.: How do we engage with activity trackers? A longitudinal study of habito. In: UbiComp 2015, pp. 1305–1316. ACM (2015)
14. Grudin, J.: From tool to partner: the evolution of human-computer interaction. Synth. Lect. Hum.-Centered Inf. **10**(1), i-183 (2017). https://doi.org/10.2200/S00745ED1V01Y201612HCI035
15. Hollenbeck, J.R., Williams, C.R., Klein, H.J.: An empirical examination of the antecedents of commitment to difficult goals. J. Appl. Psychol. **74**(1), 18 (1989)
16. Jakicic, J.M., et al.: Effect of wearable technology combined with a lifestyle intervention on long-term weight loss: the idea randomized clinical trial. Jama **316**(11), 1161–1171 (2016)
17. Labroo, A.A., Patrick, V.M.: Psychological distancing: why happiness helps you see the big picture. J. Consum. Res. **35**(5), 800–809 (2008)
18. Lieberman, H., Selker, T.: Agents for the user interface. In: Handbook of Agent Technology, pp. 1–21 (2003)
19. Locke, E.A., Latham, G.P.: New directions in goal-setting theory. Curr. Dir. Psychol. Sci. **15**(5), 265–268 (2006)
20. Nass, C., Steuer, J., Tauber, E.R.: Computers are social actors. In: CHI 1994, pp. 72–78. ACM, New York, NY, USA (1994). https://doi.org/10.1145/191666.191703
21. Niess, J., Diefenbach, S.: Communication styles of interactive tools for self-improvement. Psychol. Well-Being **6**(1), 3 (2016). https://doi.org/10.1186/s13612-016-0040-8
22. Niess, J., Woźniak, P.W.: Supporting meaningful personal fitness: the tracker goal evolution model. In: CHI 2018, pp. 171:1–171:12. ACM, New York, NY, USA (2018). https://doi.org/10.1145/3173574.3173745
23. Paolacci, G., Chandler, J., Ipeirotis, P.G.: Running experiments on amazon mechanical turk. Judgm. Decis. Making **5**(5), 411–419 (2010)
24. Pekrun, R., Perry, R.P.: Control-value theory of achievement emotions. In: International Handbook of Emotions in Education, pp. 120–141 (2014)
25. Skalski, P., Tamborini, R.: The role of social presence in interactive agent-based persuasion. Media Psychol. **10**(3), 385–413 (2007)
26. Trope, Y., Liberman, N.: Construal-level theory of psychological distance. Psychol. Rev. **117**(2), 440 (2010)
27. Williams, L.E., Stein, R., Galguera, L.: The distinct affective consequences of psychological distance and construal level. J. Consum. Res. **40**(6), 1123–1138 (2013)

Persuading from the Start: Participatory Development of Sustainable Persuasive Data-Driven Technologies in Healthcare

Julia Keizer[1], Nienke Beerlage-de Jong[1,2]([⊠]), Nashwan Al Naiemi[3,4], and J. E. W. C. van Gemert-Pijnen[1,2]

[1] Centre for eHealth and Wellbeing Research, University of Twente, Enschede, The Netherlands
n.beerlage-dejong@utwente.nl
[2] Department of Medical Microbiology and Infection Control, University Medical Centre Groningen, Groningen, The Netherlands
[3] Department of Medical Microbiology and Infection Control, Hospital Group Twente, Almelo, Hengelo, The Netherlands
[4] LabMicTA, Hengelo, The Netherlands

Abstract. Data-driven technologies can persuade humans to optimize their behavior and context based on objective data. However, current data-driven technologies have limited persuasive powers, because of a misfit between technology, end-users and context. Neglecting end-users in the development process contributes to this misfit and to limited engagement with the to-be-developed technology. This threatens sustainable (long-term) implementation. Therefore, this paper demonstrates how a bottom-up participatory development approach can improve the persuasive design of data-driven technologies and simultaneously increase engagement of end-users to foster sustainable implementation. This is done by describing part of the development of an Audit & Feedback system for healthcare workers at a Dutch regional general hospital. The system intends to contribute to reducing antimicrobial resistance. The rationale for, questions asked at and results of a questionnaire and two focus groups are described.

Keywords: Participatory development · Bottom-up · Data · Antimicrobial resistance (AMR)

1 Introduction

Society faces wicked problems that threaten the quality and safety of healthcare and harm public and individual health [1]. Humans (unintentionally) contribute to these problems by behaving suboptimal (e.g. not complying with guidelines) or creating suboptimal contexts (e.g. creating a messy work environment) [2]. At the same time, there is no doubt that humans and their behavior are vital in developing and implementing successful solutions [3]. However, to cope with the complexity of modern-day challenges, humans require substantial support. Persuasive technologies that take advantage of the potentials that (big) data offer are promising for efficient and sustainable solutions. Data-driven

© Springer Nature Switzerland AG 2020
S. B. Gram-Hansen et al. (Eds.): PERSUASIVE 2020, LNCS 12064, pp. 113–125, 2020.
https://doi.org/10.1007/978-3-030-45712-9_9

technologies can persuade people to optimize their behavior (i.e. individual actions) and context (e.g. working routines) based on objective data [4].

From previous studies in hospitals, we know that (big) data are routinely collected for each individual patient to make diagnostic and treatment decisions and to monitor the patient's status (e.g. result of diagnostic tests) [4]. However, these data are not optimally used for improvement strategies [5]. This relinquishes the opportunities of reflecting on one's work and work processes, disallowing healthcare workers (HCW) to learn from mistakes and to identify good-practices [6]. Especially this reflective form of reusing routinely collected data promises to be a feasible, cost-effective way to support humans: the (big) data are already available, yet not smartly combined, translated and communicated to persuade HCW to improve their behavior and context [4]. This principle is not new. Audit and feedback (AF) has been widely used in healthcare [7]. By summarizing data about aspects of care (i.e. audit) and reporting the findings back (i.e. feedback) to HCW, AF encourages behavior and practice changes. This makes AF an interesting case to study data-driven persuasive technologies.

Although AF is widely used in healthcare, it yields variable and modest effects in practice [7]. AF is mostly organized in a top-down (e.g. audits by healthcare inspectorate [8]) and expert-driven (e.g. indicators created by quality-experts [9]) way. Thereby, feedback, often provided at hospital-level, is hardly useful for HCW to improve their behavior and working routines [4]. Because of this misfit between the datadriven technology, the end-users and their context, current AF have little persuasive powers. The limited persuasiveness and thus added value of AF might be caused by neglecting end-users (in this case HCW) in the AF development process [10]. Making AF persuasive requires extensively studying users and their context throughout the development process. Therefore, the first aim of this paper is to demonstrate **how a bottom-up participatory development approach can improve the persuasive design of data-driven technologies** for their end-user (i.e. HCW), and within their context.

However, this is not enough for sustainable solutions that are used and have an effect in the long-term. Persuasively designed technologies do not guarantee adoption and acceptance in practice. Often, factors that determine successful implementation are studied after the design of the technology. But, implementation is not a post-design step; extensively discussing success factors for implementation from the start of the development process with relevant stakeholders is crucial [11]. As mentioned before, they are the ones responsible for implementing successful solutions in practice. Therefore, the second aim of this paper is to demonstrate **how bottom-up participatory development is a necessary precondition for the development of persuasive datadriven technologies that foster sustainable implementation**. We do this, by showing how our bottom-up participatory approach persuaded end-users (i.e. HCW) from the start to get engaged by and take ownership of the persuasive technology.

Our studies have focused on the application of persuasive data-driven technologies for a striking modern-day example of behavior-inflicted wicked problems: antimicrobial resistance (AMR) [4, 12, 13]. AMR is a threat to global health(care). It is largely caused by humans and relies on human actions to be solved [14]. Persuasive data-driven technologies can inform, support and persuade HCW to optimize their diagnostic, antibiotic (AB) prescription and infection control behavior to limit AMR [15].

We used the CeHRes-roadmap, which guides the holistic development (from problem definition to evaluation) of persuasive technology [11]. Drawing from participatory development, persuasive design and business modelling, it assumes that people, technologies and their contexts are always interrelated. By using this multidisciplinary, socio-technical behavioral approach, we gained deep understanding of the relevant stakeholders, their think- and work-processes and their context, including success factors for future implementation. By studying these, we aim to better match HCW' and other stakeholders' perspectives to optimally benefit from the vast amount of routinely collected data, to improve the quality and safety of healthcare. Incorporating these findings into future AF strategies ensures that they match HCW' needs and their context, thereby increasing the likelihood of uptake and integration in practice [16]. Simultaneously, it builds towards a methodological and conceptual guide for good-practice bottom-up participatory development and implementation processes of persuasive technologies.

2 Methods

A participatory development approach requires multiple complementary methods to grasp the breadth of wicked problems. Therefore, this study used a mixed-methods sequential explanatory design [17]. Quantitative results from a questionnaire provided input for two consecutive (qualitative) focus groups. Since the persuasiveness of a technology largely depends on the **content**, **functionalities** and **design**, this research focused mostly on these aspects. Additionally, attention was paid to implementation factors (e.g. what is the **added value**, how it be **used in practice** and what are **preconditions** for uptake and sustainable use?). In a second focus group, specific attention was paid to the bottom-up participatory research approach in relation to fostering implementation (see Table 1 for rationales and the respective goals of the sub-studies).

Table 1. Elucidating the mixed-methods sequential explanatory design

Method	Method rationale	Sub-study goal
Questionnaire	Specify topics for the focus groups, while integrating AMR-expert views	Prioritize *what* topics for AF, derived from national AMR guidelines, are most relevant to the end-users/HCW
Focus group 1	Realize in-depth discussions (no consensus needed)	Gain insight in *what* audit & feedback topics would be of added value and *why*
Focus group 2	Realize in-depth discussions (no consensus needed)	(1) Gain insight in *how* AF would be used in practice, identify *technology requirements*. (2) Discuss *experiences* via the bottom-up participatory research approach

The study was performed in a Dutch regional general hospital (687 beds) by a research team of three health sciences/psychology researchers, a clinical microbiologist and a pharmacist. End-users (i.e. urologists, residents and co-assistants) from a high-risk AMR department (urology) were included. The University's ethical committee approved the study (190008), all respondents signed an informed consent prior to participating in this study.

2.1   Step 1: Questionnaire (Prioritizing Topics for AF Content)

To prioritize what topics for AF were deemed most relevant, "top-down" content from national AB stewardship guideline [18], infection control audits of the national healthcare inspectorate [19] and key publications on AMR [20–25] were translated into 27 AMR quality-indicators (e.g. "Were cultures taken before the start of empirical treatment?"). To end up with a feasible number of AF topics to be discussed within the hour time-frame of the focus groups, HCW answered the following questions about each predetermined indicator: "Would you like to have in-sight in this indicator? ("No/Yes") and "How relevant would insight in this indicator be for the treatment of individual patients/for limiting AMR?" (5-point Likert items: "Limited – High relevance").

A pilot-test was held with two AMR-experts and a urologist to ensure comprehension and clarity of the questions. All attendees of a regular weekly educational session (n = 7, ± 50% of department) filled in the questionnaire after a short presentation about the research. Descriptive analyses were performed in Microsoft Excel (v2016). Responses were summarized in means and standard deviations and the research team discussed the quality-indicators for which more than 75% of respondents saw relevance to avoid individual preferences in the small number of respondents. Through discussion, four AF topics were selected for the consecutive focus groups.

2.2   Step 2: Focus Group 1 (*Content & Added Value*)

The second step was to determine *why* HCW would want to use audit and feedback and *what* (kind of) AF they need for it to be relevant and meaningful. Therefore, the first semi-structured focus group used the results of the questionnaire to discuss the following questions for each topic: (1) "*Why* would you want to have this insight?", (2) "Currently, *what* insight do you use to determine quality of X?", (3) "Which *additional insight* would you need to determine quality of X?". Probing questions were used to gain deeper insight in perceived relevance of and to find preconditions for successful AF.

2.3   Step 3: Focus Group 2 (*Practical Use & Requirements*)

The third step within this study was to determine how HCW would want to use AF in practice and to identify technology requirements (e.g. functionalities and design) for AF, using three examples in the form of low-fidelity prototypes. The first example was the prototype based on focus group 1. For the second and third example, screenshots of existing AMR-tools were requested and attained from the first authors of published papers. The second example was an interactive open-source software app for infection management and antimicrobial stewardship: Rapid Analysis of Diagnostic and Antimicrobial Patterns in R (RadaR), developed to support AMR-experts in analyzing AMRdata [26].

The third example was an existing tool to measure the quality of infection control and antimicrobial use: the Infection Risk Scan (IRIS), developed to easily and transparently communicate risks and improvement areas to HCW and managers [27].

The following three questions (and subsequent probing questions) were asked for each example: (1) "What is your first impression?", (2) "How would you use this in your work?", (3) "How would you like the AF system to support you in doing so?". Furthermore, experiences with the bottom-up participatory research approach and expectations of how this approach might influence the persuasiveness, usefulness and effectivity of the to-be-developed technology, its development and implementation were discussed.

For both focus groups pilot-tests were held with a urologist to ensure clarity and comprehension of the questions. All urologists and urology-residents who work at the studied Dutch regional general hospital were invited for the meetings. One hour of each meeting was dedicated to audit and feedback (April & October 2019). Participants were specifically asked not to think in limitations by data/IT-systems. The focus groups were audio-recorded and transcribed verbatim. Transcripts were coded in Excel by researcher JK. The first round of coding was deductive based on the focus group schemes and was succeeded by open and axial coding to establish sub-codes and variations. Analyst triangulation was applied (independent coding of 25% by another researcher (BB)) [28] and kappa statistic were used to test interrater reliability [29].

3   Results

Sociodemographic characteristics of the questionnaire (QNR) respondents and focus group participants are shown in Table 2. Completing the questionnaire took 20 min on average, and both focus groups took one hour. Interrater reliability was found to be substantial for focus group 1 (Kappa = 0.685, $p < 0.001$) and moderate for focus group 2 (Kappa = 0.479, p 0.017). Participants were unfamiliar with qualitative research in the form of focus groups and with participating in a participatory research project.

Table 2. Respondents'/Participants' characteristics

	n	Age mean (SD)	Gender n		Function n (%)		Experience mean (SD)	
			F	M	Physician	Resident	Function	Hospital
Questionnaire	7*	34.1 (12.4)	4	3	2	2	4.7 (8.3)	4.7 (8.5)
Focus group 1	5	42.0 (10.8)	3	2	3	2	8.8 (8.4)	8.2 (8.8)
Focus group 2	5	41.8 (11.0)	3	2	3	2	8.6 (8.5)	8.0 (9.0)

*Co-assistants (n = 2) were excluded from the focus groups due to their limited experience in urology. Note. Four out of five participants of focus groups 1 and 2 were the same individuals.

118   J. Keizer et al.

The results section of this paper focuses on **content, functionalities and design,** which are all relevant to the persuasive design of data-driven technologies [30]. Results are structured in *HCW needs* and *contextual considerations* (e.g. perceived added value, anticipated use in practice and preconditions), both relevant to the persuasive design of data-driven technologies and for fostering implementation through persuasive development. Main findings are shown in bold and illustrative quotes in italic.

3.1 Content

The Sequential Explanatory Design Enabled Prioritizing HCW' Content Needs

Questionnaire. Table 3 shows five quality-indicators that were rated as being most relevant. They were discussed in the research team to select the final four AF topics. Indicators three and four were combined into "Updating the (empirical) AB treatment plan once new information (e.g. culture results or advice from colleague) is available".

Table 3. Questionnaire results (most relevant quality indicators)

Most relevant quality-indicators (k = 27)	Relevance patient (n = 5)		Relevance AMR (n = 5)	
	Mean	SD	Mean	SD
Taking cultures before the start of (empirical) AB	4.43	0.79	4.43	0.79
Adequate AB use (e.g. quantity and duration of AB treatment)	3.86	0.69	4.57	0.53
Following advices from other health care professionals	4.00	0.58	4.29	0.49
Adapting the (empirical) AB treatment based on culture results	4.14	0.90	4.43	0.98
Resistance patterns (e.g. surveillance of micro-organisms)	4.29	0.95	4.86	0.38
AB = Antibiotic				

Focus Group 1. In focus group 1, participants expressed their need to have insight in process indicators, such as the **quantity and quality of their diagnostics and AB treatment**. Participants would like insight in outcomes relevant to their patients:

"Whether you used an AB that allows patients to go home sooner." (R3). Both positive (how often do we do it right?) and negative insight are relevant. Also, participants were interested in **resistance patterns for specific sub-groups** to tailor their (empirical) AB treatment to individual patients. These insights would have to be **benchmarked** against some standard, such as local policies, guidelines or comparisons to other hospitals. Lastly, participants expressed the need for information **tailored to function groups**.

HCW Could Easily Envision the Added Value of and Preconditions for AF

Focus Group 1. Respondents saw clear added value of AF **to evaluate and improve the status quo** and consequently **proactively change current policies and practices**. Furthermore, AF can **facilitate objective discussions** about performance. Lastly, it creates **room for discussions on innovations** (e.g. phage therapy). For AF to be useful in practice, respondents warned that some content was more relevant for inpatients than for outpatients (e.g. changing empirical treatments after receiving culture results). In consultation with the pharmacist and the hospital data-manager, the decision was made to focus on inpatients in the rest of the studies, because there would be many missing data for the outpatient population that are crucial for meaningful audits (e.g. GP cultures). Furthermore, participants urged the need to, **from the early development phases, start thinking about practical issues and consequences for policies and working routines that insights could convey**: *"What if the patient is on your OR table, you are doing the time-out and your culture results are not known yet. Do you cancel the operation? ... Then we have to be honest: if the results are not in yet, you willingly and knowingly take a risk, how small that risk may be." (R1)*. Therefore, participants wanted to extensively discuss goals to make them realistic and relevant for their patients and for limiting AMR. Also, participants mentioned data management, including their own registration behavior, and ICT-support as a crucial precondition for successful AF. Lastly, participants require an open culture, in which quality of their work can be discussed safely.

HCW Required Examples to Envision and Verbalize Technological Needs

Creating The Prototype. Results of focus group 1 were translated into a lo-fi prototype together with a creative company specialized in developing serious games (see Fig. 1 for detailed description). The prototype consisted of screenshots and was not interactive. The prototype was merely used to show what an AF technology could entail to help participants to envision and verbalize their needs.

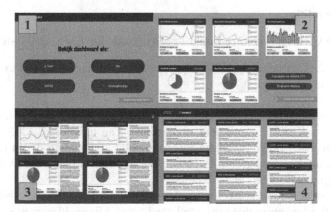

Fig. 1. Prototype quality dashboard based on findings of focus group 1.

Screen 1: specific user-roles (e.g. physician, AMR-expert). Screen 2: overview of the five topics that were deemed important (i.e. quality & quantity of cultures/AB treatment, resistance patterns). Trends over time are shown in graphs and coloured scores below (e.g. results relative to the past 12 months). A benchmark with other regional hospitals is shown below the graphs in coloured scores. When clicking on a graph, screen 3 opens: more details and background information (e.g. justification of score calculations). Screen 4: discussion mode, HCW can upload interesting cases, improvement plans or innovations to discuss.

Could Easily Envision the Anticipated Use in Practice

Focus Group 2. To realize the potential added value as envisioned in the first focus group, participants indicated that elaborate AF, such as the examples provided, would be interesting to use in practice. However, participants envisioned that the examples would **not be used in daily practice**, but could be used in three "modes":

(1) In **(half) yearly meetings dedicated to AMR** aiming to evaluate status quo, discuss improvement strategies and strive for innovation. More frequent meetings were not deemed relevant, since resistance patterns and working routines (incl. individual behaviors) do not change fast, nor feasible, because of time-constraints.
(2) In **ongoing educational meetings of residents** (e.g. monthly) aiming to create AMR awareness and to reflect upon one's individual impact on quality and safety of care through their own diagnostic and AB treatment behaviors.
(3) As a **decision-support system** to make more proactive decisions both on individual patient level (e.g. choosing the right AB given the culture results) and on policy level (e.g. regularly changing empirical treatment policy).

The three modes could coexist in practice with different target groups, for whom the technological functionalities should differ.

3.2 Functionalities

HCW Could Clearly Verbalize Functionality Needs for Each AF Mode

Focus Group 2. Consequently, HCW expressed needs with regards to AF content within the before mentioned modes:

(1) Quality management: participants required an **overview** to quickly see what does (not) go well and improvement suggestions. The task force, AMR-experts and other interested HCW should be able to dive into the data **in-depth** (e.g. filtering and zooming in on subgroups/-topics). Both trends over time and benchmarks with other regional hospitals were required.
(2) Education: additional needs for educational purposes were the possibility to **zoom in to individual cases** that can be reflected upon. AF should support reconstructing and improving the reasoning underlying decisions (i.e. declarative information).
(3) Decision-support: participants required **timely advice** to optimize diagnostic and AB treatments for individual patients (i.e. personalized medicine) and warnings to proactively change empirical treatment.

HCW Could Clearly Envision Preconditions to Foster Implementation

Focus Group 2. Participants thought that AF alone would not improve outcomes. Additional activities are required **to engage HCW** in accepting and using AF in one or various modes such as creating a **task force**, having a **consensus meeting** and **training** on how to use AF. Participants did not want responsibility for collecting, analyzing and interpreting data, due to time constraints, insufficient data management skills and AMR knowledge: *"I think it can be dangerous for us to look at this ourselves... it is difficult to assess quality." (R3).* To come to **substantiated improvement strategies** that fit AF data and HCW working routines, and that contribute to improved individual patient care and limiting AMR, participants required **help from data-, quality-, and AMR-experts**.

3.3 Design

HCW Could Clearly Verbalize Design Needs

Focus Group 2. Participants appreciated a **clear and structured overview**, with **easily interpretable graphs** and an easy-to-use **navigation structure** (e.g. using workbook tabs per topic): *"Yes, I find it nicely structured. You still have to be careful not to present too much information on one tab, but it works nice with the tabs." (R4).* Participants preferred **graphs over numbers**, especially for scores that were too complicated to be represented with a single score. Furthermore, there must be **coherence between visuals and scores** (e.g. use green for positive). One participant indicated that choices on for example colors and lay-out should be based on generic design rules for dashboards.

3.4 Participatory Research

Participants were **enthusiastic** about the participatory research, because it incorporates their perspective from the start of development: *"You start from the user groups that you want to reach. From the whole process you learn if and how they are open for that and how they want to be persuaded." (R5).* At first, participants had some doubts about the qualitative and open nature of the focus groups. Along the way, participants realized its added value, because the abstracted findings and **prototype matched their needs and context**. However, concerns remained regarding **generalizability** of the findings: *"It could well be that it does not work in other hospitals ... We cannot just translate our findings to the rest of the country." (R3).* Finally, planning focus groups with as many HCW as possible was difficult, reflecting the **time- and resource-intensive** characteristics of focus groups.

4 Discussion

This paper demonstrated how participatory, bottom-up development can serve as the foundation for persuasive design and simultaneously increase engagement of end-users to foster sustainable implementation. The approach allowed for continuous formative evaluations to iteratively elicit and sharpen HCW' needs, contextual considerations and their interdependencies to design persuasive technology. The participatory bottom-up development persuaded end-users to remain engaged throughout the development process. By paying attention to needs and contextual considerations from the start of the persuasive development process, a fostering implementation context was provoked.

4.1 Persuasive Data-Driven Technologies

From the discussions on HCW' needs and contextual considerations, persuasiveness of AF technology mostly relied on content, functionalities and design. These are also of importance to the Persuasive System Design (PSD) Model [31]. Our bottom-up participatory approach revealed an additional layer to the PSD's design principles, thereby supporting the PSD postulates. By matching "top-down"-context requirements with bottom-up HCW' needs from the start of the development process, credibility support elements (e.g. expertise) are incrementally and transparently integrated in the content of the technology ánd in the end-users' perceptions. Primary task support elements (e.g. personalization) should be adaptable to the anticipated mode of use (e.g. quality management or training), while preconditions for successful AF use required changes in current working and training schemes. Users and their context thus shape the process of persuasive development and implementation, while reversely, the process shapes its users and context. For each wicked behavior-inflected problem, the users and context vary, requiring iteratively adaptable persuasive features and implementation strategies. Thus, the PSD should be complemented with models and strategies from the early development phases to increase persuasiveness and foster sustainable implementation, such as via actionable AF [32] and the multidimensional benefit framework [33].

4.2 Bottom-Up Participatory Approach to Foster Engagement/Ownership

To optimize the fit between humans, their context and the persuasive technology, an agile development process is required [34]. In this paper, we demonstrated why iterative phases are crucial for successful development: both HCW and the research team needed and used several sessions to clearly envision and verbalize their needs and the direction of the project. Additionally, we believe that the iterative nature of the bottomup participatory approach persuaded end-users (i.e. HCW) to engage with and take ownership of the development of the persuasive technology. Engagement needs to grow, especially for subjects that are not within the primary tasks of HCW, such as AMR [35]. We saw increased engagement with the subject (i.e. AMR), but also with reflecting on one's work (i.e. embracing quality management). The focus groups provided time to discuss matters that otherwise would have not been discussed. Also, the participatory approach created enthusiasm among the participants for the research topic and a stronger working relationship with the researchers. With that, it created more willingness to facilitate other research activities, such as data collection. Effect on implementation has yet to be determined, but participatory research has persuaded HCW to be closely engaged with this research. We are convinced that this is a crucial precondition to realize ownership and nurture local champions, which are highly recommended for successful sustainable implementation [36]. This study concretized ownership by showing that

HCW still require top-down support from data-, quality-, and AMR-experts to come to substantiated and sustainable improvement strategies. Rethinking ownership in terms of shared-ownership is thus required to embrace the true multidisciplinary nature of the complex wicked problems that the world faces today.

4.3 Professionalizing Persuasive Design

The bottom-up participatory approach allowed us to continuously adapt the persuasive design of the technology to HCW' needs and contextual considerations. In the persuasive design field, the need to match user, context and technology is not new [11]. However, few studies explicitly report on how this match can be realized. This study adds to this knowledge base by demonstrating the dependencies between HCW' needs and contextual considerations, and how the persuasive design can incorporate them. Furthermore, it showed how a bottom-up participatory approach can help in iteratively optimizing the user, context, technology fit. Crystallizing values and requirements from mixed-methods and transparently reporting on the taken steps are required to further professionalize the field of persuasive technology. First steps in that direction have already been taken by Kip et al. [37] and Van Velsen et al. [30].

4.4 Strengths and Limitations

A limitation to this bottom-up approach is that top-down considerations were mostly ignored. For example, only minimal efforts were taken to match Inspectorate audits that are a legal obligation. Matching new to existing initiatives is one of the key-factors of implementation and we did take actions to avoid 'discovering the wheel all over again'. We included top-down content by basing the discussions on existing quality-indicators from AMR-experts. Also, top-down considerations were incorporated in the questionnaire and focus group schemes by including AMR-experts in our research team. Including the top-down perspective indirectly thus was an explicit choice within our development project, because we were interested in studying the bottom-up approach (i.e. letting the HCW' needs and context guide the development process). Starting with a small and homogeneous target-group allowed us to gain in-depth insights at the cost of generalizability. This reflects a methodological issue apparent in all (pilot-) development processes and urges the need for local adaptations to the to-be-developed technology.

5 Conclusion

A bottom-up participatory development approach has the potential to improve the persuasive design of data-driven technologies and simultaneously increase engagement of end-users. This is a necessary precondition for the development of persuasive datadriven technologies that foster sustainable implementation.

References

1. World Health Organization [WHO]: World health statistics 2018: monitoring health for the SDGs, sustainable development goals. WHO, Geneva, p. 47

2. Holden, R.J., et al.: SEIPS 2.0: a human factors framework for studying and improving the work of healthcare professionals and patients. Ergonomics **56**(11), 1669–1686 (2013)
3. Lorencatto, F., et al.: Driving sustainable change in antimicrobial prescribing practice: how can social and behavioural sciences help? J. Antimicr. Chemother. **73**(10), 2613–2624 (2018)
4. Keizer, J., et al.: Finding the match between user and expert for optimal audit and feedback: sense-making of routinely collected antimicrobial data Journal of Antimicrobial Resistance and Infection Control (2019). p. Manuscript submitted for publication (copy with author)
5. Micallef, C., et al.: Secondary use of data from hospital electronic prescribing and pharmacy systems to support the quality and safety of antimicrobial use: a systematic review. J. Antimicrob. Chemother. **72**(7), 1880–1885 (2017). https://doi.org/10.1093/jac/dkx082
6. Van Mourik, M.S.M., et al.: Designing surveillance of healthcare-associated infections in the era of automation and reporting mandates. Clin. Infect. Dis. **66**(6), 970–976 (2018)
7. Ivers, N., et al.: Audit and feedback: effects on professional practice and healthcare outcomes. Cochrane Database Syst. Rev. **13**(6), CD000259 (2012)
8. Mitchell, B.G., et al.: Time spent by infection control professionals undertaking healthcare associated infection surveillance: a multi-centred cross sectional study. Infect. Dis. Health **21**(1), 36–40 (2016). https://doi.org/10.1016/j.idh.2016.03.003
9. Bal, A.M., Gould, I.M.: Antibiotic stewardship: overcoming implementation barriers. Curr. Opin. Infect. Dis. **24**(4), 357–362 (2011). https://doi.org/10.1097/QCO.0b013e3283483262
10. Colquhoun, H.L., et al.: Advancing the literature on designing audit and feedback interventions: identifying theory-informed hypotheses. Implement Sci. **12**(1), 117 (2017)
11. Van Gemert-Pijnen, J.E.W.C., et al.: eHealth Research, Theory and Development: A Multidisciplinary Approach. Routledge, London (2018)
12. Keizer, J., et al.: Antimicrobial Resistance Safety Stewardship (AMSS): empowering healthcare workers through quality management. In: International Forum on Quality & Safety in Healthcare: People Make Change (2019)
13. Keizer, J., et al.: Cross-border comparison of antimicrobial resistance (AMR) and AMR prevention measures: the healthcare workers' perspective. Antimicrob. Resist. Infect. Control **8**(1), 123 (2019). https://doi.org/10.1186/s13756-019-0577-4
14. World Health Organization [WHO]: Global Action Plan on Antimicrobial Resistance. WHO, Geneva (2015)
15. Kullar, R., et al.: The "epic" challenge of optimizing antimicrobial stewardship: the role of electronic medical records and technology. Clin. Infect. Dis. **57**(7), 1005–1013 (2013)
16. Baysari, M.T., et al.: The effectiveness of information technology to improve antimicrobial prescribing in hospitals: a systematic review and meta-analysis. Int. J. Med. Inform. **92**, 15–34 (2016). https://doi.org/10.1016/j.ijmedinf.2016.04.008
17. Creswell, J.W., et al.: Advanced mixed methods research designs. In: Tashakkori, A., Teddlie, C. (eds.) Handbook on Mixed Methods in the Behavioral and Social Sciences. Sage, Thousand Oaks (2003)
18. Stichting Werkgroep Antibioticabeleid [SWAB]: SWAB Guidelines for Antimicrobial Stewardship. SWAB, Bergen (2017)
19. Inspectorate, H.a.Y.C.: Toetsingskader TIP3. Ministry of Health, Welfare and Sports (2016)
20. World Health Organization [WHO]: Diagnostic stewardship: A guide to implementation in antimicrobial resistance surveillance sites. WHO (2016)
21. Filice, G., et al.: Antimicrobial Stewardship Programs in Inpatient Settings: A Systematic Review (2013)
22. Dellit, T.H., et al.: Infectious diseases society of America and the society for healthcare epidemiology of America guidelines for developing an institutional program to enhance antimicrobial stewardship. Clin. Infect. Dis. **44**(2), 159–177 (2007)
23. Centers for Disease Control and Prevention [CDC]: Core Elements of Hospital Antibiotic Stewardship Programs. US Department of Health and Human Services, Atlanta, GA (2014)

24. Storr, J., et al.: Core components for effective infection prevention and control programmes: new WHO evidence-based recommendations. Antimicr. Resist. Infect. Control **6**, 6 (2017)
25. Zingg, W., et al.: Hospital organisation, management, and structure for prevention of healthcare-associated infection: a systematic review and expert consensus. Lancet Infect. Dis. **15**(2), 212–224 (2015). https://doi.org/10.1016/s1473-3099(14)70854-0
26. Luz, C.F., et al.: Rapid analysis of diagnostic and antimicrobial patterns in R (RadaR): interactive open-source software app for infection management and antimicrobial stewardship. J. Med. Internet Res. **21**(6), e12843 (2019). https://doi.org/10.2196/12843
27. Willemsen, I., Kluytmans, J.: The infection risk scan (IRIS): standardization and transparency in infection control and antimicrobial use. Antimicr. Resist. Infect. Control **7**, 38 (2018)
28. Patton, M.Q.: Enhancing the quality and credibility of qualitative analysis. Health Serv. Res. **34**(5 Pt 2), 1189–1208 (1999)
29. Landis, J.R., Koch, G.G.: The measurement of observer agreement for categorical data. Biometrics **33**(1), 159–174 (1977). https://doi.org/10.2307/2529310
30. Van Velsen, L., et al.: Designing eHealth that matters via a multidisciplinary requirements development approach. JMIR Res. Protoc. **2**(1), e21 (2013). https://doi.org/10.2196/resprot.2547
31. Oinas-Kukkonen, H., Harjumaa, M.: Persuasive systems design: key issues, process model, and system features. Commun. Ass Inf. Syst. **24**, 28 (2009)
32. Hysong, S.J., et al.: Audit and feedback and clinical practice guideline adherence: making feedback actionable. Implement Sci. **1**, 9 (2006). https://doi.org/10.1186/1748-5908-1-9
33. Wang, Y., et al.: Big data analytics: understanding its capabilities and potential benefits for healthcare organizations. Technol. Forecast. Soc. Change **126**, 3–13 (2018)
34. Hekler, E.B., et al.: Agile science: creating useful products for behavior change in the real world. Transl. Behav. Med. **6**(2), 317–328 (2016). https://doi.org/10.1007/s13142-016-0395-7
35. Charani, E., Holmes, A.H.: Antimicrobial stewardship programmes: the need for wider engagement. BMJ Qual. Saf. **22**, 885–887 (2013). https://doi.org/10.1136/bmjqs-2013-002444
36. Zimmerman, B., et al.: Front-line ownership: generating a cure mindset for patient safety. Healthcare Pap. **13**(1), 6–22 (2013)
37. Kip, H., et al.: Putting the value in VR how to systematically and iteratively develop a value-based VR application with a complex target group. In: CHI Conference on Human Factors in Computing Systems Proceedings (CHI 2019), Glasgow, Scotland (2019)

HeartHealth: A Persuasive Mobile App for Mitigating the Risk of Ischemic Heart Disease

Oladapo Oyebode(✉) ⓘD, Boma Graham-Kalio, and Rita Orji ⓘD

Faculty of Computer Science, Dalhousie University, Halifax, NS B3H 4R2, Canada
{oladapo.oyebode,bm435858,rita.orji}@dal.ca

Abstract. Ischemic Heart Disease (IHD) is the leading cause of early deaths globally. It has been named as the leading cause of deaths in the United States and the second in Canada. The key risk factors of IHD include high blood cholesterol and high blood pressure, both of which can be prevented and managed through heart-healthy diets containing low saturated fats, trans fats, and sodium. Therefore, the goal of our work is to design a persuasive mobile app (called HeartHealth) that motivates people, especially adults, to keep their blood cholesterol and blood pressure at safe levels by eating heart-healthy diets. Our approach is in four stages. First, we create a low-fidelity prototype that implements ten persuasive strategies, and then assess the perceived persuasiveness of selected users towards the strategies through an online survey. Second, we analyze the responses collected and then select the most effective strategies which, in turn, are used to design the high-fidelity prototype. Third, we conduct another study on the high-fidelity prototype which requires participants to interact with the prototype and provide comments through an online survey. Fourth, we perform thematic analysis on the comments and then refine the prototype based on the results.

Keywords: Heart disease · Heart-healthy diet · Persuasive strategies · Mobile app design · Persuasive technology

1 Introduction

Ischemic Heart Disease (IHD), also called coronary heart disease, is the buildup of plaque in the heart's arteries which can lead to heart attack, heart failure, or death [1]. According to the Institute for Health Metrics and Evaluation (IHME)'s Global Burden of Disease (GBD) study, the IHD is the leading cause of early deaths globally and projected to occupy the top spot till 2040 [2]. Similarly, the World Health Organization (WHO) stated that cardiovascular diseases (CVDs), an example of which is IHD, cause 17.9 million deaths annually [3]. IHD can be effectively managed by reducing its key risk factors, especially high blood pressure and high blood cholesterol, through heart-healthy lifestyle choices [1, 4]. Specifically, preventing unhealthy diets that are high in saturated fats, trans fats, and sodium is one of the most effective lifestyle changes that reduce the risk of IHD [4, 5]. Thus, a solution is required that motivates people to monitor saturated

© Springer Nature Switzerland AG 2020
S. B. Gram-Hansen et al. (Eds.): PERSUASIVE 2020, LNCS 12064, pp. 126–138, 2020.
https://doi.org/10.1007/978-3-030-45712-9_10

fats, trans fats, and sodium in their diets in order to maintain their blood cholesterol and blood pressure at normal levels as a preventive and control measure. While many existing research has investigated persuasive technology (PT) usage for health and well-being, including healthy eating [6–8], little work has been done regarding the use of PT to motivate people with or without IHD to maintain normal blood cholesterol and blood pressure levels through heart-healthy diets.

Therefore, the purpose of our work is to design a persuasive mobile app, called HeartHealth, that motivates people to eat heart-healthy diets that contain low saturated fat, trans fat, and sodium with the goal of maintaining their blood cholesterol and blood pressure at normal levels.

Our approach is to first conduct a study that enables us to answer the following research question: *Which persuasive strategies are most effective in motivating people to eat diets containing low saturated fat, trans fat, and sodium?* We created a low-fidelity prototype that implement ten persuasive strategies and then assessed the perceived persuasiveness of selected users towards the strategies through an online survey. Afterwards, we analyzed the responses collected and then selected the most effective strategies which, in turn, are used to design the high-fidelity prototype. Furthermore, we conducted another study on the high-fidelity prototype which requires participants to interact with the prototype and provide comments through an online survey. We performed thematic analysis on the comments received and then refined the prototype based on the results.

The contributions of our work are: (1) The perceived persuasiveness assessment led to the design of an app that implements the most effective strategies for preventing and managing ischemic heart disease, thereby keeping its users engaged, focused, and motivated; (2) The refinements done as a result of user comments on the high-fidelity prototype will boost the app's usability, as well as the overall user experience.

2 Background

2.1 Dietary Levels, Blood Cholesterol Levels, and Blood Pressure Levels

The American Heart Association (AHA) and other credible health sources have explicitly stated the heart-healthy daily limit for saturated fat, trans fat, and sodium intake in their online reports [9–12]. In addition, the heart-healthy blood cholesterol and blood pressure levels were also mentioned [13, 14] to facilitate adequate monitoring. Table 1 shows the

Table 1. Recommended daily heart-healthy dietary levels

	Daily value	Remark
Saturated fat	13 g or 5–6% of total calories	Recommended total calories per day is 2000
Trans fat	2 g or less than 1% of total calories	Recommended total calories per day is 2000
Sodium	1,500 mg	Sodium comes from salt and other sodium-containing ingredients

recommended heart-healthy dietary values, Table 2 shows the healthy blood cholesterol levels based on age group and gender, and Table 3 shows the normal blood pressure level. These tables informed the design of the proposed HeartHealth mobile app.

Limiting saturated and trans fats intake without exceeding the recommended daily values shown in Table 1 will help lower or control high blood cholesterol [15]. Similarly, reducing sodium intake will curb high blood pressure [11].

Table 2. Healthy blood cholesterol levels by age and gender

Age group	Total cholesterol (mg/dL[a])	Non-HDL (mg/dL)	LDL (mg/dL)	HDL (mg/dL)
0–19	<170	<120	<100	>45
20 and above (Male)	125–200	<130	<100	≥40
20 and above (Female)	125–200	<130	< 100	≥50

[a]milligrams per deciliter of blood

Doctors use lipid panel to measure the total cholesterol, high-density lipoprotein (HDL) cholesterol[1], and the non-HDL cholesterol levels. The Non-HDL cholesterol, which includes low-density lipoprotein (LDL) cholesterol[2], is calculated by subtracting the HDL cholesterol level from the total cholesterol level. Thus, the blood cholesterol is high if either the total cholesterol or non-HDL level is higher than the healthy cholesterol level for the age groups and gender specified in Table 2 [13]. Table 3 shows the heart-friendly blood pressure level according to AHA [14]. Systolic is the upper number of a blood pressure reading (e.g., 110 mmHg/70 mmHg), while diastolic is the lower number.

Table 3. Healthy blood pressure level

Level	Systolic (mmHg)	Diastolic (mmHg)
Normal	<120	<80

2.2 Persuasiveness Versus Usability

According to Orji et al., *"Persuasiveness is a term used in describing a system's persuasive capability to motivate behaviour change. The perceived persuasiveness of a persuasive strategy or a system is an estimation of its ability to motivate behaviour change."* [16]. On the other hand, *"Usability is the extent to which a product can be used by specified users to achieve specified goals with effectiveness, efficiency and satisfaction in a specified context of use."* [17].

---

[1] also called good cholesterol.
[2] also called bad cholesterol.

3   Related Work

Many existing works have designed persuasive technologies (PTs) to motivate healthy eating [18, 19]. However, little work has been done in designing PTs targeted at IHD or CHD to encourage heart-healthy diets and ultimately help in maintaining heart-friendly blood cholesterol and blood pressure levels. One of the relevant works is that of Neubeck et al. [20]. They conducted a review of existing literature on cardiovascular disease (CVD) using persuasive technology. One of their findings is that real-time tracking of biometric data enables reflection on current habits and encourages pursuit of long-term goals. This also allows users to engage with a bigger picture of their health when they see the patterns and connections in the collected data. Finally, they summarized the importance of CVD app features during various life stages. Regarding persuasive strategies, they concluded that self-monitoring is moderately important for adults and older adults, but of low importance to adolescents or teenagers. Reward, however, is highly important for children, adolescents and adults. While personalization is moderately important for adolescents and older adults, it is highly important for adults but of low importance to children. Lastly, social comparison is highly important for adolescents, moderately important for adults, but of low importance to older adults.

These findings provide useful insights in designing our PT to prevent or manage IHD, since IHD is a type of CVD. For instance, we included the strategies mentioned in the literature above as part of the persuasive strategies to be evaluated by users in our first study.

4   Method

To answer the research question stated in Sect. 1, we designed a low-fidelity prototype implementing 10 persuasive strategies and then conducted an online survey involving 8 participants. The aim of the survey is to assess participants' perceived persuasiveness [21] towards the implemented strategies, and to determine and select the most effective strategies that will promote the intended behaviour. The selected persuasive strategies are used in designing the high-fidelity prototype which, in turn, is evaluated by the participants and then refined based on their feedback.

4.1   Prototype and Persuasive Strategies

The low-fidelity prototype implemented 10 persuasive strategies proposed by Oinas-Kukkonen et al. [22] and widely-used in health apps [20, 23, 24]. The strategies are *personalization, self-monitoring, reward, tunneling, reminder, authority, suggestion, reduction, praise*, and *social comparison*. The low-fidelity prototype, which constitutes a mobile app in its mockup form, is designed using the Balsamiq wireframing tool [25]. We created at least two screens modelling a typical user interaction with the proposed HeartHealth app for each strategy. Figures 1, 2, 3 and 4 show the low-fidelity prototype for *self-monitoring, suggestion, reduction,* and *reminder* respectively. Once the low-fidelity prototype has been evaluated and responses analyzed, the high-fidelity prototype is designed using only the most effective persuasive strategies. The high-fidelity prototype was designed using the Fluid UI tool [26].

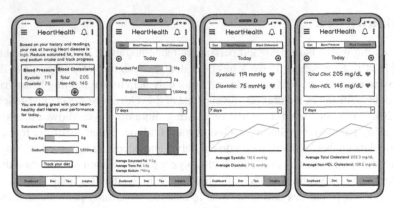

Fig. 1. Low-fidelity prototype for *Self-monitoring*

Fig. 2. Low-fidelity prototype for *Suggestion*

Fig. 3. Low-fidelity prototype for *Reduction*

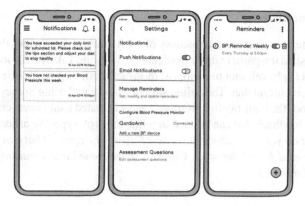

Fig. 4. Low-fidelity prototype for *Reminder*

4.2 Participants

Since the proposed mobile app (HeartHealth) is most suited for adults, participants recruited for the two studies were adults between 18 and 44 years old. Tables 4 and 5 show the demographic information of the participants and the sample size for the first and second online surveys respectively. The first survey (which focuses on assessing perceived persuasiveness) was completed by 9 participants, but 1 was excluded from analysis due to incomplete responses (i.e. majority of the strategies were not evaluated by the participant). The average completion time for the first survey was 6.23 min.

Table 4. Demographics of participants for the first online survey

Age	18–24 (12.5%), 25–34 (62.5%), 35–44 (25%)
Gender	Male (37.5%), Female (62.5%)
Sample size	8

On the other hand, 8 participants completed the second survey, which focuses on evaluating the high-fidelity prototype. 2 participants were excluded from analysis due to incomplete responses (i.e. questions were skipped by the participants). The average completion time for the second survey was 8.14 min.

Table 5. Demographics of participants for the second online survey

Age	18–24 (16.7%), 25–34 (83.3%)
Gender	Male (33.3%), Female (66.7%)
Sample size	6

4.3 Survey Questions

In measuring the perceived persuasiveness of each strategy [21] using the low-fidelity prototype, we asked the participants to indicate on a 7-point Likert scale to which degree the strategy will (a) be relevant to them, (b) motivate them to change their diet, (c) make them rethink their current diet. The online survey was created using SurveyMonkey [27]. On the other hand, the high-fidelity prototype was evaluated using open-ended questions to elicit holistic feedback that can be used to refine the prototype. We asked the following questions: *What do you think about the ease-of-use of the app?*, *What can you say about the overall look-and-feel of the app?*, *Can you share some ideas regarding how the app can be further improved?*

4.4 Survey Procedure

We conducted two online surveys each of which were made available to participants on different days. The uniform resource locator (URL) of the surveys were sent to participants' email boxes and also shared on Slack. Once the first survey, which evaluates the low-fidelity prototype, is opened by the participants, they were presented with a short introduction about the objective of the evaluation, and then a screen requesting their gender and age group. Afterwards, the participants were presented with a screen for each of the 10 persuasive strategies. Each screen shows the low-fidelity prototype in order of interaction, followed by the three questions for assessing participants' perceived persuasiveness of that strategy. On the other hand, the second survey, which evaluates the high-fidelity prototype, presents a screen showing a link to an environment where participants can interact with the prototype, followed by three open-ended questions for eliciting user comments.

4.5 Data Analysis

To assess the most effective persuasive strategies for HeartHealth, we first computed the mean score of three items measuring the perceived persuasiveness for each strategy per participant. Using R language, we created boxplots showing the perceived persuasiveness score for each strategy. The boxplots allowed us to visualize the differences in the persuasiveness of the strategies with respect to the neutral rating (which is the value 4 on the 7-point Likert scale). Moreover, thematic analysis was conducted on the comments provided by participants of the second survey.

5 Results

5.1 Perceived Persuasiveness of the Strategies

We compared the perceived persuasiveness scores to determine the strategies perceived to persuade users the most using the neutral rating as benchmark. In other words, we selected only the persuasive strategies whose scores are above the neutral rating. As shown in Fig. 5 and Table 6, perceived persuasiveness scores of the 10 strategies are above the neutral rating of 4. In decreasing order of persuasiveness, we found that *self-monitoring* followed by *suggestion, reminder, authority, personalization,* and *reduction* are the most effective strategies. On the other hand, *praise, reward, tunneling,* and *social comparison* emerged as the least persuasive strategies, listed in decreasing order of persuasiveness.

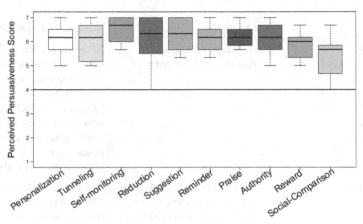

Fig. 5. Boxplots showing perceived persuasiveness of the 10 strategies on a scale of 1 to 7. The blue horizontal line represents the neutral rating. (Color figure online)

Table 6. Means and standard deviations of perceived persuasiveness towards the 10 strategies

Persuasive strategy	Mean	Standard deviation
Self-monitoring	6.500	0.534
Suggestion	6.292	0.700
Reminder	6.125	0.589
Authority	6.125	0.665
Personalization	6.083	0.636
Reduction	6.083	1.095
Praise	6.042	0.806
Reward	5.833	0.564
Tunneling	5.625	1.618
Social comparison	5.125	1.469

Since all the strategies were perceived to be effective based on the results above, we implemented the 10 strategies in the high-fidelity prototype.

5.2 Thematic Analysis of User Comments

The outcome of the thematic analysis conducted on the comments provided by the participants who evaluated the high-fidelity prototype are summarized in Table 7.

Table 7. Themes, descriptions, and example of comments

Theme	Description	Example of comments
Ease of use	How easy the app is to perform intended tasks	*"The app is clear and easy to navigate it also personalize your experience which I really love"* (C1) *"Fairly easy. I didn't know what to do on the dashboard when I first opened the app. A pointer to the action I should take may be necessary."* (C2)
User interface	Appearance and functionality in terms of colours, images, layout, fonts, and behaviour of controls	*"look almost like a real app; love the overall theme and colour and how these match the topic "* (C3) *"overall, it is simple and well organized"* (C4)
Data sharing with Healthcare Providers/Doctors	Ability to share data/reports with healthcare providers or doctors	*"...export or share functions to share collected data with a health provider"* (C5) *"the app may be linked with your family doctor, so he/she also check your progress "* (C6)
Additional navigation	Request for specific navigation elements for moving between certain features	*"...when starting the app there is only one arrow to move forward, there is no way to go back to fix input information."* (C8)
Theme customization	Ability to change the app's theme	*"...allow users to change the theme of the app"* (C9)

While 100% of respondents are satisfied with the app's user interface, 66.67% believe the app is very easy to use and 33.33% believe it is fairly easy to use. Majority of the changes recommended by the respondents (covering data sharing, theme customization, additional navigation, and ease of use) have been implemented and more refined high-fidelity prototype produced as a result. Some of the high-fidelity prototype for *self-monitoring*, *suggestion*, *reduction*, and *reminder* strategies are shown in Figs. 6, 7, 8 and 9.

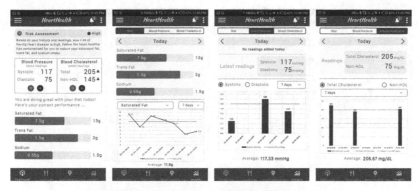

Fig. 6. High-fidelity prototype for *Self-monitoring*

Fig. 7. High-fidelity prototype for *Suggestion*

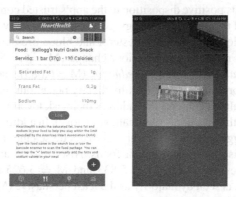

Fig. 8. High-fidelity prototype for *Reduction* strategy

Fig. 9. High-fidelity prototype for *Reminder*

6 Discussion

The results of the perceived persuasiveness study revealed interesting information about the extent to which intended users are persuaded by each strategy. For instance, *self-monitoring* is perceived as the most persuasive of the 10 strategies (M = 6.5). Thus, the proposed mobile app (HeartHealth) has a strong likelihood of motivating users to eat heart-healthy diets since it allows them to monitor their diets and also measure the effect of their diets on blood cholesterol and blood pressure levels through daily performance tracking and trend analysis. Furthermore, users want to receive suggestions regarding the right diets that can keep their heart healthy, hence the reason *suggestion* is the second most persuasive strategy (M = 6.292). Users are also motivated by the app's compliance with heart-healthy recommendations from world-class and highly respected organizations such as the American Heart Association (AHA) and National Heart, Lungs, and Blood Institute (NHLBI). This positive disposition to the app's trusted contents was reflected in the high mean score of the *authority* strategy (M = 6.125). Moreover, being *reminded* or notified of their food logging, blood cholesterol and blood pressure readings is equally perceived by users as required for behaviour change (M = 6.125). With mean scores above 6.0, *personalization* (M = 6.083), *reduction* (M = 6.083), and *praise* (M = 6.042) are also effective for promoting heart-healthy dietary behaviour. For instance, users are provided with personalized contents that address their risk level (which is influenced by their age, gender, health condition(s), and family history). In addition, users are provided quicker means for logging their foods (through barcode scanner and intelligent search feature), and also praised for logging their foods. Also, *reward* and *tunneling* are also persuasive but with lesser impact (M = 5.833 and M = 5.625 respectively). *Social comparison*, however, is seen by majority as the least persuasive (M = 5.125) compared to other strategies.

Although the sample size of the studies may not be enough to draw strong conclusions about the perceived persuasiveness of the strategies, the perceived persuasiveness assessment led to the design of an app that implements the most effective strategies for preventing and managing ischemic heart disease, thereby keeping its users engaged, focused, and motivated. In addition, the refinements done as a result of user comments on the high-fidelity prototype will boost the app's usability, as well as the overall user experience.

7 Conclusion and Future Work

We designed a persuasive mobile app, called HeartHealth, that motivates people to eat heart-healthy foods containing low saturated fat, trans fat, and sodium using only the persuasive strategies perceived to be the most effective for this purpose. We created low-fidelity prototype implementing 10 strategies and then conducted an online survey to assess participants' perceived persuasiveness towards the strategies. Our results revealed that all the strategies are effective to achieve our goal since their perceived persuasiveness scores are above the neutral rating of 4. Furthermore, we created high-fidelity prototype using the 10 strategies and conducted another online survey so that participants can evaluate the prototype and provide feedback or comments which were then used to refine the prototype.

Our future work is to conduct wider studies involving many participants that meet at least one of the following recruitment criteria: (1) *without heart disease nor with related health condition(s)*, (2) *without heart disease but with related health conditions (such as diabetes, hypertension, or stroke)*, and (3) *with heart disease*. Also, we will introduce physical activity tracking and allow users to integrate HeartHealth with their favourite workout devices (such as Fitbit) or apps (such as Google Fit) since physical activity helps to burn fats. We also plan to introduce coaching feature so that users can share their progress directly with heart doctors, specialists, and nutritionists and receive real-time advice or diagnosis. Finally, introducing features that discourage smoking habit, which is detrimental to the heart, will also be considered.

References

1. Public Health Agency of Canada: Heart Disease in Canada (2017). https://www.canada.ca/en/public-health/services/publications/diseases-conditions/heart-disease-canada.html
2. Institute for Health Metrics & Evaluation: Findings of the Global Burden of Disease Study (2018). http://www.healthdata.org/sites/default/files/files/policy_report/2019/GBD_2017_Booklet.pdf
3. World Health Organization (WHO): Noncommunicable diseases key facts. World Health Organization (2018)
4. National Heart Lung and Blood Institute (NHLBI): Ischemic Heart Disease. https://www.nhlbi.nih.gov/health-topics/ischemic-heart-disease
5. National Center for Chronic Disease Prevention & Health Promotion: Behaviors That Increase Risk for Heart Disease (2019). https://www.cdc.gov/heartdisease/risk_factors.htm
6. Orji, R., et al.: Modeling gender differences in healthy eating determinants for persuasive intervention design BT. In: Persuasive Technology, pp. 161–173 (2013)
7. Orji, R., Moffatt, K.: Persuasive technology for health and wellness. Health Inform. J. **24**, 66–91 (2018)
8. IJsselsteijn, W., de Kort, Y., Midden, C., Eggen, B., van den Hoven, E.: Persuasive technology for human well-being: setting the scene. In: IJsselsteijn, W.A., de Kort, Y.A.W., Midden, C., Eggen, B., van den Hoven, E. (eds.) PERSUASIVE 2006. LNCS, vol. 3962, pp. 1–5. Springer, Heidelberg (2006). https://doi.org/10.1007/11755494_1

9. American Heart Association: Saturated Fat. https://www.heart.org/en/healthy-living/healthy-eating/eat-smart/fats/saturated-fats
10. American Heart Association (AHA): Trans Fats. https://www.heart.org/en/healthy-living/healthy-eating/eat-smart/fats/trans-fat
11. American Heart Association (AHA): How much sodium should I eat per day? https://www.heart.org/en/healthy-living/healthy-eating/eat-smart/sodium/how-much-sodium-should-i-eat-per-day
12. A.D.A.M. Medical Encyclopedia: Facts about trans fats. https://medlineplus.gov/ency/patientinstructions/000786.htm
13. National Heart Lung and Blood Institute (NHLBI): High Blood Cholesterol. https://www.nhlbi.nih.gov/health-topics/high-blood-cholesterol
14. American Heart Association (AHA): Understanding Blood Pressure Readings. https://www.heart.org/en/health-topics/high-blood-pressure/understanding-blood-pressure-readings
15. American Heart Association (AHA): Prevention and Treatment of High Cholesterol. https://www.heart.org/en/health-topics/cholesterol/prevention-and-treatment-of-high-cholesterol-hyperlipidemia
16. Orji, et al.: Deconstructing persuasiveness of strategies in behaviour change systems using the ARCS model of motivation. Behav. Inf. Technol. **38**, 319–335 (2019)
17. Jokela, T., et al.: The standard of user-centered design and the standard definition of usability: analyzing ISO 13407 against ISO 9241-11. In: ACM International Conference Proceeding Series, vol. 46, pp. 53–60 (2003)
18. Chu, H., et al.: Persuasive technology to improve eating behavior using a sensor-embedded fork. In: ACM International Joint Conference on Pervasive and Ubiquitous Computing, pp. 319–329 (2014)
19. Kaptein, et al.: Adaptive persuasive systems: a study of tailored persuasive text messages to reduce snacking. ACM Trans. Interact. Intell. Syst. **2**, 1–25 (2012)
20. Neubeck, et al.: The mobile revolution-using smartphone apps to prevent cardiovascular disease. Nat. Rev. Cardiol. **12**, 350–360 (2015)
21. Drozd, F., Lehto, T., Oinas-Kukkonen, H.: Exploring perceived persuasiveness of a behavior change support system: a structural model. In: Bang, M., Ragnemalm, E.L. (eds.) PERSUASIVE 2012. LNCS, vol. 7284, pp. 157–168. Springer, Heidelberg (2012). https://doi.org/10.1007/978-3-642-31037-9_14
22. Harri, O., Marja, H.: Persuasive systems design: key issues, process model, and system features. Commun. Assoc. Inf. Syst. **24**, 96 (2009)
23. Nurcan, A., Duygu, F.: Use of Persuasion Strategies in Mobile Health Applications. Springer, Cham (2018). https://doi.org/10.1007/978-3-319-73135-3_2
24. Wais-Zechmann, B., Gattol, V., Neureiter, K., Orji, R., Tscheligi, M.: Persuasive technology to support chronic health conditions: investigating the optimal persuasive strategies for persons with COPD. In: Ham, J., Karapanos, E., Morita, P.P., Burns, C.M. (eds.) PERSUASIVE 2018. LNCS, vol. 10809, pp. 255–266. Springer, Cham (2018). https://doi.org/10.1007/978-3-319-78978-1_21
25. Balsamiq Studios: Quick and Easy Wireframing Tool. https://balsamiq.com/wireframes/
26. Fluid: Fluid UI - Create Web and Mobile Prototypes in Minutes. https://www.fluidui.com/
27. SurveyMonkey: SurveyMonkey: How It Works. https://www.surveymonkey.com/mp/take-a-tour/?ut_source=megamenu

Learning to Stop Smoking: Understanding Persuasive Applications' Long-Term Behavior Change Effectiveness Through User Achievement Motivation

Jaap Ham[1](✉) and Sitwat Usman Langrial[2,3]

[1] Eindhoven University of Technology, Eindhoven, The Netherlands
j.r.c.ham@tue.nl
[2] Sur University College, Sur, Oman
Dr.Sitwat.Langrial@suc.edu.om
[3] Namal Institute, Mianwali, Pakistan
Sitwat@namal.edu.pk

Abstract. Compromising smoking cessation applications' effectiveness, many users relapse. We propose that long-term adoption of persuasive technology is (partly) dependent on users' motivational orientation. Therefore, we studied the potential relationship between user's achievement motivation and the long-term behavior change effectiveness of persuasive technology. One-hundred users of a smoking cessation app filled out a questionnaire assessing their motivational orientation and (long-term) behavior change rates. Based on research findings, we expected that *participants with stronger learning goal orientation* (who are focused on self-improvement and persistent when facing failure) would report a *higher* long-term behavior change success rate. In contrast, we expected that *participants with a stronger performance goal orientation* (focused on winning, for whom solitary failures can undermine intrinsic motivation) would report *lower* long-term success. Results confirmed our hypotheses. This research broadens our understanding of how persuasive applications' effectiveness relates to user achievement motivation.

Keywords: Smoking cessation · Behavior change · Persuasive technology · Health · Achievement orientation

1 Introduction

Health risks associated with smoking are well studied and reported. Research shows that smoking is one of the factors leading to acute conditions such as lung cancer and cardiovascular diseases [1]. A high majority of smokers realize health risks associated with smoking, and consequently try to quit, however, fails in the effort [2]. There are different methods available for smokers to quit, for example, instructional and conditioning methods. A recent trend in helping smokers quit is through the use of smoking cessation applications (apps). These apps are designed to support smokers quit smoking through

© Springer Nature Switzerland AG 2020
S. B. Gram-Hansen et al. (Eds.): PERSUASIVE 2020, LNCS 12064, pp. 139–149, 2020.
https://doi.org/10.1007/978-3-030-45712-9_11

tracking, self-monitoring and distracting them from smoking [3]. It can be reasoned that most of the smoking cessation apps are designed based on the principles of Persuasive Technology (PT). PTs are technologies that are designed to change peoples' attitudes and/or behaviors without the use of coercion or deception [4, 5]. PTs have the potential to be used as a tool for preventive health engineering. PTs have already shown potential in supporting people to live with healthy lifestyle and can therefore help prevent a wide range of medical conditions [6, 7]. Although PTs are promising in promoting healthy behaviors, actual behavior change effectiveness is often limited. The limited effectiveness of smoking cessation apps could be explained by the finding that most of these apps are not grounded in theory [8]. Still, recent research indicates that smoking cessation apps that are designed using behavior change theories are also not proving to be very successful [9].

One major challenge for preventive health through the use of PT is to be able to change human behavior over a longer period of time. It is frequently highlighted in literature that PTs for smoking cessation show promise however the effect is rather short-term. To date, it is hard to find a study that has evaluated and reported long-term effectiveness of smoking cessation apps. Some of the research studies underscore that long-term effectiveness of PTs for behaviors such as smoking does not even exist [10]. Therefore, the area relating to the long-term effectiveness of PTs in behavior change still calls for further research. In this study, we investigated whether there was a correlation between users' motivations and long-term effectiveness of PTs.

Smoking remains the common most preventable cause of acute illnesses in the modern world [11, 12]. PTs can play an important role in addressing this problem. This could be, for example, done through developing apps to support individuals to quit. Fogg [4], explains the mechanisms of using computing devices through the functional triad. The functional triad can be easily incorporated in a smoking cessation apps. As a tool, an app can help individuals track statistics on the number of cigarettes smoked, as a media, an app can present immediate feedback on health-related consequences and as a social actor, an app can provide support, for example, through goal-setting, rewards, feedback and even social support. One of the challenges for smoking cessation is that it cannot be studied as a "single act of observable behavior". In contrast to less frequent behaviors, smoking brings in the factor of behavior change process and it is therefore that some researchers argue that persuasion through technology should be studied as a long-term process [13].

To the best of our knowledge, research on the long-term effectiveness of PTs is scarce. Among the few, one study examined long-term effectiveness of wearable devices for promoting fitness. This study concludes that users who adhere with PTs for a longer period of time have different needs especially because they are expected to move a step further towards maintaining a positive behavior [10]. The same could be the case with users of smoking cessation apps. However, it is a highly contextualized and personalized area of study. Ubhi et al. [9] studied smoking cessation apps and observed that 81% of the users stopped using the app after just four weeks, which is an evidence of a low adherence rate. Extended adherence is essential for any kind of behavior change as it is inherently a long-term process. Experts from other disciplines including psychology and social sciences have worked to understand the reasons for short-term adoption of technologies that promote healthy behaviors. The most cited work in this area is Technology Acceptance Model (TAM). According to TAM, whether an individual has an intention to adopt a technology depends on two major factors i.e. perceived usefulness and perceived ease of use [13]. TAM has been extended by including a third factor called social influence and it has been further integrated with models of technology acceptance [14] and used for investigating acceptance of persuasive robots [28]. We argue that TAM is not particularly useful when it comes to determining why people stay motivated in using PTs in the long run. Firstly, TAM explains only about 40% of variance in adoption [15]. Secondly, the model is used to explain whether or not an individual has an intention to start using a specific technology. Our argument is that initial adoption of a technology is not sufficient enough to help understand why individuals continue or discontinue to use that particular technology. It is therefore that we believe that long-term adoption of a given PT leading to achievement of sustained behavior change largely depends on individual users' motivations. To investigate our hypothesis, we referred to the theory of Achievement Motivation [16].

Little if any research is available on what motivates people to use and adhere with PTs. Earlier researchers have postulated that adaptive motivational patterns play an important role in long term success of a certain goal [17]. These patterns are behavioral in nature and facilitate founding, continuing and achieving those goals that have high value for individuals [17]. Dweck's framework highlights two types of achievements: *Learning Goals* and *Performance Goals*. Of the two, learning goals aim at improving one's abilities to perform better. For example, to quit smoking could be seen as a learning goal for an individual to quit smoking would mean that the individual has to prepare to quit smoking by learning and mastering the skills needed for such a behavior change. Performance goals on the other hand can be seen as making a stricter target. For example, planning to quit smoking by the end of the month. According to [18], adoption of learning goals generally leads to better motivational patterns as compared with adoption of performance goals [18]. Another, related theoretical framework distinguishes three types of goals i.e. (i) Learning Goals, (ii) Performance-approach Goals and Performance-avoidance Goals [19]. According to this framework, individuals position themselves either around improving their competence or display an avoidance attitude. Simply put, the two approaches are either aimed at achieving a goal with self-confidence to be successful (through a learning goal or a performance-approach goal) or avoiding working towards a goal anticipating fear of failure (through a performance-avoidance goal) [19]. They argue that adoption of approach-oriented goals often leads to high motivation when compared with adoption of avoidance-oriented goals [19].

Subsequently, approach-oriented goals lead to formation of behaviors that are centered on positive outcomes. If this stands true, then it can be safely argued that approach-oriented goals improve task engagement and greater potential of mastering a skill. According to [20], the approaches towards goals depend on the context. One possible explanation would be that performance approach goals are more likely to avoid failures. However, changing from a learning goal to performance goal is less likely to happen as failures do not necessarily undermine learning goals. In the context of smoking cessation, if an individual with a *performance* goal experiences relapse after quitting, there is a chance that in the next attempt the individual might focus on avoiding another relapse rather than focusing on continuing quitting. On the contrary, if the same individual had set a *learning* goal, the chance of shifting towards performance avoidance might be far less because a relapse would not undermine the original goal. On the other hand, performance-approach goals can lead to high performance and adaptive motivational patterns when individuals experience a phase of success. One study shows that those individuals who had set performance-approach goals actually scored higher grades than those who had set learning goals [21]. This is an interesting finding and reveals that learning goals are not always as effective as advocated.

To sum up, learning goals are linked with high intrinsic and adaptive motivational patterns that is characterized by high persistence. The performance-avoidance goals have a detrimental effect on motivational patterns and performance and lastly, performance-approach goals can result in either negative or positive outcomes in terms of motivational behaviors. It is important to note that majority of research on achievement goals was carried out in the field of Education, Workplace and Sports [22, 23]. Adoption of achievement goals and its relation to sustained success in the area of PT for healthy behaviors is not yet studied.

2 Objectives

This paper sets the first step towards investigating a possible connection between achievement motivation and PT behavior change effectiveness. Theories on achievement motivation assert that challenges in behavior change could be tackled if individuals had adaptive motivational patterns. Such motivational patterns are linked to setting learning goals, and goals that are approach oriented. We therefore inferred that there might be a link between the type of goal and the long-term success that an individual might experience through the use of PTs. We also investigated a possible connection between goal types and success that individuals experience when using smoking cessation apps. The objective is to identify whether there is any correlation between the type of achievement goals and their long-term success through the use of PT. The following research question is therefore developed:

What is the relationship between users' achievement motivation and the effectiveness of Persuasive Technology (smoking cessation app) for attaining sustained (long-term) behavior change?

To investigate the research question, we conducted an online survey where participants reported their smoking cessation success, the type of achievement motivation that they had and their demographical contexts. Through the analysis of a possible relationship between participants' smoking cessation success and their achievement motivation helped come up with the following hypotheses:

Hypothesis 1a: Individuals who score higher on learning goals and performance-approach goals also have a higher success rate in smoking cessation.
Hypothesis 1b: Individuals who score higher on performance-avoidance goals have a lower success rate in smoking cessation.

Earlier studies have shown that adoption of performance-avoidance goals is unfavorable for intrinsic motivation and task performance when compared with the adoption of performance-approach goals and learning goals [19, 20]. We assumed that people who score high on performance avoidance goals to have less chance to quit smoking when compared with people who score higher on performance approach and learning goals. Our assumption creates further hypotheses:

Hypothesis 2a: Individuals who score higher on learning goals stay smoke free for longer period of time.
Hypothesis 2 b: Individuals who score higher on performance approach and performance avoidance approach goals stay smoke free for shorter period of time.

3 Methods

An a priori power analysis using G* Power [24] indicated that we needed no less than 82 participants in order to have 80% power for detecting a medium sized correlation with a two-tailed significance level of .05. A total of 100 (32 M, 68 F) participants took part in the study. All the participants were proficient at the English language. In addition, all participants were trying to quit smoking or had tried to quit. In addition, all participants used a smoking cessation app to receive support in quitting smoking.

Recruitment was carried out through two different channels. First, participants were recruited through a social media page "Smoke Free" from Facebook. This page hosted a community who can find support to quit smoking. We posted a link to the survey on this page regularly for a period of two months describing the objectives of the research. Second, a group of participants were recruited at shopping malls and public transport stations. Potential participants were asked if they had ever used a smoke cessation app. Those who had used such apps were given access to the link to the survey and requested to register their responses. Participants who clicked the link were directed to the survey where a brief overview of the research was presented advising the participants about the objectives, expected duration to complete the survey and data confidentiality policy. To ensure that data is not duplicated, participants had to log in using their emails in order to fill out the survey. Subsequently, participants were asked about the type/s of apps that they had used for smoking cessation. An option of "None" was included for those who had never used an app. The following three pages of the survey, participants responded to questions about their smoking behaviors, achievement goals, and their demographic context. On an average, it took six (6) minutes for the participants to complete the survey. No monetary rewards were offered to the participants.

To examine participants' smoking behaviors while using the Smoke Free app, we included questions on smoking behavior in the survey. The questions were based on previous studies [25, 26]. As there was no clear consensus in earlier studies on how smoking cessation is measured, we decided to use a combination of questions to construct a reliable measure. In all, seven (7) questions targeted smoking behaviors to measure success and persistence. A factor analysis and analysis of Cronbach's Alpha rendered two (2) measures for smoking cessation performance. The first measure of performance was the sum of answers to four (4) questions that indicated the success rate experienced by participants. These measures showed high internal consistency (Cronbach Alpha = .84) based on the following four questions:

How many relapses did you experience while using the app?
Did you smoke since the intended day of quitting?
Do you smoke less after adopting to use the app?
Did you successfully quit smoking using the app?

The second measure of performance indicated the length of duration that participants managed to stay smoke free. Participants responded whether they had remained smoke free for less than a week, from a week to one month and from one to three months. The duration of staying smoke free was used to measure the long-term performance in order to test our second hypothesis. The third measure focused on participants' adoption of learning, performance-approach and performance-avoidance goals while trying to quit smoking. For this purpose, we applied an adaptation of the Achievement Goal Questionnaire developed by [21]. This questionnaire was used to examine the types of achievement goals that university students adopted for a Psychology class while the performance goal items measured their motivation to perform well in the class compared to other students and contained six questions per goal types. While the classroom context is highly different from smoking cessation context however we believe that it suited our study as participants could still be motivated to perform well when compared to other people in their quest to quit smoking. Further, the subject at hand is unique in the sense that instead of learning Psychology, participants of this study had an opportunity to learn more about smoking cessation. For these reasons, we rephrased the items developed by [21] in order to fit the study context.

A factor analysis confirmed that the items could be divided into three independent groups. Some of the items from the Achievement Goal questionnaire did not load high on either of the three factors and were therefore dropped. Subsequent calculations of Cronbach's Alpha showed that the adaption of achievement goals questionnaire rendered three internally consistent measures. First, a learning goal was calculated by averaging the score on five learning goal questions with a high reliability (Cronbach Alpha = .94). A performance-approach goal measure was calculated by averaging the scores on five performance-approach goal items that showed high reliability (Cronbach Alpha = .91). A performance-avoidance goal measure was calculated by averaging the scores on two performance-avoidance goal items that showed significant reliability (Cronbach Alpha = .84). Since the achievement goal items were rephrased versions of the original items constructed by [21], the items were developed slightly different from the original ones based on the context of the study. The factor analyses for internal consistency helped us come up with three components. According to [27] several demographic measures are closely connected to the success rate for to smoking cessation. Participants answered 11 questions on the demographical circumstances that might impact their smoking behavior. These items were used for control variables as well as for validating measures that we developed by comparing results to earlier studies. Important demographic variables include the participant's age, whether or not they have other smokers in their family, their desire to quit smoking and whether or not they have invested money to buy the smoking cessation app.

4 The Smoking Cessation App

All participants [n = 100] used a smoking cessation app in their quest to quit smoking. Majority of participants (89%) used the Smoke Free app that had main features comprising of a dashboard, diary and progress screen. Table 1 presents the means, standard deviation, observed ranges, possible ranges and reliabilities for the main areas of interest for this study. On an average, participants were highly successful in their quest to quit smoking using the app. Three quarters of the participants indicated to be not smoking at the time they completed the survey. In addition, most of the participants seemed to have a learning goal-oriented approach with a mean average learning goal score of 3.92 on a scale from 1 to 5.

Table 1. Means, standard deviation, observed ranges, possible ranges and reliabilities.

Variable	Mean	SD	Observed range	Possible range	Cronbach's alpha
Rate of cessation success	9.22	3.70	0.00–12.00	0.00–12.00	.84
Performance-approach goal	2.39	1.31	1.00–5.00	1.00–5.00	.91
Performance-avoidance goal	3.41	1.38	1.00–5.00	1.00–5.00	.94
Learning goal	3.92	1.15	1.40–5.00	1.00–5.00	.84
Time not smoked	1.29	1.27	0–3*	0–3	–

*0 = Less than one week; 1 = One week to one month; 2 = One month to three months; 3 = More than three months

5 Results

Results of the study provided partial support for hypothesis 1a, which stated that individuals who score high on learning goals and performance-approach goals are more likely to have higher success rate in smoking cessation. In line with hypothesis 1a, participants who scored higher on the *learning goal measure* also scored higher on success rate, as indicated by a first order Spearman rank correlation which is controlled for the effects of performance-avoidance goals, r(97) = .17, p = .092. Not confirming hypothesis 1a, we observed no meaningful correlation between *performance-approach goal scores* and *success rate*. Likewise, we observed insignificant zero-order correlations between success rate and learning goals or performance-approach goals. Results supported hypothesis 1b that stated that individuals who score higher on performance-avoidance goals will have lower success rate in smoking cessation. In line with hypothesis 1b, participants who scored higher on performance-avoidance goals scored lower success rates as indicated by a first order Spearman rank correlation r(97) = −.18, p = .074. There was no support for hypothesis 2a which stated that individuals who score higher on learning goals to be smoke free for longer time period. That is, results showed no meaningful correlation between learning goals scores and the amount of time that participants reported to be smoke free. Finally, results showed partial evidence supporting hypothesis 2b, which stated that individuals who score higher on performance-approach and performance-avoidance goals to be smoke free for a shorter time period. In line with hypothesis 2b, participants who scored higher on *performance-avoidance goals* reported less often to be smoke free for a long period of time, as indicated by partial Spearman rank correlation $r(96) = -.18$, $p = .078$. Contrary to hypothesis 2b results did not show a correlation between *performance-approach goals* and the amount of time that participants reported to be smoke free.

The results indicate that the recruitment strategy had a highly significant relationship with success rate, $t(98) = -5.21$, $p < .00001$, with participants who were recruited through social media having higher scores. On an average, participants in the study were successful with 54 out of 100 scoring the maximum 12 points on our measure for success rate. On average, the participants had a success rate of 9.22 on a scale from 0 to 12. Most of these participants were recruited through social media. A small group of participants were recruited by approaching them in person. Highly significant zero order correlations were found between measures for smoking cessation success rate and four items from the demographic questionnaire. Firstly, participants who had indicated high desire to quit smoking scored high on success rate, $r = .54$, $p < .01$. Secondly, participants with a higher income also scored high on success rate, $r = .35$, $p < .01$. Thirdly, older participants scored high success rates, $r = .27$, $p < .01$. Fourthly, participants who smoked more cigarettes prior to the quitting attempt had a higher success rate, $r = .38$, $p < .01$. Except for the number of cigarettes smoked per day, the findings of this study are in line with previous research on smoking cessation. In the presented study, we noticed that participants who smoked more cigarettes before attempting to quit had higher income, a higher desire to quit and more often used a paid app. This could be one explanation for why participants who smoke more were more successful. We also found significant differences in success rates for gender and whether participants used a free app or a paid one. Females were more successful when compared with males, $t(97) = -2.93$, $p < .001$. In addition, participants who indicated that they paid for the apps were more successful when compared with those who used free smoking cessation apps, $t(98) = -3.81$, $p < .001$.

6 Discussion

In this study, we investigated achievement goals and whether they can contribute to quit smoking for a longer period of time. Our major focus was on the first three months of effects of achievements goals because the majority of smokers give up their pursuit and get back to smoking during this time period. Previous research on achievement goals shows that certain types of goals are more beneficial for persistent behaviors. Learning goals [21] have shown to lead to higher performance and intrinsic motivation. We conducted an online survey with participants who had used a smoking cessation app. The participants reported on their smoking behaviors while using the app, and we measured their achievement goals (learning goal and performance goals) and demographic contexts. Supporting our hypotheses, results showed that participants who scored higher on the learning goal measure also reported to have a higher success rate. Results also indicated that participants who scored higher on performance-avoidance goals reported to have a lower success rate. Additionally, participants who scored higher on performance-avoidance goals reported less often to be smoke free for a long period of time. Overall, the results from the current study suggest that the existing theories of achievement goals [21] can be generalized to the context of smoking cessation and PT.

Based on the results, we propose that people in the early stage of smoking cessation can benefit more from adopting learning goals. Learning about smoking cessation could prepare people to quit by developing quitting strategies that they could later apply in the process of quitting and in case of relapse. When people are fully prepared to quit smoking, they might benefit from performance-approach goals. However, further studies are called for to validate this proposition. In this study, we did not make any distinction between different stages of smoking cessation that is indeed a limitation. This study adds significant value to the field of PT as a first step towards investigating a possible relationship between achievement goals and long-term success of PTs (apps). The majority of research in the area of PT focuses on short term adoption, which we believe is a limitation to the field itself. Furthermore, studies that investigated success rates of smoking cessation apps do not investigate why some people are more successful than others using the same app or technology and long-term effect and use of PTs is also not well studied [10]. By recruiting both recent adopters and long-term users of a smoking cessation app, we took the first step towards investigating reasons of failure within the first few months of using such technologies. However, since we did not follow up participants for a longer period of time, extended duration remains another limitation of this study. However, we did try to include people with different levels of success and found indicators that achievement goals of users to impact long term success.

Also, the current results suggest that personalization of persuasive technology (see e.g., [29]) improves its effectiveness. That is, included in the design of technology (and all contexts) are elements that activate certain goals. The current results show that fitting (personalizing) this technology to user characteristics might be beneficial.

This study provides evidence that partitioning of learning goals, performance-avoidance goals and performance-approach goals [21] can be applied in the field of behavior change and PT. The results indicate that further research on the relationship between achievement goals and quality of life could be promising. Finally, this study highlights the negative effects of performance-avoidance goals and that these can be applied in the context of behavior change and PT. The results confirm these effects in the short term and provide an indication of the same for medium to long term. We believe that these findings add value for PT researchers who investigate ways to improve quality of life through continued long-term healthy behaviors.

Acknowledgements. We would like to thank Ahmet Aman (Eindhoven University of Technology) for important contributions and for running the study, and Mila Davids (Eindhoven University of Technology) for her valuable comments.

References

1. Bauer, U.E., Briss, P.A., Goodman, R.A., Bowman, B.A.: Prevention of chronic disease in the 21st century: elimination of the leading preventable causes of premature death and disability in the USA. Lancet **384**(9937), 45–52 (2014)
2. Chapman, S., MacKenzie, R.: The global research neglect of unassisted smoking cessation: causes and consequences. PLoS Med. **7**(2), e1000216 (2010)
3. Valdivieso-López, E., et al.: Efficacy of a mobile application for smoking cessation in young people: study protocol for a clustered, randomized trial. BMC Public Health **13**(1), 704 (2013). https://doi.org/10.1186/1471-2458-13-704
4. Fogg, B.J., Fogg, B.: Persuasive Technology: Using Computers to Change What We Think and Do. Morgan Kaufmann Publishers, Amsterdam (2003)
5. Oinas-Kukkonen, H.: Behavior change support systems: a research model and agenda. In: Ploug, T., Hasle, P., Oinas-Kukkonen, H. (eds.) PERSUASIVE 2010. LNCS, vol. 6137, pp. 4–14. Springer, Heidelberg (2010). https://doi.org/10.1007/978-3-642-13226-1_3
6. Halko, S., Kientz, Julie A.: Personality and persuasive technology: an exploratory study on health-promoting mobile applications. In: Ploug, T., Hasle, P., Oinas-Kukkonen, H. (eds.) PERSUASIVE 2010. LNCS, vol. 6137, pp. 150–161. Springer, Heidelberg (2010). https://doi.org/10.1007/978-3-642-13226-1_16
7. Klasnja, P., Consolvo, S., McDonald, D.W., Landay, J.A., Pratt, W.: Using mobile and personal sensing technologies to support health behavior change in everyday life: lessons learned. In: AMIA Annual Symposium Proceedings, vol. 2009, p. 338. American Medical Informatics Association (2009)
8. Abroms, L.C., Westmaas, J.L., Bontemps-Jones, J., Ramani, R., Mellerson, J.: A content analysis of popular smartphone apps for smoking cessation. Am. J. Prev. Med. **45**(6), 732–736 (2013)
9. Ubhi, H.K., Kotz, D., Michie, S., van Schayck, O.C., Sheard, D., Selladurai, A., West, R.: Comparative analysis of smoking cessation smartphone applications available in 2012 versus 2014. Addict. Behav. **58**, 175–181 (2016)
10. Fritz, T., Huang, E.M., Murphy, G.C., Zimmermann, T.: Persuasive technology in the real world: a study of long-term use of activity sensing devices for fitness. In: Proceedings of the SIGCHI Conference on Human Factors in Computing Systems, pp. 487–496. ACM, April 2014
11. Mannino, D.M., Buist, A.S.: Global burden of COPD: risk factors, prevalence, and future trends. The Lancet **370**(9589), 765–773 (2007)
12. Oinas-Kukkonen, H., Harjumaa, M.: A systematic framework for designing and evaluating persuasive systems. In: Oinas-Kukkonen, H., Hasle, P., Harjumaa, M., Segerståhl, K., Øhrstrøm, P. (eds.) PERSUASIVE 2008. LNCS, vol. 5033, pp. 164–176. Springer, Heidelberg (2008). https://doi.org/10.1007/978-3-540-68504-3_15
13. Davis, F.: A technology acceptance model for empirically testing new end-user information systems. Theory and results, Doctoral dissertation. Massachusetts Institute of Technology (1986)
14. Venkatesh, V., Davis, F.D.: A theoretical extension of the technology acceptance model: four longitudinal field studies. Manage. Sci. **46**(2), 186–204 (2000)
15. Legris, P., Ingham, J., Collerette, P.: Why do people use information technology? A critical review of the technology acceptance model. Inf. Manage. **40**(3), 191–204 (2003)
16. Weiner, B.: An attributional theory of achievement motivation and emotion. Psychol. Rev. **92**(4), 548 (1985)
17. Dweck, C.S.: Motivational processes affecting learning. Am. Psychol. **41**(10), 1040 (1986)

18. Heyman, G.D., Dweck, C.S., Cain, K.M.: Young children's vulnerability to self-blame and helplessness: relationship to beliefs about goodness. Child Dev. 63(2), 401–415 (1992)

19. Elliot, A.J., Harackiewicz, J.M.: Approach and avoidance achievement goals and intrinsic motivation: a mediational analysis. J. Pers. Soc. Psychol. 70(3), 461 (1996)

20. Cury, F., Elliot, A., Sarrazin, P., Da Fonseca, D., Rufo, M.: The trichotomous achievement goal model and intrinsic motivation: a sequential mediational analysis. J. Exp. Soc. Psychol. 38, 473–481 (2002)

21. Elliot, A.J., Church, M.A.: A hierarchical model of approach and avoidance achievement motivation. J. Pers. Soc. Psychol. 72(1), 218 (1997)

22. Van Yperen, N.W., Orehek, E.: Achievement goals in the workplace: conceptualization, prevalence, profiles, and outcomes. J. Econ. Psychol. 38, 71–79 (2013)

23. Abrahamsen, F.E., Roberts, G.C., Pensgaard, A.M.: Achievement goals and gender effects on multidimensional anxiety in national elite sport. Psychol. Sport Exerc. 9(4), 449–464 (2008)

24. Faul, F., Erdfelder, E., Buchner, A., Lang, A.G.: Statistical power analyses using G* Power 3.1: tests for correlation and regression analyses. Behav. Res. Methods 41(4), 1149–1160 (2009)

25. Freund, K.M., Belanger, A.J., D'Agostino, R.B., Kannel, W.B.: The health risks of smoking - the framingham study: 34 years of follow up. Ann. Epidemiol. 3(4), 417–424 (1993)

26. Hughes, J.: Motivating and Helping Smokers to Stop Smoking. University of Vermont, Vermont (2003)

27. Hymowitz, N., Cummings, K.M., Hyland, A., Lynn, W.R., Pechacek, T.F., Hartwell, T.D.: Predictors of smoking cessation in a cohort of adult smokers followed for five years. Tob. Control 6(suppl 2), S57 (1997)

28. Ghazali, A.S., Ham, J., Barakova, E., Markopoulos, P.: Persuasive Robots Acceptance Model (PRAM): roles of social responses within the acceptance model of persuasive robots. Int. J. Soc. Robot. 1–18 (2020). https://doi.org/10.1007/s12369-019-00611-1

29. Masthoff, J., Grasso, F., Ham, J.: Preface to the special issue on personalization and behavior change. User Model. User-Adap. Interact. 24(5), 345–350 (2014). https://doi.org/10.1007/s11257-014-9151-1

Mobile-based Text Messages for Improved Pediatric Health in Rural Areas of Pakistan: A Qualitative Study

Sitwat Usman Langrial[1]([⊠]) and Jaap Ham[2]

[1] Namal Institute, Mianwali, Pakistan
Sitwat@namal.edu.pk
[2] Eindhoven University of Technology, Eindhoven, The Netherlands
j.r.c.ham@tue.nl

Abstract. Persuasive Technology (PT) as a field of research provides tremendous opportunities for helping people improve their health and wellbeing. This paper highlights opportunities for empowering rural female population through a simple text-based persuasive intervention. The study was performed in June 2019 in a remotely located population in North-Eastern Pakistan. The target population were young mothers who were frequent users of mobile phones and able to read text messages. The study investigated whether simple Mobile-based Text Messages based on Integrated Management of Childhood Illness (IMCI) could bring a positive behavior change in mothers such as breastfeeding, avoiding self-medication when a child is sick and having the child immunized regularly. For data collection, we opted to conduct Focus Group Discussions in order to gain richer insights. The findings revealed that a high majority of the participants found the text messages to be useful. More interestingly, just over the span of one month, these participants reported to have a natural change in their behaviors.

Keywords: Persuasive Technology · Integrated Management of Childhood Illness · Text- based messages · Pediatric health · Rural population · Focus group · Qualitative findings

1 Introduction

1.1 Persuasive Technology

Persuasive Technology (PT) are interactive technologies (systems, applications) that are designed and developed to motivate and support people in adopting and maintaining positive/ desirable behaviors [1]. Dedicated research in the area of PT over the past years has shown promising results in an array of research domains especially health and wellness [1]. Using PT as a tool for bringing desirable behavior change through shaping and reinforcing became more prominent when Behavior Change Support Systems (BCSS) were introduced [2–4]. Recent years have witnessed a plethora of PTs aiming at various aspects of health, wellness and general wellbeing. Some of the common examples

© Springer Nature Switzerland AG 2020
S. B. Gram-Hansen et al. (Eds.): PERSUASIVE 2020, LNCS 12064, pp. 150–159, 2020.
https://doi.org/10.1007/978-3-030-45712-9_12

include enhanced physical activity [5], healthy eating [6], smoking cessation [7], safe sexual behavior [8], dental hygiene [9], safe driving [10] and mental health [11]. We are now witnessing an increasing number of research projects in health and wellness domain that is without doubt encouraging. However, a quick overview of available literature indicates that investment in the area of PT for health and wellness is predominantly being made in the western world. There could be several reasons for this shortcoming. For instance, lack of funding, and lack or very little knowledge of PT. Therefore, it is of high significance that PT and its likely impact is studied in low-income countries especially targeting rural population. This is the main reason that a very narrow research problem is targeted in this work that focuses on the very basics of PT i.e. Mobile – based messages for mothers with an aim to educate them in looking after their children's health. Before designing the research procedure, a situation analysis was performed that revealed that there was a dire need to educate mothers about raising healthy children.

1.2 Childhood Illness in Low-Income Countries

Mothers play a central role in children's health that has been studied and reported as a key communal and anthropological factor that can directly influence mortality rates in children under five years of age [12]. Among others, a common reason for high infant mortality rate in Pakistan is delayed medical help. This is because of several reasons including lack of education, insufficient knowledge, and mere negligence [13, 14]. Infant illness and high mortality rate are a continuous cause of concern for families and healthcare systems in low-income countries subsequently adding to the global disease burden [15]. Literature reveals that a high number of infant mortality is caused by improper assessment and lack of knowledge amongst parents and/ or immediate caregivers [16]. Poor or substandard healthcare facilities, distant location from primary healthcare units and high treatment costs also contribute to the problem in low-income countries [17]. Growing popularity and acceptance of PT provides us with a unique and cost-effective opportunity to address this critical problem. It is disappointing to note that there are almost no research studies reported that highlight use of PT in low-income countries. This is despite the fact that numerous articles have emphasized its effectiveness. It is therefore that simple Mobile-based Text Messages could be delivered as an intervention with an aim to enhance parents' knowledge, understanding and skills that are necessary for immediate primary health support to a sick child.

1.3 Integrated Management of Childhood Illness

The World Health Organization (WHO) introduced Integrated Management of Childhood Illness (IMCI) with an aim to overcome the obstinate problem of substandard child healthcare especially in low – and middle – income countries [18, 19]. IMCI focuses on improving children's health through well-timed and suitable case management (for common diseases). The objective is to induce an integrated child health education and training for parents and immediate caregivers. Such trainings are meant to be delivered through Primary Health Care units [20]. More importantly, trainings based on IMCI have to be delivered through multidisciplinary teams as all members of a given primary health care unit are interrelated. IMCI strongly emphasizes on the importance of community in improved child healthcare [21], which makes perfect sense. We strongly argue that it is time to focus on parents and immediate caregivers especially now that we have cost-effective and simple to use technologies such as PT. Our argument is supported by [22]. Presented work is narrow and purposefully focused to explore the potential of Mobile-based Text Messages on improving parents' education and understanding on children's health. The content of the text messages was developed from IMCI guidelines to educate parents by increasing their knowledge and improving skills when they are dealing with a sick child with no immediate professional health support in the nearby vicinity. It must be noted that PT has advanced over the past decade however using Mobile-based Text Messages is more like taking a step back for contextual reasons. In addition, the founding father of PT advocates simple steps for behavior change [23].

2 Related Work

Dedicated research can be found that shows how researchers and practitioners have contributed to uplifting child healthcare standards [24, 25]. According to a study, IMCI training and education has led to a significant improvement in assessment of danger signs, assessment of co-morbidity and correct medical prescription [26]. Other studies underscore that IMCI helps healthcare providers in superior health assessment, providing better advice and prescribing right medication [27]. Literature also shows that medical students who receive IMCI training perform much better in a community medicine setting [28]. IMCI guidelines have been implemented and examined in a number of countries and results show that there is a noticeable improvement in child health, however more work needs to be done. As a matter of fact, the protocol (IMCI) has been (fully or partially) implemented in more than 100 countries [15] yet the prime issue of high child mortality rate persists to date. A good number of studies on child health have been carried out in Pakistan. One study outlines that low female education is one of the major reasons behind high mortality rates in rural areas [29]. Other researchers call for a separate clinical setting for IMCI implementation [30], which is certainly a good proposition however not really practical in a low-income country. Sadly, Pakistan has the world's 3rd highest infant mortality rate [31] and mothers' inability to assess a sick child's situation is one of the leading factors. This makes our study of great significance as it aims to find a way (in this work using PT) to reach out distantly located, less educated mothers through a cost-effective approach based on the guidelines set out by IMCI.

3 Procedures

3.1 Recruitment

The study was conducted in June 2019. Local Primary Health Units' administrators were contacted to inform perspective participants about the study. In addition, recruitment pamphlets (in Urdu language) were distributed to households and local higher secondary schools. The pamphlets explained in detail that the participation was voluntary and that we were trying to seek support from young mothers who have children under 5 years of age and that they had access to mobile phones. In response, we received expression of interest from 263 young mothers. An initial screening was performed and 68 were excluded from the study as they were either medical assistants or had children above the age of five years. Therefore, the total sample size of this study was 195.

3.2 Ethical Approval

Adhering with the international best practices and ethical code of conduct, we obtained ethical approval from the local district's authority. The ethical approval application entailed aim of the study, detailed information for the perspective participants, informed consent forms and an undertaking about the confidentiality of the participants' data. The study had no psychological or physical implications for the participants. We did not initiate the study until having received the informed consent forms. Lastly, participants were advised and explained that they had no obligation to complete their participation and could opt out at any point of time.

3.3 Data Collection

The study lasted for one month. At the end of the study, participants were invited for focus group discussions. The purpose of the focus groups was explained with the invitation. The first author acted as a mediator of the focus group. The idea behind having focus group discussions was to try and collect participants' experiences and opinions about the Mobile-based Text Messages. In other words, we wanted to observe whether a simple intervention (based on the principles of PT) had a any influence on the participants' behaviors towards child healthcare. And that if they had observed a gradual change in their children's health related behaviors. Out of the 195 participants who completed the study, 30 agreed to take part in the focus group discussions. This is because Pakistan's rural population is a highly conservative society [32] and women hesitate or avoid speaking out. It was logical to arrange three focus group discussions on the 3rd, 4th and 5th of July 2019 in a local high school for females. Each focus group comprised of ten participants. The moderator was accompanied by a female teaching staff so that the participants felt comfortable. Each focus group lasted for approximately 60 min. Participants were welcomed and thanked for their support. Refreshments were served and discussion started with the question about their experience with the Mobile-based Text Messages. They were advised and encouraged to give comments, suggestions openly as this was going to help mothers. The moderator explained to the participants that the content of the messages was designed using IMCI guidelines and that the language was oversimplified for their understanding. Table 1 shows three of IMCI's guidelines, a brief description and examples of text messages.

Table 1. Three IMCI recommended practices that were incorporated in the mobile-based text messages for this study.

IMCI guidelines	Brief description	Simplified message example
Breastfeeding	Breastfeed the infant for at least four months	*"Your child's health depends on the best food and that is through breast feeding"*
Health professionals' advice	Always follow your doctor's advice and do not forget to follow up	*"Your child deserves the best available treatment. Do not try self-medication. Always consult the nearest primary health care unit"*
Immunization	Ensure to complete entire immunization before the first birthday	*"Immunization saves lives. Never neglect the mobile teams that reach you for immunization. Keep a record of completed and upcoming immunizations"*

4   Findings

The study was conducted to investigate whether simple Mobile-based Text messages could bring a positive behavior change in mothers such Breastfeeding, avoiding self-medication when a child is sick and getting the child immunized regularly. The assumption was that text messages will improve mothers' knowledge and skills leading to improved child health. We also assumed that such a simple intervention based on PT would be well received by the participants. Finally, we expected that simple interventions are going to shape up positive behavior amongst parents (especially mothers). We emphasized on mothers because men in rural areas of Pakistan do not play equal parental role.

We were happy to receive the feedback from the participants of the focus group discussions. All the participants from the three groups supported such interventions. In other words, the intervention was well received by all the participants of the focus groups. Indeed, one cannot ignore the fact that the intervention was focused on children's health. Participants were happy that the messages were simple yet informative, which is in line with the proposition made by Fogg [23]. Below are some of the representative comments:

4.1   Breastfeeding

"I have learnt that no matter what, I will breastfeed my baby. I will never compromise on her health". (Mother, 20 Years)

"Sometimes I used to delay feeding my baby. The messages were helpful in a way that I started giving first preference to my child (baby)". (Mother, 18 Years)

"I am a year 12 student and have one baby boy (smiles). I think that the messages about breastfeeding are going to help a lot of mothers". (Mother, 19 Years)

"I am not good at reading text messages (giggles). But my elder daughter would run to me and say it is time to feed the baby (her brother). I think this was so beautiful". (Mother, 25 Years)

"I am a bachelor's student with a 3 months old girl. While the messages were really good, it would have been even better, had you included the importance of cleanliness". (Mother, 22 Years)

4.2 Self-medication

"Having three kids is not easy. We live in a remote area and my babies suffer from diarrhea regularly. I used to give them a lot of water but now I have started consulting the lady health worker and use ORS. Also, I have started seeking advice about cleaning, liquid intake and mosquito bite protection. Thank you." (Mother, 26 Years)

"I used to give my baby cough syrup without any medical advice, but not now. I see a doctor or a nurse and act accordingly." (Mother, 22 Years)

"Because of the medical advice, I avoid giving any medicine at my own. I keep my child clean, watch her and if she is not well, I immediately call the local doctor". (Mother, 20 Years)

"My sister and I are both mothers and we have a habit of giving our kids (babies) Panadol whenever they are sick. From the last month, we have started following the messages and realized that we were so wrong. I am so thankful and so is my sister." (Mother, 24 Years)

"The messages to avoid self-medication is (was) very good. Is there not a way to interact with the sender to seek immediate advice?" (Mother, 21 Years)

4.3 Immunization

"I got married when I was 17 and I go to high school. My baby girl (5 months) stays with my mom. The messages about immunization are (were) of great help. I have already formed a diary for the entire year." (Mother, 17 Years)

"The messages were really helpful as I had to get immunizations for my two boys on different dates. Now I have started telling my friends too (smiles". (Mother, 23 Years)

"Thank you. I will not forget my baby girl's immunization." (Mother, 20 Years)

"I think you should increase the length of the study (research). We have a lot of things (chores) to do and one month was too short of a period." (Mother, 22 Years)

"Is it possible to send a message about immunization one day before? If that is done, I am sure no child will be left out. In any case, I like this idea of sending text messages". (Mother, 21)

Having gone through the feedback received from participants, there are a number of deductions that can be made. First, that the simple intervention was well received by the participants. It was also encouraging to see that some of the participants wanted a longer and interactive version of intervention. This small-scale yet significant study and its results further support the scope and potential of Persuasive Technology (PT) as the Mobile-based Text Based messages were actually what the PT community knows as "Reminders" [33]. While designing the text messages (reminders) we paid detailed attention to the target population and kept them simple. Mobile phones were purposefully used as a delivery platform as mobile phone usage in Pakistan is very high [34]. It is noticeable from this study that PT through simple interventions in rural areas can make a positive impact. Reminders are already known to make a difference and the findings from this study are no exception.

5 Discussion

The study was conducted to investigate whether simple Mobile-based Text messages could bring a positive behavior change in mothers such as breastfeeding, avoiding self-medication when a child is sick and having the child immunized regularly. Participants' comments and feedback endorse the effect of Mobile-based Text Messages. Not only did the participants of the focus group discussions find the intervention useful but they also showed a desire for a long term and interactive study. This is highly encouraging as we did not anticipate that kind of response. The findings also indicate that there is no real need to develop and employ complicated interventions that supports previous research findings [35]. On the contrary, simple interventions could perhaps be more effective. One limitation of this study is that the entire focus was on children's health that lead to such a positive response. The other important limitation of the study is that only 30 participants agreed to take part in focus group discussions. However, we are preparing questionnaires for those who did not feel comfortable in focus group discussions. It might be argued that there is a lack of novelty in the work as it focuses on reminders that has been deeply studied, however, it is worth noting that the impact of this study stands out. The study follows Fogg's recommendations by focusing on what might be seen as a simple target behavior, applying persuasive techniques and trying to build on small success [36]. Most importantly, presented work outlines that applicability of PT in countries such as Pakistan where the very idea of persuasion through technology is undermined. We therefore believe that this study and future research will broaden the acceptance and applicability of PT in countries such as Pakistan and beyond.

6 Conclusions

The paper presented qualitative findings of a relatively small-scale study that employed Mobile-based Text Messages (Reminders) using Persuasive Technology (PT) and Integrated Management of Childhood Illness (IMCI). Participants showed a positive attitude towards the intervention and made useful suggestions that can be implemented in future research. It was interesting to see that some of the participants had already shown a sign of positive behavior change. Almost all the participants gave positive and supportive feedback despite being from a rural area, which encourages us to design further studies with a broader focus on IMCI-recommended practices. Lastly, findings from this study indicate that simple PT intervention with meaningful messages is a significant trigger that can lead to behavior change, which is certainly an interesting finding and calls for future work.

Acknowledgements. We would like to thank all participants for their time and valuable feedback that made this study possible. Our special thanks to the local health care units for their support.

References

1. Orji, R., Moffatt, K.: Persuasive technology for health and wellness: state-of-the- art and emerging trends. Health Inf. J. **24**(1), 66–91 (2018)
2. Karppinen, P., et al.: Opportunities and challenges of behavior change support systems for enhancing habit formation: a qualitative study. J. Biomed. Inf. **84**, 82–92 (2018)
3. Kelders, S.M., Oinas-Kukkonen, H., Oörni, A., van Gemert-Pijnen, J.E.: Health behavior change support systems as a research discipline; a viewpoint. Int. J. Med. Inf. **96**, 3–10 (2016)
4. Win, K.T., Oinas-Kukkonen, H.: Introduction to the minitrack on health behavior change support systems. In: Proceedings of the 51st Hawaii International Conference on System Sciences, January 2018
5. Matthews, J., Win, K.T., Oinas-Kukkonen, H., Freeman, M.: Persuasive technology in mobile applications promoting physical activity: a systematic review. J. Med. Syst. **40**(3), 72 (2016)
6. Pollak, J., Gay, G., Byrne, S., Wagner, E., Retelny, D., Humphreys, L.: It's time to eat! Using mobile games to promote healthy eating. IEEE Pervasive Comput. **9**(3), 21–27 (2010)
7. Ghorai, K., Akter, S., Khatun, F., Ray, P.: mHealth for smoking cessation programs: a systematic review. J. Personal. Med. **4**(3), 412–423 (2014)
8. Stibe, A., Cugelman, B.: Persuasive backfiring: when behavior change interventions trigger unintended negative outcomes. In: Meschtscherjakov, A., De Ruyter, B., Fuchsberger, V., Murer, M., Tscheligi, M. (eds.) PERSUASIVE 2016. LNCS, vol. 9638, pp. 65–77. Springer, Cham (2016). https://doi.org/10.1007/978-3-319-31510-2_6
9. Anderson, C.N., Noar, S.M., Rogers, B.D.: The persuasive power of oral health promotion messages: a theory of planned behavior approach to dental checkups among young adults. Health Commun. **28**(3), 304–313 (2013)
10. Miranda, B., Jere, C., Alharbi, O., Lakshmi, S., Khouja, Y., Chatterjee, S.: Examining the efficacy of a persuasive technology package in reducing texting and driving behavior. In: Berkovsky, S., Freyne, J. (eds.) PERSUASIVE 2013. LNCS, vol. 7822, pp. 137–148. Springer, Heidelberg (2013). https://doi.org/10.1007/978-3-642-37157-8_17

11. Doherty, G., Coyle, D., Sharry, J.: Engagement with online mental health interventions: an exploratory clinical study of a treatment for depression. In: Proceedings of the SIGCHI Conference on Human Factors in Computing Systems, pp. 1421–1430. ACM,, May 2012

12. Durrani, H.M., Kumar, R., Durrani, S.M.: Recognizing the danger signs and health seeking behaviour of mothers in childhood illness in Karachi, Pakistan. Univers. J. Public Health 3(2), 49–54 (2015)

13. Jehan, I., et al.: Neonatal mortality, risk factors and causes: a prospective population-based cohort study in urban Pakistan. Bull. World Health Organ. 87, 130–138 (2009)

14. Liu, L., et al.: Global, regional, and national causes of child mortality in 2000–13, with projections to inform post- 2015 priorities: an updated systematic analysis. Lancet 385(9966), 430–440 (2015)

15. Mushi, D., Mpembeni, R., Jahn, A.: Effectiveness of community based safe motherhood promoters in improving the utilization of obstetric care. The case of Mtwara Rural District in Tanzania. BMC Pregnancy Childbirth 10(1), 14 (2010). https://doi.org/10.1186/1471-2393-10-14

16. Al-Araimi, F.A., Langrial, S.U.: A hypothetical model to predict nursing students' perceptions of the usefulness of pre-service integrated management of childhood illness training. Sultan Qaboos Univ. Med. J. 16(4), e469 (2016)

17. World Health Organization. Implementation tools: package of essential noncommunicable (PEN) disease interventions for primary health care in low-resource settings. World Health Organization (2013)

18. Gove, S.: Integrated management of childhood illness by outpatient health workers: technical basis and overview. The WHO working group on guidelines for integrated management of the sick child. Bull. World Health Organ. 75(1), 7 (1997)

19. Nicoll, A.: Integrated management of childhood illness in resource-poor countries: an initiative from the World Health Organization. Trans. Roy. Soc. Trop. Med. Hyg. 94(1), 9–11 (2000)

20. Shouly, B.A.J.M. Quality Assessment of Primary Health Care Delivered to Children Under 5 Years Old in North West-Bank/Palestine, Doctoral dissertation (2011)

21. Thompson, M.E., Harutyunyan, T.L.: Impact of a community-based integrated management of childhood illnesses (IMCI) programme in Gegharkunik, Armenia. Health Policy Plann. 24(2), 101–107 (2009)

22. Araimi, A., Fannah, F.A.: A hypothetical model to predict the potential impact of government and management support in implementing integrated management of childhood illness practices. Oman Med. J. 32(3), 221 (2017)

23. Fogg, B.J.: A behavior model for persuasive design. In: Proceedings of the 4th International Conference on Persuasive Technology, p. 40. ACM, April 2009

24. Kiplagat, A., Musto, R., Mwizamholya, D., Morona, D.: Factors influencing the implementation of integrated management of childhood illness (IMCI) by healthcare workers at public health centers & dispensaries in Mwanza, Tanzania. BMC Public Health 14(1), 277 (2014)

25. Kalu, N., Lufesi, N., Havens, D., Mortimer, K.: Implementation of World Health Organization Integrated Management of Childhood Illnesses (IMCI) guidelines for the assessment of pneumonia in the under 5 s in rural Malawi. PLoS ONE 11(5), e0155830 (2016)

26. Chopra, M., Patel, S., Cloete, K., Sanders, D., Peterson, S.: Effect of an IMCI intervention on quality of care across four districts in Cape Town, South Africa. Arch. Dis. Child. 90(4), 397–401 (2005)

27. Maramagi, C.A., Lubanga, R.G., Kiguli, S., Ekwaru, P.J., Heggenhougen, K.: Health providers' counselling of caregivers in the Integrated Management of Childhood Illness (IMCI) programme in Uganda. Afr. Health Sci. 4(1), 31–39 (2004)

28. Patwari, A.K., Raina, N.: Integrated Management of Childhood Illness (IMCI): a robust strategy. Indian J. Pediatr. 69(1), 41–48 (2002)

29. Agha, A., Younus, M., Kadir, M.M., Ali, S., Fatmi, Z.: Eight key household practices of Integrated Management of Childhood Illnesses (IMCI) amongst mothers of children aged 6 to 59 months in Gambat, Sindh, Pakistan. J. Pak. Med. Assoc. **57**(6), 288 (2007)
30. Akber Pradhan, N., Rizvi, N., Sami, N., Gul, X.: Insight into implementation of facility-based integrated management of childhood illness strategy in a rural district of Sindh, Pakistan. Global Health Action **6**(1), 20086 (2013)
31. Khan, A., et al.: Newborn survival in Pakistan: a decade of change and future implications. Health Policy Plann. **27**(suppl_3), iii72–iii87 (2012)
32. Maheen, H., Hoban, E.: Rural women's experience of living and giving birth in relief camps in Pakistan. PLoS Curr. **9** (2017)
33. Lappalainen, P., Langrial, S., Oinas-Kukkonen, H., Tolvanen, A., Lappalainen, R.: Web-based acceptance and commitment therapy for depressive symptoms with minimal support: a randomized controlled trial. Behav. Modif. **39**(6), 805–834 (2015)
34. Kazi, A., et al.: Effect of mobile phone text message reminders on routine immunization uptake in Pakistan: randomized controlled trial. JMIR Public Health Surveill. **4**(1), e20 (2018)
35. Langrial, S.U., Lappalainen, P.: Information systems for improving mental health: six emerging themes of research. In: Pacific Asia Conference On Information Systems (PACIS). Association for Information System (2016)
36. Fogg, B.J.: Creating persuasive technologies: an eight-step design process. In: Proceedings of the 4th international conference on persuasive technology, pp. 1–6 (2009)

Persuasive Solutions for a Sustainable Future

Persuasive Mobile Apps for Health and Wellness: A Comparative Systematic Review

Oladapo Oyebode$^{(\boxtimes)}$ (ID), Chinenye Ndulue (ID), Mona Alhasani, and Rita Orji (ID)

Faculty of Computer Science, Dalhousie University, Halifax, NS B3H 4R2, Canada
{oladapo.oyebode,cndulue,mona.alhasani,rita.orji}@dal.ca

Abstract. While majority of previous research focus on reviewing mobile health (mHealth) apps targeting specific health domain, this paper provides a comparative systematic review of mHealth apps across multiple health domains with the aim of deconstructing the persuasive strategies employed and their implementation. Specifically, we targeted four health domains (i.e., *physical activity and fitness*, *diet*, *emotional and mental health*, and *health assessment and healthcare*). We retrieved a total of 639 apps from Google Play out of which 80 popular apps were extracted (20 apps in each category). Three expert reviewers coded the apps using 32 persuasive strategies (PSs) based on Persuasive System Design (PSD) Model and Cialdini's Principles of Persuasion. Overall, out of the 80 mHealth apps reviewed, *personalization* is the most commonly employed PS (n = 77), followed by *surface credibility* (n = 69), *trustworthiness* (n = 66) and *self-monitoring* (n = 64). How the apps are implemented varies depending on the domain. Based on our findings, we offer suggestions for designing mHealth apps to improve their persuasiveness.

Keywords: Health · Wellness · Mobile apps · Persuasive strategies · Behaviour change · Systematic review

1 Introduction

The proliferation of smartphones has made it possible to share millions of life-enriching mobile apps to billions of people worldwide [1]. Many of these apps are health-related and help in managing chronic or mild health conditions [2], supporting the adoption of a healthy lifestyle or promoting healthy behaviours [3]. Specifically, these mobile health (mHealth) apps are effective in promoting physical activity [3, 4], weight management [5], dietary interventions [3], disease management [2], mental well-being [6], and so on. However, for behaviour change to occur, developers of mHealth apps need to employ persuasive principles or strategies [7, 8].

While previous research has conducted literature review on the persuasiveness of mHealth apps [9, 10] or review apps targeting specific health domain [11–14], existing work has not conducted a comparative systematic review of mHealth apps (on Google Play or App Store) across multiple health domains (such as fitness, diet, mental health, etc.) at the same time to the best of our knowledge.

© Springer Nature Switzerland AG 2020
S. B. Gram-Hansen et al. (Eds.): PERSUASIVE 2020, LNCS 12064, pp. 163–181, 2020.
https://doi.org/10.1007/978-3-030-45712-9_13

To fill this gap, we conduct a comparative systematic review of 80 mHealth apps across four different categories with each category having 20 popular apps. The categories include *physical activity and fitness, diet, emotional and mental health*, and *health assessment and healthcare*. The goal of this review is to identify and compare the persuasive strategies employed by the apps and how they were implemented. Three expert reviewers coded the apps using 32 persuasive strategies (PSs) based on the Persuasive System Design (PSD) Model [7] and Cialdini's Principles of Persuasion [8].

Our findings show that for the Physical Activity and Fitness category, *personalization* (n = 20) and *trustworthiness* (n = 20) PSs are the most commonly employed, followed by *self-monitoring* (n = 19). For the Diet category, *personalization* (n = 20), *commitment/consistency* (n = 20) and *suggestion* (n = 20) PSs emerged as the most commonly employed, followed by *reminders* (n = 19). Moreover, under the Emotional and Mental Health category, *personalization* (n = 19) and *surface credibility* (n = 19) PSs are the most commonly employed, followed by *liking* (n = 17). For the Health Assessment and Healthcare category, *personalization* (n = 18) is the most commonly employed PS, followed by *surface credibility* (n = 16), and *self-monitoring* (n = 15). Overall, out of the 80 mHealth apps reviewed, *personalization* emerged as the most commonly employed PS (n = 77), followed by *surface credibility* (n = 69), *trustworthiness* (n = 66), and *self-monitoring* (n = 64). Based on our findings, we offer suggestions for designing mHealth apps to improve their persuasiveness.

2 Related Work

Existing research has evaluated mobile health apps to determine the persuasive features they provide. For instance, Langrial et al. [15] conducted a review to identify the persuasive features in twelve mobile apps for personal well-being using the PSD model. Similarly, Chang et al. [6] evaluated twelve mobile apps for mental well-being using the 28 principles of the PSD model. They reviewed the apps based on user acceptance of mobile services, mobile intervention design, and persuasive design. Furthermore, Azar et al. [16] assessed the intervention strategies present in 23 weight management mobile apps using four behavioural theories or models, which are the health belief model, transtheoretical model, theory of reasoned action/planned behaviour, and the social cognitive or social learning theory. They also assessed the persuasive nature of the applications using the Fogg Behavioural Model (FBM).

Rather than targeting a specific health domain, our work provides a comparative systematic review of 80 mHealth apps across multiple health domains using both the PSD model and Cialdini's Principles of Persuasion. Specifically, we targeted four health domains: *physical activity and fitness, diet, emotional and mental health*, and *health assessment and healthcare* to uncover new insights and enrich the literature.

3 Methodology

In this section, we discussed the app selection criteria and coding process.

3.1 Selection of MHealth Apps

We developed a Python script to automate the app selection process which involves two stages. First, we searched for health-related apps that are free or free with in-app purchases on Google Play using keywords appropriate for each category, as defined in Table 1. We filtered our search results by selecting apps that belong to at least one of the following relevant Google Play groups: health and fitness, medical, social, and lifestyle. Second, we selected 20 most popular apps after sorting the total apps in each category in descending order of number of installations, followed by average ratings and number of reviews. Table 2 shows the apps summary per category based on number of installations, average ratings and number of reviews. We ensure that none of the 20 apps in a category is repeated in another category. In other words, we selected 80 unique apps in total for coding and analysis. 92.5% of the 80 apps were updated in 2019.

Table 1. App Categories and Search Keywords, and the corresponding number of Unique Apps retrieved.

App Category	Description	Keywords	No. of Apps
Physical Activity and Fitness	Apps that promote any form of physical activity or exercises, such as walking, running, cycling, etc.	*fitness, physical activity, exercise, running, walking, cycling, etc.*	195
Diet	Apps targeted at healthy eating such as tracking diet or food intake, as well as water consumption	*diet, drink, food, nutrition, water, etc.*	120
Emotional and Mental Health	Apps for mental health and emotion regulations such as helping users control their feelings and thoughts, as well as anxiety, depression, stress and sleep disorders	*mental, emotion, anxiety, depression, sleep, stress, etc.*	167
Health Assessment and Healthcare	Apps that help with health assessment and/or diagnosis, as well as provide access to qualified healthcare professionals	*healthcare, health assessment, symptom, diagnosis, doctor, etc.*	157

Table 2. Summary of 20 Popular Apps in each Category based on the Number of Installations, Average Ratings, and Number of Reviews

App category	No. of installations (range)	Average ratings (range)	No. of reviews (range)
Physical Activity and Fitness	10000000–500000000	3.7–4.8	60788–930822
Diet	1000000–50000000	3.4–4.8	8699–2165194
Emotional and Mental Health	1000000–10000000	3.6–4.8	8686–298437
Health Assessment and Healthcare	500000–10000000	4.1–4.8	5133–303407

3.2 Coding and Analysis of Selected Apps

In the coding phase, we identified the persuasive strategies (PSs) employed in designing each of the 80 mHealth apps including how the strategies were implemented using the PSD model [7] and Cialdini's Principles of Persuasion [8]. Both frameworks have been widely used in deconstructing persuasive technologies over the years. From the PSD model, we used all the PSs under the primary task support, dialogue support, system credibility support and social support categories for coding purposes. From the Cialdini's Principles of Persuasion, we selected four out of the six available PSs since two strategies (i.e., *authority* and *liking*) already exist in the PSD model. Table 3 shows the 32 persuasive strategies and their categories.

Figure 1 describes the coding process. Three expert reviewers installed the apps on their Android smartphones and used the app features to perform various tasks while taking note of the PSs and how they were implemented in their coding sheets. Afterwards, the reviewers discussed the information captured on the coding sheets.

Table 3. Persuasive Frameworks, Categories and Descriptions, as well as the individual Persuasive Strategies

Framework	Category	Description	Persuasive strategies
PSD	Primary task support	Support users in performing their intended tasks	Reduction, Tunneling, Tailoring, Personalization, Self-monitoring, Simulation, Rehearsal

(continued)

Table 3. (*continued*)

Framework	Category	Description	Persuasive strategies
	Dialogue support	Provide feedback that moves users toward the target behaviour	Praise, Rewards, Reminders, Suggestion, Similarity, Liking, Social role
	System credibility support	Support the development of systems that are more credible	Trustworthiness, Expertise, Surface credibility, Real-world feel, Authority, Third-party endorsements, Verifiability
	Social support	Motivate users through social influence	Social learning, Social comparison, Normative influence, Social facilitation, Cooperation, Competition, Recognition
Cialdini's Principles of Persuasion	–	Set of principles or strategies that influence people's behaviour	Reciprocity, Scarcity, Social proof, and Commitment/consistency

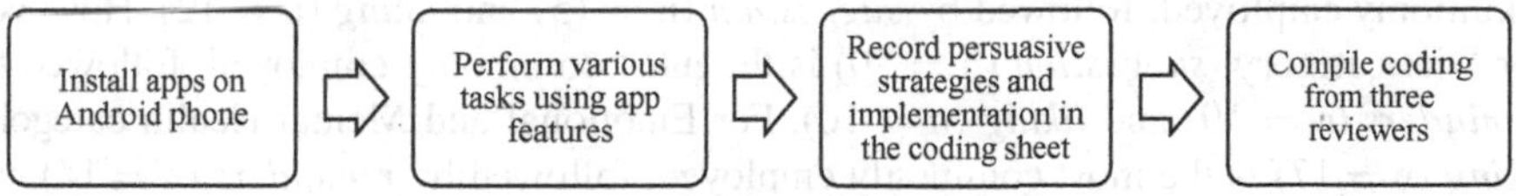

Fig. 1. The Process of Coding Apps

4 Results

In this section, we present the apps review results. We discussed the persuasive strategies identified in the apps and how they were implemented.

4.1 Persuasive Strategies Employed by Apps in Various Health Domains

Figure 2 shows the primary task support PSs employed by apps in the four health domains or categories (i.e., Physical Activity and Fitness, Diet, Emotional and Mental Health, and Health Assessment and Healthcare). Of the seven primary task support PSs, *personalization* is the most commonly employed strategy in all four categories, followed by *self-monitoring*. Specifically, for Physical Activity and Fitness category, *personalization* is the most commonly employed strategy (n = 20), followed by *self-monitoring* (n = 19) and *reduction* (n = 18). For Diet category, *personalization* is the most commonly employed strategy (n = 20), followed by *self-monitoring* (n = 19) and *reduction* (n = 19). However, for Emotional and Mental Health category, *personalization* is the most commonly implemented strategy (n = 19), followed by *self-monitoring* (n = 11) and *tunneling* (n = 11). For Health Assessment and Healthcare category, *personalization* is the most commonly implemented strategy (n = 18), followed by *self-monitoring* (n = 15) and *tunneling* (n = 11).

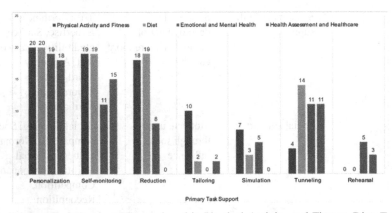

Fig. 2. Primary Task Support PSs employed in Physical Activity and Fitness, Diet, Emotional and Mental Health, and Health Assessment and Healthcare categories

Furthermore, Fig. 3 shows the dialogue support PSs employed by apps in the four categories. For Physical Activity and Fitness category, *reminders* (n = 17) is the most commonly employed, followed by *suggestion* (n = 15) and *liking* (n = 12). However, for Diet category, *suggestion* (n = 20) is the most commonly employed, followed by *reminders* (n = 19) and *liking* (n = 10). For Emotional and Mental Health category, *liking* (n = 17) is the most commonly employed, followed by *reminders* (n = 14) and

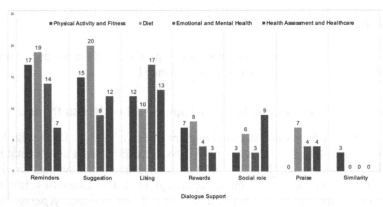

Fig. 3. Dialogue Support PSs employed in Physical Activity and Fitness, Diet, Emotional and Mental Health, and Health Assessment and Healthcare categories

suggestion (n = 9). Finally, for Health Assessment and Healthcare category, *liking* (n = 13) is the most commonly employed, followed by *suggestion* (n = 12) and *social role* (n = 9).

Moreover, Fig. 4 revealed the system credibility PSs employed by apps in the four categories. For Physical Activity and Fitness category, *trustworthiness* (n = 20) is the most commonly employed PS, followed by *real-world feel* (n = 17), *surface credibility* (n = 16) and *expertise* (n = 16). For Diet category, *trustworthiness* (n = 19) and *expertise* (n = 19) are the most commonly employed PSs, followed by *surface credibility* (n = 18). For Emotional and Mental Health category, *surface credibility* (n = 19) is the most commonly employed, followed by *trustworthiness* (n = 13) and *real-world feel* (n = 12). Finally, for Health Assessment and Healthcare category, *surface credibility* (n = 16) is the most commonly employed, followed by *real-world feel* (n = 15) and *trustworthiness* (n = 14).

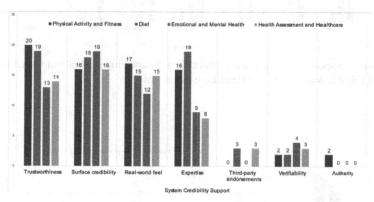

Fig. 4. System Credibility Support PSs employed in Physical Activity and Fitness, Diet, Emotional and Mental Health, and Health Assessment and Healthcare categories

Furthermore, Fig. 5 shows the social support PSs employed by apps in the four categories. For Physical Activity and Fitness category, *competition* is most commonly employed (n = 10), followed by *social learning* (n = 5) and *recognition* (n = 5). For Diet category, *normative influence* is most commonly employed (n = 8), followed by *social learning* (n = 7) and *competition* (n = 7). For Emotional and Mental Health category, only *social facilitation* (n = 1) and *social learning* (n = 1) were employed. Interestingly, for Health Assessment and Healthcare category, none of the apps employed the social support PSs. Also, none of the four categories employed the *cooperation* PS.

Finally, Fig. 6 revealed the Cialdini's Principles of Persuasion employed by apps in the four categories. For *commitment/consistency* (n = 18) is the most commonly employed, followed by *reciprocity* (n = 9) and *social proof* (n = 6). For Diet category, *commitment/consistency* (n = 20) is the most commonly employed, followed by *social proof* (n = 10) and *scarcity* (n = 7). For Emotional and Mental Health category, *reciprocity* (n = 6) is the most commonly employed, followed by *commitment/consistency* (n = 5) and *social proof* (n = 3). Interestingly, for Health Assessment and Healthcare category, *commitment/consistency* (n = 4) is the only strategy employed.

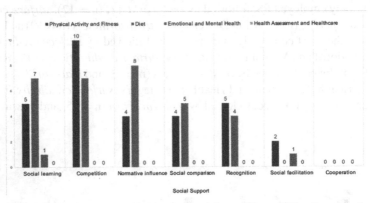

Fig. 5. Social Support PSs employed in Physical Activity and Fitness, Diet, Emotional and Mental Health, and Health Assessment and Healthcare categories

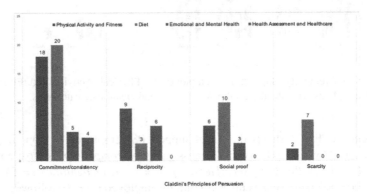

Fig. 6. Cialdini's Principles of Persuasion employed in Physical Activity and Fitness, Diet, Emotional and Mental Health, and Health Assessment and Healthcare categories

4.2 Persuasive Strategies Implementation in the Apps

Table 4 presents how the various persuasive strategies are implemented in the apps.

Table 4. Persuasive Strategies and how they are Implemented in the Apps

Persuasive Strategy	Physical Activity and Fitness Apps	Diet Apps	Emotional and Mental Health Apps	Health Assessment and Healthcare Apps
Personalization	Personalized contents based on users' gender, age, weight and height; customizable language, sound, music, etc.	Personalized contents based on users' demographics, height, weight, location; customizable notification, sound and triggers, widgets, language, etc.	Personalized contents based on users' demographics; customizable theme, alarm, sound, music, language, etc.	Use personal information to assign doctors; customizable theme, font size and language
Self-monitoring	Graphs and texts that show users' progress, including current and past activities	Graphs and texts that show users' progress, including current and past activities	Graphs/charts showing sleep, mood, and emotion analysis	Heartrate analysis, symptom tracking, sugar-level analysis, doctors' report, self-assessment report, etc.
Reduction	Predetermined lists of exercise/sport types and training plans	List of popular restaurants and recipes with their respective calories; cup sizes for drinking water; barcode scanner for food logging	Meditation, sleep, relaxation and happiness goals are broken down into smaller achievable tasks	–
Tunneling	After question answering steps, suitable exercise, fitness or training plans are provided	After question answering steps, suitable exercise, fitness or training plans are provided	Step-by-step guides on proper meditation and emotional health	Guide users on addressing symptoms
Tailoring	Exercise plans are based on users' fitness level	Users can set dietary preferences and get matching recipes	–	Medical scenarios and learning contents are based on area of specialty

(continued)

Table 4. (*continued*)

Persuasive Strategy	Physical Activity and Fitness Apps	Diet Apps	Emotional and Mental Health Apps	Health Assessment and Healthcare Apps
Simulation	Pictures show the before and after effects of performing various exercises	Uses fat and slim avatars reflect the impact of performing target behaviour	Animated images and avatars demonstrate transitions towards good sleeping habits	–
Rehearsal	–	–	Rehearse meditation and gratitude leading to happiness	Healthcare professionals can rehearse medical cases (such as surgery-related cases)
Reminders	Remind user to workout using push notifications with sound and text	Reminds users to track meals and water using push notifications with sound and text	Remind or notify users to meditate, sleep and wakeup, etc. using push notifications with sound and text	Remind users about finishing pills using push notifications with sound and text
Suggestion	Suggest number of calories to burn, fitness plan, daily steps, etc.	Suggest daily calories, ounce of water, nutrition values, food quantity, etc.	Provide tips on how to have better sleep and relaxation; suggest better meditation modes	Suggest solutions to skin diseases and certain health issues or symptoms
Praise	–	Offer praises using texts, symbols and images after users log food and drinks	Praise users for completing meditation audios and other activities	Healthcare professionals are praised for managing medical cases
Liking	Well-organized and attractive user interfaces with relevant pictures and videos	Well-organized, attractive, simple, and easy-to-use user interfaces	Attractive icons/avatars and illustrations, great animations and cool colours	Well-organized, attractive, simple, and easy-to-use user interfaces

(*continued*)

Table 4. (*continued*)

Persuasive Strategy	Physical Activity and Fitness Apps	Diet Apps	Emotional and Mental Health Apps	Health Assessment and Healthcare Apps
Rewards	Virtual rewards in form of badges and trophies	Virtual rewards in form of points, stars, badges, etc.	Virtual rewards in the form of stickers, badges, and activity streaks	Scores awarded for completing medical cases
Similarity	Girl avatar with pink colours provide necessary information to female users	–	–	–
Social role	Forum supports conversations between users	Forum and chat features support conversation with other users	Virtual therapist and life coach to respond to users' queries or questions	Nurse, doctor and advisor's role to provide medical assistance
Trustworthiness	Contents are related to the target behaviour, with privacy policy statements to gain user trust	Contents are related to the target behaviour, with privacy policy statements and relevant health notices	Contents are related to the target behaviour, with privacy policy statements; user have control over data	Contents are related to the target behaviour, with privacy policy statements to gain user trust
Expertise	Exercise types, fitness plans and training contents reflect specialist knowledge	Meal plans, drink suggestions, recipes and calorie content reflect specialist knowledge	Audios and videos from experts (e.g., licensed therapists), etc.	Doctors are licensed experts
Surface credibility	Professional interface with limited or no ads	Professional interface with limited or no ads	Professional interface with limited or no ads	Professional interface with limited or no ads

(*continued*)

Table 4. (*continued*)

Persuasive Strategy	Physical Activity and Fitness Apps	Diet Apps	Emotional and Mental Health Apps	Health Assessment and Healthcare Apps
Real-world feel	Contact names, email and mailing addresses, and phone numbers of people behind the apps are revealed	Contact names, email and mailing addresses, and phone numbers of people behind the apps are revealed	Contact names and email addresses of people behind the apps are revealed	Contact names, email and mailing addresses, and phone numbers of people behind the apps are revealed
Authority	World Health Organization and National Institutes of Health are referenced in app	–	–	–
Third-party endorsements	–	Endorsement by British Medical Journal and University of Sydney's Medical Centre and other organizations	–	Endorsement/accreditation by URAC, TRUSTe Certified Privacy, HiTrust, ClearHealth Quality Institute, etc.
Verifiability	Links to external websites from training contents to provide further details	Links to external websites for supporting videos; links to websites for more recipes	Links to web resources to verify information	Links to web resources to verify information
Social learning	Forum for sharing success stories and experiences so other users can learn	Sharable food journal, community and newsfeed features allow users to share progress and experiences	Users can chat in groups to learn from one another	–

(*continued*)

Table 4. (*continued*)

Persuasive Strategy	Physical Activity and Fitness Apps	Diet Apps	Emotional and Mental Health Apps	Health Assessment and Healthcare Apps
Social comparison	In a challenge, compare performance with that of participating users	Compare hydration and calorie levels with friends; compare progress with that of others during a challenge	–	–
Normative influence	Community, groups and clubs for users with similar goals or interests (e.g., running, walking, or cycling)	Groups and community for users with similar goals or targets	–	–
Social facilitation	Users can see friends running with them virtually	–	Users can see the number of people also meditating at the same time	–
Cooperation	–	–	–	–
Competition	Users compete in running, walking or cycling challenges	Users compete in food-related challenges (e.g., no chocolate, no fatty food, etc.) for specified duration	–	–
Recognition	Leaderboard reveals top runners for public recognition	Leaderboard reveals top performers for public recognition	–	–

(*continued*)

Table 4. (*continued*)

Persuasive Strategy	Physical Activity and Fitness Apps	Diet Apps	Emotional and Mental Health Apps	Health Assessment and Healthcare Apps
Commitment/consistency	Users commit to daily, weekly or monthly workout or exercise goals/plans	Users commit to daily, weekly or monthly water drinking and weight reduction goals	Users commit to daily and weekly sleep goals, as well as mood-based and meditation programs	Users commit to daily plans and health goals
Scarcity	65% discount on premium offers that expire in 24 h	Limited time, large discount offers for plan/subscription upgrade and premium features	–	–
Social proof	Each active challenge shows number of participants; groups/clubs show number of runners, cyclers, etc.	Number of users who joined an active challenge; number of group members; etc.	Shows the number of users currently meditating; shows number of members in a chat group	–
Reciprocity	7 days and 30 days free access to premium features	7 days and 30 days free access to premium features	7 days trial period for premium features	–

4.3 Persuasive Strategies and App Effectiveness

For each category, we performed a bivariate Pearson Correlation (using SPSS version 25) to determine whether a relationship exists between the number of persuasive strategies implemented in an app and the perceived app effectiveness (based on average ratings). We also performed the same computation for all apps combined. The results, as shown in Table 5, revealed that for each category, there is no correlation (though not significant) between the number of strategies employed and app effectiveness. Overall, no relationship exists between the number of persuasive strategies employed in an app and its effectiveness.

Table 5. Relationship between Number of Persuasive Strategies and App Effectiveness based on Pearson Correlation Coefficient (r)

Physical Activity and Fitness Apps	Diet Apps	Emotional and Mental Health Apps	Health Assessment and Healthcare Apps	Overall (all apps)
$r(20) = 0.188, p = 0.428$	$r(20) = -0.037, p = 0.877$	$r(20) = -0.126, p = 0.598$	$r(20) = 0.048, p = 0.841$	$r(80) = 0.044, p = 0.697$

5 Discussion

We conducted a comparative systematic review of 80 mHealth apps across four categories (see Table 1) with the aim of deconstructing the persuasive strategies employed and their implementation, and then provide suggestions on how the persuasiveness of mHealth apps can be further improved using the insights.

5.1 Persuasive Strategies Employed Overall

Out of the 80 mHealth apps reviewed, *personalization* emerged as the most commonly employed PS (n = 77), followed by *surface credibility* (n = 69), *trustworthiness* (n = 66), *self-monitoring* (n = 64), *real-world feel* (n = 59), *reminders* (n = 57), *suggestion* (n = 56), *liking* (n = 52), *expertise* (n = 52), *commitment/consistency* (n = 47), *reduction* (n = 45) and *tunneling* (n = 40). Other strategies were employed by less than 23 apps. Research has shown that the *personalization* strategy was effective in promoting health-related behaviours [9, 17] which, in turn, explains why 96% of the total apps implemented it.

5.2 Persuasive Strategies for Physical Activity

Based on our findings, all the reviewed apps under the physical activity and fitness category employed both the *personalization* and *trustworthiness* PSs. Moreover, 95% of the apps employed *self-monitoring*, 90% employed *commitment/consistency* and *reduction*, 85% employed *reminders* and *real-world feel*, 80% employed *surface credibility* and *expertise*, and 75% employed *suggestion*. 65% or less employed other strategies. Existing research supported our findings. For instance, *self-monitoring* and *reminders* were found to be commonly implemented in physical activity apps by [18, 19]. Another study found that users are more persuaded by physical activity apps that implement primary task support and dialogue support PSs [20], including goal-setting [21] which correlates well with the *commitment/consistency* strategy [22].

5.3 Persuasive Strategies for Healthy Eating

Our findings revealed that *personalization*, *commitment/consistency*, and *suggestion* PSs were implemented in all the reviewed apps under the Diet category. 95% of the apps employed *self-monitoring*, *reduction*, *reminders*, *expertise* and *trustworthiness* PSs, while 90% and 75% of the apps employed *surface credibility* and *real-world feel* respectively. This shows that most mHealth apps rely on a mix of these strategies to promote healthy diets among users.

5.4 Persuasive Strategies for Emotional and Mental Health

Our findings showed that 95% of the reviewed apps employed the *personalization* and *surface credibility* PSs under emotional and mental health category, while 85% and 70% implemented the *liking* and *reminders* strategies respectively. This outcome is corroborated by previous research on persuasive mental health apps which shows that primary task support PSs are the most commonly implemented, followed by system credibility and dialogue support strategies [6].

5.5 Persuasive Strategies for Health Assessment and Healthcare Delivery

In health assessment and healthcare category, 90% and 80% of the reviewed apps implemented the *personalization* and *surface credibility* PSs respectively. However, 75% of the apps implemented *real-world feel* and *self-monitoring*, while 70% implemented the *trustworthiness* PS. Only 60% and 45% of the apps employed *suggestions* and *social role* PSs which are equally important to provide medical advice and facilitate doctor-patient conversations.

5.6 Comparative Analysis

Table 6 shows the three most dominant persuasive strategies and the least dominant strategies for each of the four categories.

In a world where precision medicine has become prominent, personalization is unarguably critical to tailor healthcare (such as treatment and prevention of diseases or ailments) to individual patient. It is therefore not surprising personalization is the most dominant in mHealth apps. Surface credibility is important for emotional and mental health, as well as health assessment and healthcare delivery, due to the sensitive nature of these issues. Users tend to be skeptical and critical of apps in these areas and that makes it really necessary that the apps must be professionally looking, responsive, and with visually appealing interface to be adopted. Any app that lacks these attributes may be deemed incredible. Hence, surface credibility is a popular strategy in these domains. Furthermore, self-monitoring is dominant in physical activity and fitness apps since technological advancements in these areas have made it possible to automatically track movements (while walking, running, cycling, etc.) in real-time through various sensors on smartphones or wearable devices. Same applies to health assessment and healthcare delivery apps, where various sensors can be used to track vital signs, such as heart rate, blood pressure, temperature, etc. However, it is difficult to monitor food intake and dietary levels in diet apps unless users supply this information manually, and that explains why self-monitoring is not among the top in the domain of dieting.

5.7 Design Suggestions

Research has shown that social interaction can motivate individuals to achieve their target behaviours [18, 23, 24]. However, only 21% of the 80 mHealth apps employed at least one of the social support PSs. Designers of persuasive mHealth apps should consider implementing social support strategies in their apps by providing features allowing users

Table 6. Comparative Analysis of Persuasive Strategies across the four Categories

	Physical Activity and Fitness	Diet	Emotional and Mental Health	Health Assessment and Healthcare
Most Dominant Persuasive Strategies	Personalization Trustworthiness Self-monitoring	Personalization Suggestion Commitment/consistency	Personalization Surface credibility Liking	Personalization Surface credibility Self-monitoring
Least Dominant Persuasive Strategies	Rehearsal, Praise, Third-party endorsements, Cooperation	Rehearsal, Similarity, Authority, Cooperation, Social facilitation	Tailoring, Similarity, Third-party endorsements, Authority, Cooperation, Social comparison, Competition, Normative influence, Recognition, Scarcity	Reduction, Simulation, Similarity, Authority, Competition, Cooperation, Social comparison, Social learning, Normative influence, Social facilitation, Recognition, Scarcity Social proof, Reciprocity

to: (1) invite their friends to perform the target behaviour together, (2) compare their performance with others performing the same activities, (3) be publicly recognized after achieving important milestones that move them closer to their health goals, (4) learn from other users' experiences or success stories, (5) team up with (or join) other users in performing a common healthy activity.

Designers should also introduce *praise* in their apps such that users are praised or appreciated for every milestone achieved even if it seems small or trivial.

Finally, the relationship between the number of persuasive strategies employed in persuasive app design and their effectiveness is an open area of research. Although many existing persuasive apps employ multiple strategies, this analysis suggests that there is no relationship between the number of strategies employed in persuasive app for health design and app effectiveness as operationalized by the app rating. Hence, persuasive app developers could employ fewer strategies and still be effective. This will reduce the app complexity and reduce overall cognitive load on the user. This is in line with Orji et al. [25] which shows that persuasive apps employing a single strategy can be effective.

6 Conclusion and Future Work

We conducted a comparative systematic review of 80 mHealth apps across four categories with each category having 20 popular apps. The categories include physical activity and fitness, diet, emotional and mental health, and health assessment and healthcare. The goal of this review is to identify and compare the PSs employed and how they were implemented, and then offer design suggestions to improve persuasiveness of mHealth apps.

Our future work will be a broader review involving additional mHealth apps from both Google Play and App Store, spanning more health domains. In addition to PSs in PSD and Cialdini's Principles of Persuasion frameworks, others such as *punishment* would be considered. We also plan to investigate the effectiveness of apps employing multiple strategies in comparison to those employing a single strategy in actual app.

References

1. Gu, T.: Insights into the World's 3.2 Billion Smartphone Users, the Devices They Use & the Mobile Games They Play (2019). https://newzoo.com/insights/articles/newzoos-global-mobile-market-report-insights-into-the-worlds-3-2-billion-smartphone-users-the-devices-they-use-the-mobile-games-they-play/
2. Martínez-Pérez, B., et al.: Mobile health applications for the most prevalent conditions by the world health organization: review and analysis. J. Med. Internet Res. **15**, e120 (2013)
3. Dute, D.J., et al.: Using mobile apps to promote a healthy lifestyle among adolescents and students. JMIR mHealth uHealth. **4**, e39 (2016)
4. Dallinga, J.M., et al.: App use, physical activity and healthy lifestyle: a cross sectional study. BMC Public Health **15**, 1–9 (2015)
5. Rivera, J., et al.: Mobile apps for weight management. JMIR mHealth **4**, e87 (2016)
6. Chang, T.-R., Kaasinen, E., Kaipainen, K.: Persuasive design in mobile applications for mental well-being: multidisciplinary expert review. In: Godara, B., Nikita, K.S. (eds.) MobiHealth 2012. LNICST, vol. 61, pp. 154–162. Springer, Heidelberg (2013). https://doi.org/10.1007/978-3-642-37893-5_18
7. Harri, O., Marja, H.: Persuasive systems design: key issues, process model, and system features. Commun. Assoc. Inf. Syst. **24**, 96 (2009)
8. Cialdini, R.B.: Harnessing the science of persuasion. Harvard Bus. Rev. **79**(9), 72–81 (2001)
9. Nurcan, A., Duygu, F.: Use of Persuasion Strategies in Mobile Health Applications. Springer, Cham (2018). https://doi.org/10.1007/978-3-319-73135-3_2
10. Pinzon, O.E., Iyengar, M.S.: Persuasive technology and mobile health: a systematic review. In: Persuasive Technology, pp. 45–48, Linköping, Sweden (2012)
11. Meedya, S., Sheikh, M.K., Win, K.T., Halcomb, E.: Evaluation of breastfeeding mobile health applications based on the persuasive system design model. In: Oinas-Kukkonen, H., Win, K.T., Karapanos, E., Karppinen, P., Kyza, E. (eds.) PERSUASIVE 2019. LNCS, vol. 11433, pp. 189–201. Springer, Cham (2019). https://doi.org/10.1007/978-3-030-17287-9_16
12. Geuens, J., et al.: A review of persuasive principles in mobile apps for chronic arthritis patients: opportunities for improvement. JMIR mHealth **4**, e118 (2016)
13. Thach, K.S., Phan, T.P.N.: Persuasive design principles in mental health apps. In: IEEE-RIVF International Conference on Computer and Communication Technology, pp. 1–6 (2019)
14. Tiffany, B., et al.: Mobile apps for oral health promotion. JMIR **6**, e11432 (2018)
15. Langrial, S., et al.: Native mobile applications for personal well-being: a persuasive systems design evaluation. In: PACIS 2012 Proceedings (2012)
16. Azar, K.M., et al.: Mobile applications for weight management. Am. J. Prev. Med. **45**, 583–589 (2013)
17. Orji, R., Moffatt, K.: Persuasive technology for health and wellness: state-of-the-art and emerging trends. Health Inform. J. **24**, 66–91 (2018)

18. Matthews, J., et al.: Persuasive technology in mobile applications promoting physical activity: a systematic review. J. Med. Syst. **40**, 1–13 (2016)
19. Wang, Y., et al.: Persuasive technology in reducing prolonged sedentary behavior at work: a systematic review. Smart Heal. **7–8**, 19–30 (2018)
20. Bartlett, Y.K., et al.: Using persuasive technology to increase physical activity in people with chronic obstructive pulmonary disease by encouraging regular walking. J. Med. Internet Res. **19**, 124 (2017)
21. Consolvo, S., et al.: Goal-setting considerations for persuasive technologies that encourage physical activity. In: ACM International Conference Proceeding Series, p. 350 (2009)
22. Cham, S., Algashami, A., McAlaney, J., Stefanidis, A., Phalp, K., Ali, R.: Goal setting for persuasive information systems: five reference checklists. In: Oinas-Kukkonen, H., Win, K.T., Karapanos, E., Karppinen, P., Kyza, E. (eds.) PERSUASIVE 2019. LNCS, vol. 11433, pp. 237–253. Springer, Cham (2019). https://doi.org/10.1007/978-3-030-17287-9_20
23. Orji, R., et al.: Socially-driven persuasive health intervention design: competition, social comparison, and cooperation. Health Inform. J. **25**, 1451–1484 (2018)
24. Orji, R.: Why are persuasive strategies effective? Exploring the strengths and weaknesses of socially-oriented persuasive strategies. In: de Vries, P.W., Oinas-Kukkonen, H., Siemons, L., Beerlage-de Jong, N., van Gemert-Pijnen, L. (eds.) PERSUASIVE 2017. LNCS, vol. 10171, pp. 253–266. Springer, Cham (2017). https://doi.org/10.1007/978-3-319-55134-0_20
25. Orji, R., et al.: Improving the efficacy of games for change using personalization models. ACM Trans. Comput. Interact. **24**, 32 (2017)

Persuasive Mobile Apps for Sustainable Waste Management: A Systematic Review

Banuchitra Suruliraj[1]([⊠]), Makuochi Nkwo[2], and Rita Orji[1]

[1] Faculty of Computer Science, Dalhousie University, Halifax, NS, Canada
Banuchitra.suruliraj@dal.ca
[2] Department of Computer Science, Ebonyi State University, Abakaliki, Nigeria

Abstract. This paper provides a systematic review of mobile apps for waste management with the main aim of uncovering the persuasive strategies employed, their operationalizations, the relationship between the number of persuasive strategies employed and the apps' effectiveness to achieve specific target behavior. Specifically, we systematically investigated 125 mobile apps for waste management and identified distinct persuasive strategies, from the primary task support category of the PSD model. Furthermore, we classified these strategies based on the kind of waste management activities that the app was designed to support. Secondly, we uncovered how each of the persuasive strategies was implemented in the waste management apps to achieve the targeted outcome. Thirdly, we evaluated the relationship between the number of persuasive strategies employed in the apps design and the effectiveness of the apps (measured by user ratings). The results show that the apps cumulatively employed 251 persuasive strategies spread across the seven distinct primary task support persuasive strategies as follows: reduction (n = 76), tunneling (n = 9), tailoring (n = 37), personalization (n = 75), self-monitoring (n = 31), simulation (n = 7) and rehearsal (n = 16). In addition, our findings show that appropriate waste disposal, collection, recycling, and general waste management challenges were some of the waste management issues that the mobile apps targeted. Based on our results, we offer some design recommendations for operationalizing persuasive strategies in waste management app to increase their effectiveness.

Keywords: Waste management · Mobile apps · Persuasive strategies · Persuasive technology

1 Introduction

Proper waste management plays a significant role in ensuring the health and wellbeing of the people [8, 14, 16, 18]. Efforts by governments and stakeholders around the world, aimed at ensuring that citizens adopt positive waste disposal behaviors have been largely ineffective [17, 20]; hence the calls for a new approach, which can be achieved via the combined powers of technologies and persuasive strategies [8, 9]. As a result, there is an unprecedented increase in the design and adoption of persuasive technologies (PTs), which are capable of promoting a clean and sustainable environment. PTs are interactive

© Springer Nature Switzerland AG 2020
S. B. Gram-Hansen et al. (Eds.): PERSUASIVE 2020, LNCS 12064, pp. 182–194, 2020.
https://doi.org/10.1007/978-3-030-45712-9_14

systems that persuade users to accomplish desired behaviors as they use these digital technologies [1, 3, 4]. The advancement and ubiquitous nature of mobile technologies have created opportunities for users to interact with one another, learn new behaviors, and accomplish targeted tasks [6, 7, 10, 12]. These advancements have inspired researchers and designers to develop mobile interventions that target a variety of environmental sustainability issues [15, 19].

Persuasive strategies are the building block of PTs that enables then motivate, influence, and assist users in adapting the desired behaviors [11]. As a result, they are progressively being implemented in a variety of systems or apps to engage users and support them to achieve desired outcomes [2, 15]. Many apps exist, targeted at various forms of waste management challenges such as waste trashing, collection, recycling, etc. [9]. However, there is a dearth of research about what persuasive strategies are implemented by these apps and how they are operationalized to achieve the desired objective of promoting sustainable waste management behavior.

Therefore, this paper provides a systematic review of mobile apps for waste management with the main aim of uncovering the persuasive strategies employed their operationalizations, the relationship between the number of persuasive strategies employed and the apps' effectiveness, the specific target behavior of the apps. Specifically, we systematically reviewed 125 apps from the app store (Android and Apple), to identify distinct persuasive strategies implemented on the apps. In addition, we distinguished these strategies according to the kind of waste management activities that the apps were designed to promote. Secondly, we uncovered how the persuasive strategies were implemented in the waste management apps to achieve the target outcomes. Thirdly, we evaluated the relationship between the number of persuasive strategies employed in the apps design and the effectiveness of the apps.

The results show that the apps cumulatively employed 251 persuasive strategies spread across the seven distinct primary task support persuasive strategies as follows: reduction (n = 76), tunneling (n = 9), tailoring (n = 37), personalization (n = 75), self-monitoring (n = 31), simulation (n = 7) and rehearsal (n = 16). In addition, our findings show that appropriate waste disposal, collection, recycling, and general waste management challenges were some of the waste management issues that the mobile apps targeted. Based on our results, we offer some design recommendations for operationalizing persuasive strategies in waste management app to increase their effectiveness. This study is significant to the various stakeholders in the waste management business as its findings will potentially inform the design of waste management interventions that will be effective and promote clean and sustainable behavior.

To the best of the authors' knowledge, no existing studies have conducted a systematic review of apps or interventions for waste management to uncover the persuasive strategies employed and their operationalization. This is essential to inform future research in this area.

2 Literature Review

Persuasive strategies are techniques, which are implemented on persuasive technologies to help users achieve sustainable behaviors [7, 10]. Persuasive technologies are interactive applications (mobile and desktop systems) that are designed to motivate a change of behavior among users without coercion or deception [3, 4, 19]. Fogg (2009) designed an eight-step process to building persuasive technologies [3], Oinas-Kukkonen and Harjumaa (2009) developed design strategies which could be employed in developing and evaluating persuasive systems [13]. They described twenty-eight strategies otherwise referred to as the persuasive system design (PSD) model. These persuasive strategies are grouped into four categories Based on the kind of support that they provide to users of a system: the primary task, dialogue, system credibility, and social support [6, 11] categories. In contrast to other categories, the primary task support strategies aid system users in carrying out their tasks directly. The persuasive strategies in this group are Reduction, Tunneling, Tailoring, Personalization, Self-monitoring, Simulation, and Rehearsal [11]. The **reduction** strategy motivates system users to perform target behaviors by breaking down complex activities into simple tasks. The **tunneling** strategy motivates users to carry out target behaviors by guiding them through a process or experience during system use, hence reducing deviations. While **tailoring** information displays to the potential interests, personality, context and other factors relevant to the user(s) will potentially motivate system users to perform target behaviors, providing personalized content and services will also influence users to carry out target behaviors within the system. The **self-monitoring** strategy motivates users to achieve target behaviors by helping them to keep track of their individual performances or status along the way. The **simulation** strategy motivates system users by enabling them to see the relationship between cause-and-effect and their behaviors. The **rehearsal** strategy provides a means for users to rehearse a target behavior before performing it in the real world [13].

A review of related literature shows that several researchers have employed the PSD model to deconstruct the persuasive strategies implemented in apps in different domains [1, 5, 6, 11, 16]. The persuasive strategies from the primary task emerged as the commonly employed PTs, hence our decision to focus on it in this paper.

In the health and wellness domain, Orji and Moffatt (2018) conducted an empirical review of 85 papers to understand the effectiveness of PTs for health and wellness among others [16]. Results show that tracking and monitoring (primary task support strategies) are the most frequently used strategies [16]. Similarly, Kelders et al. employed the PSD model to evaluate the effectiveness of web-based health interventions [5]. Findings show that primary task support strategies were the most frequently implemented strategies when compared to others [5].

Fewer studies have designed and evaluated PT interventions for a sustainable environment. For instance, Rahuvaran designed mobile applications for water conservation and power consumption in Denmark [19]. In addition, Nkwo et al. discuss a waste management app for encouraging students to adopt clean and sustainable behaviors and protect the university environment via the provision of various personalized persuasive displays and support [9]. There are a growing number of persuasive apps targeted at motivating sustainable waste management behaviors. However, no research has investigated the persuasive strategies employed by these apps to make them effective. Therefore, we extend research in these analysis 125 apps to uncover the persuasive strategies from the primary task support employed to promote intended behavior; sustainable waste management. This will inform future research in this area.

3   Methods

This section describes the methods we employed in our study. Here, we show the persuasive app selection criteria and coding.

3.1   Selection of Sample Apps

First, we used various search terms including "waste management", "waste disposal", and "waste recycling", to search for apps on the App Store and Google Play that is related to the subject matter. In addition, we searched using various combinations of search terms using 'OR' and 'AND'. The search results show an initial list of 212 apps. We applied a number of criteria to extract the apps that best fit the objective of the study; we accepted only those apps that are designed to support waste management activities and are in English (according to the app's description and demo). In contrast, we left out the apps that failed to suit the aforementioned criteria. We ensured that apps that appeared in both App Store and Google Play were counted as one.

3.2   Coding and Analysis of Apps

The goal of coding the apps is to evaluate the number and type of persuasive strategies employed in designing persuasive apps for waste management. We coded the apps using the Persuasive System Design (PSD) model described by [13]. We chose this model because it is a widely accepted framework for deconstructing persuasive systems. Specifically, we used the persuasive strategies of the primary task support category to code the apps since they are the commonly employed strategies that directly aid in achieving the desired behavior. The primary task support strategies aid in understanding the strategies that are used in helping users to accomplish the target tasks. In order to identify the persuasive strategies used in the apps and how they were operationalized to support pro-waste management behaviors, we downloaded and reviewed 125 apps to identify the persuasive strategies using only the techniques from the primary task support category of the PSD model. We agreed and ensured a mutual understanding of the coding decisions at every point. In addition, we found how the strategies were operationalized on the persuasive apps to achieve expected outcomes. In the end, 125 apps were accepted and considered suitable for coding (see Fig. 1). In addition, we collected: *app name, platform* (i.e. iPhone, Android, or both), *developer, date of the last update, and* price (i.e. free, fee-based, and free with in-app purchases), *strategies implemented* and *operationalization, target outcomes, and country/region*. Moreover, we analyzed our data using the following approach:

- Categorized apps based on the purpose and target behavior.
- We carried out a descriptive analysis of the collected data and calculated count and average persuasive strategies employed in the apps.
- Calculated correlation co-efficient to find the relation between the number of strategies implemented and the effectiveness of the app based on user ratings.

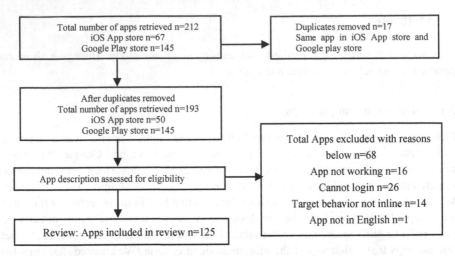

Fig. 1. Flow diagram illustrating exclusion criteria in various stages

4   Results

In this section, we present the results of our analysis. Specifically, we describe the primary Task Support strategies employed in the persuasive apps for waste management, and their implementations, the target purpose of the apps, as well as the relationship between the strategies employed and their effectiveness.

4.1   Information on Selected Apps

A summary of the reviewed apps is provided in Table 1. 65% of all the apps reviewed were updated in 2019.

Table 1. Summary of the reviewed apps

Mobile platforms	iOS (40%), Android (60%)
User ratings	5 (6%), 4–4.9 (57%), 3–3.9 (5%), 2–2.9 (3%), 1–1.9 (1%), 0 or No rating (28%)
App categories	Productivity (26%), Education (17%), Business (17%), Lifestyle (6%), Social (5%), Other 16 categories (29%)

4.2   Primary Task Support Strategies and Their Implementations in the Apps

A total of 125 shortlisted apps were reviewed from the app description in the store, the app demos, and by downloading and using each of the apps. The apps were reviewed to identify implementations of the 7 primary task support strategies (Fig. 2).

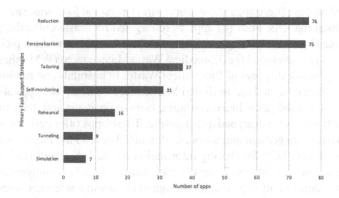

Fig. 2. Persuasive strategies and frequency of use

Among the seven strategies (see Fig. 3), Reduction (n = 76) is the most employed strategy in waste management apps followed by Personalization (n = 75), and Tailoring (n = 37). Moreover, the persuasive apps implemented Reduction strategy as suggestive search (as auto populate list), calendar view for garbage collection schedule with color coding to indicate type of waste, etc., all in a bid to reduce efforts expended by users in seeing and performing target behaviors. While many apps implemented Personalization strategy, it is operationalized as personalized language settings, notification times, email reminders, saves location, profiles, preferences and payment options, others implemented Tailoring through address-based garbage collection schedule, and location-based services. The gaming apps implemented Self-monitoring through a visual display of history; statistics etc., while gaming apps implemented it through displays of player progress, points earned, and levels completed per game session. The Rehearsal strategy is implemented mostly in gaming apps via waste sorting video games. The apps implemented the Tunneling strategy as step-by-step guides and a Do It Yourself (DIY) project where users are expected to follow a given guide. Simulation strategy is implemented via a display of city cleaning and its impacts on the environment and health, and wellness of the people. These strategies were implemented to help users carryout their most basic tasks which will potentially engender a cleaner and more sustainable environment.

4.3 App Categories by Purpose

We classified the apps into 16 categories (see Fig. 3.) based on the purpose and target behavior intended by the app. Most of the apps (n = 48) were designed to aid regional waste disposal. These apps are targeted to be used by residents of a city or municipality and primarily offer collection schedule and waste sorting guide with respect to the user's home address. 15% of the app was designed to educate people about proper waste management and waste management best practices. 10% of the apps are commercial and were owned by private organizations. They are used for on-demand services like dumpster rental in exchange for money. About 9% were designed as games that help the user to learn waste sorting by playing a waste sorting game. Some game apps offered points that can be redeemed as coupons. Five percent (5%) of the apps were designed to manage food wastes. These apps allow users to track personal food waste and buy surplus food from local markets. Four (4) apps were targeted for waste collection; these apps offer on-demand garbage pickup services and allow the user to make a pickup request. Five (5) apps were developed for Biomedical Waste Management (WM); these apps help to ensure responsible disposal of Biomedical Wastes in hospitals and relevant facilities. Five (5) apps were designed for the digital Marketplace. Marketplace apps allow its users to post listings of used items like electronics, browse for items and make an inquiry to buy. Three (3) apps were designed as Magazine. These apps offer periodical magazines related to waste management and users can download or read the magazines in the app. Three (3) apps were built for sharing information on Do It Yourself (DIY) Projects to upcycle plastics or grow plants. Three (3) apps were designed for conferences related to waste management; event apps that are designed to inform conference attendees about expected waste management practices on the venue. One (1) app was designed for Data collection. This app encourages users to report data related to waste management in the region, and in turn provide a visualization of data from across the world. One (1) app was designed as a Calculator. This app offers calculations related to wastewater treatment for professionals working in water treatment plants. One (1) app was developed for Plastic Waste Management. This app helps users to track their personal plastic usage and provide suggestions for alternatives. One (1) app was built for AI aided waste sorting. This app allows a user to take a picture of an item to be discarded and in turn provide disposal guidelines using object recognition algorithms.

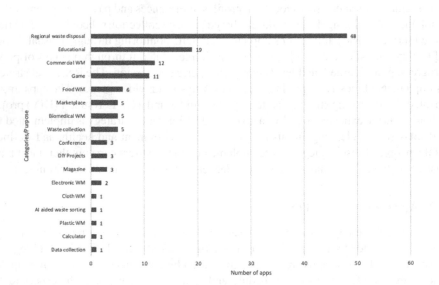

Fig. 3. Number of apps by their purpose

The top five categories discussed cover 80% of the total apps. Let us further know about persuasive strategies employed with respect to the listed categories.

4.4 Primary Task Support Strategies and App Types

As we reviewed to find the primary task support strategies employed in each app, we found that out of 48 apps in *regional waste disposal category*, 79%(38), 73%(35), 58%(28), 13%(6), 19%(9), 2%(1) and 0%(0) employed Reduction, Personalization, Tailoring, Self-monitoring, Rehearsal, Tunneling, and Simulation respectively. Out of 19 apps in the *education category*, 16%(3), 36%(7), 16%(3), 11%(2), 11%(2), 21%(4) and 0%(0) employed Reduction, Personalization, Tailoring, Self-monitoring, Rehearsal, Tunneling, and Simulation respectively. Out of 12 apps in the *Commercial WM category*, 67%(80), 25%(3), 0%(0), 50%(6), 0%(0), 8%(1) and 0%(0) employed Reduction, Personalization, Tailoring, Self-monitoring, Rehearsal, Tunneling, and Simulation respectively. Out of 11apps in the *Game category*, 27%(3), 46%(5), 9%(1), 46%(5), 36%(4), 0%(0), and 36%(4) employed Reduction, Personalization, Tailoring, Self-monitoring, Rehearsal, Tunneling, and Simulation respectively. Out of 6apps in the *Food WM category*, 83%(5), 100%(6), 17%(1), 67%(4), 0%(0), 0%(0), and 17%(1) employed Reduction, Personalization, Tailoring, Self-monitoring, Rehearsal, Tunneling, and Simulation respectively. Figure 4 highlights 16 subcategories of apps and the frequency of implementation of 7 primary task strategies. The data table highlights the number of apps implementing each strategy by category.

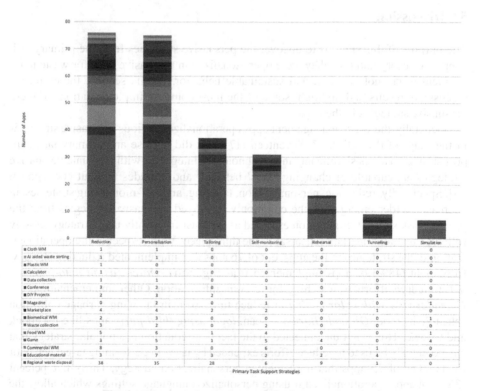

	Reduction	Personalization	Tailoring	Self-monitoring	Rehearsal	Tunneling	Simulation
Cloth WM	1	1	0	0	0	0	0
AI aided waste sorting	1	1	0	0	0	0	0
Plastic WM	1	0	0	1	0	1	0
Calculator	1	0	0	0	0	0	0
Data collection	1	1	0	0	0	0	0
Conference	3	2	0	1	0	0	0
DIY Projects	2	3	2	1	1	1	0
Magazine	0	2	0	1	0	0	1
Marketplace	4	4	2	2	0	1	0
Biomedical WM	2	3	0	0	0	0	1
Waste collection	3	2	0	2	0	0	0
Food WM	5	6	1	4	0	0	1
Game	3	5	1	5	4	0	4
Commercial WM	8	3	0	6	0	1	0
Educational material	3	7	3	2	2	4	0
Regional waste disposal	38	35	28	6	9	1	0

Primary Task Support Strategies

Fig. 4. Primary task support strategies by app categories

The graph shows the simulation strategy is mostly employed by apps in the Game category. Tunneling is the commonly used app in the educational category. DIY projects category had the highest number of strategies (3.33) employed per-app followed by food WM with 2.83 strategies per app and marketplace with 2.6 strategies per app. Regional waste disposal, game, conference, AI aided waste sorting, clothing WM, and data collection had the average number of strategies between 2 and 2.5 listed in descending order. Commercial WM, waste collection, magazine, biomedical WM, and education had an average between 1 and 1.5 also listed in descending order. Plastic WM and Calculator apps had an average of 1 strategy.

4.5   App Effectiveness and Persuasive Strategies Employed

To examine whether there is a relationship between the number of persuasive strategies employed in the app design and the perceived app effectiveness (as assessed by the app ratings), we performed Pearson's correlation between the app rating and the number of persuasive strategies. The results are $r = 0.161$ (no correlation) and $p = 0.073$ which implies there is no significant relationship between the number of primary task support strategies employed and efficacy of the app.

5   Discussion

The purpose of this study is to uncover the persuasive strategies from the primary task support category and how they were operationalized in persuasive apps for waste management to promote a clean and sustainable behavior. In this section, therefore, we discuss our results and highlight some of the most common implementations of these persuasive strategies in the apps.

Generally, the waste management apps operationalized various persuasive strategies in the range of 0 to all the 7. Seventeen (17) apps did not use any primary task support strategy. This is significant since technologies integrated with adequate persuasive strategies are capable of changing users' behavior and attitudes without coercion [4, 13]. Specifically, reduction, personalization, tailoring, and self-monitoring strategies, in decreasing order emerged as the commonly employed persuasive strategies from the primary task support. Simulation emerged as the least frequently used strategy, closely followed by tunneling and rehearsal in the third place. With respect to the operationalization of the strategies in the apps, out of 76 apps that implemented reduction strategy, forty-eight (48%) of apps implemented it as *suggestive search (as an auto-populate list)* to reduce efforts in searching for relevant information. Other implementations are *Calendar view with color-coding* to reduce time spent in knowing garbage collection schedule by type, *QR code/Bar code* scan, *login using third-party* apps like Facebook and Google. This is not unconnected to the fact that reduction is a popular strategy that can potentially be used to reduce efforts expended by users in performing target behavior [5, 11]. Out of 75 apps that implemented personalization strategy, Thirty-five percent (35%) of apps operationalized it using personalized language settings which allow the user to choose the preferred language. Other personalization implementations are *notification times, email reminders, save location, profiles, preferences* and *payment options*.

Out of 37 apps identified with Tailoring strategies, ninety-two (92%) of them implemented tailoring via the provision of *address-based garbage collection schedules and location-based services*. According to research, an interactive system which provides tailored information to users and show personalized contents could guide and persuade users to perform target behaviors [7, 10, 16].

Furthermore, the apps that implemented self-monitoring (n = 31) provided an exclusive app screen to *display history, statistics, environmental impact and amount* of CO_2 released. The gaming apps implemented self-monitoring via a real-time display of the *player progress points earned*, and *levels completed per game* session. This is in line with research suggestions that systems that allow users to keep track of their status could be effective at helping them to perform their target behaviors [2, 15]. Meanwhile, we uncovered that the Rehearsal strategy is only employed in games, and mini games included in regional waste disposal apps. A player is encouraged to rehearse waste sorting and disposal behavior by playing waste sorting games. Game tasks include *dropping each item in the appropriate bin, cleaning a city or disposing of garbage*. This is important because studies show that a system that provides a means through which a user can rehearse target behavior before actually performing it, could potentially encourage them to perform target behavior [1, 15]. Inadequate waste sorting knowledge is one of the factors affecting waste management behaviors. In addition, the Tunneling strategy is implemented to guide users in the attitude change process by providing a road map [15]. We found that tunneling was implemented in apps for waste upcycling projects via the provision of a *roadmap to complete quizzes and articles, step-by-step guides and a Do It Yourself (DIY) project of growing plants*. This enables a user to follow a given guideline to achieve a target behavior. Finally, the Simulation strategy was implemented by *simulating city cleaning and its impacts on the environment and health and wellness of the people*. Users can observe the link between inappropriate waste disposal and its hazardous effects on the environment; e.g., burning of refrigerator and propane cylinder will result in a blast or fire accident. These findings are in agreement with research [5, 8, 15].

6 Design Recommendations

Our result shows that several Waste management apps have successfully employed persuasive strategies from the primary task category to promote waste management behavior. Hence, we recommend that persuasive technology designers who want to develop a persuasive app for waste management could employ persuasive strategies from the Primary Task Support category.

The Reduction strategy should be operationalized such that users could easily perform target behaviors without expending much effort. For example, the app could list possible addresses of the nearest waste drop off locations to the user. It could be designed as automatic detection of the user's current location and suggest a closest waste drop-off location. Other intuitive ways to operationalize this strategy is by using QR code, Bar code scan for food items, Object recognition using camera to know to assist users in sorting and disposing of items appropriately, implementing Google map to direct users to the nearest waste drop-off location.

The Personalization strategy should be operationalized such that the apps will offer personalized content and services to improve user experience. This could be achieved by presenting relevant content in the user's preferred language, personalized reminder, time and date for waste disposal. The user profile could be personalized with personal photos, addresses, achievements, and payment options.

The Tailoring strategy should be operationalized such that the system delivers preferred content to specific user groups to improve user experience and facilitate the desired behavior. For instance, the display of a garbage truck collection schedule should be tailored to every zip code or perhaps, home address. This will enable users to check their schedules and waste disposal accordingly. In addition, tailoring can be operationalized in the form of player levels such as "easy", "medium" and "hard" in waste sorting game according to the user's expertise. This will potentially enable users to learn and improve their waste sorting skills.

The Self-monitoring strategy should be operationalized in apps that promote proper waste management to help users to track or see their waste management-related performances over time. The mobile app could show users a daily level of carbon-di-oxide emission around their locality. They could be provided with options to track their contribution to a clean environment by cutting down plastic use, reselling old electronics, upcycling old items, etc. In addition, an impact chart with categories of waste will potentially help the user to visualize their progress.

The Rehearsal strategy would be most effective in game environments. For instance, users can practice waste sorting in a game. This will be helpful in assisting a user to master how to appropriate sort their waste to the colored bins depending on the type of waste. The user can apply the knowledge acquired via the waste sorting game into real life by disposing garbage into the appropriate bins, thus ensuring efficient disposal and easier recycling by the municipality.

We believe that these implementations could motivate users to adopt sustainable waste behaviors and protect the environment.

7 Limitations

One of the limitations of this study is that we reviewed only apps that were provided in the English language. Since there are apps that are in other languages, the results may not generalize.

8 Conclusion

In this paper, we reviewed 125 waste management mobile applications using the Persuasive Systems Design (PSD) model to uncover the persuasive strategies from the primary task support category. Two researchers independently reviewed the apps and documented the identified strategies by first analyzing the app descriptions and demos, and eventually installing, registering, and using the apps. The apps were classified into 16 categories based on the specific target behavior and type of waste management activities it was developed for. The results of the review uncovered that *reduction, personalization, tailoring, self-monitoring,* and *rehearsal,* in decreasing order, were the most commonly used strategies from the primary task category. Surprising, we found no connection between the number of persuasive strategies employed in the apps and apps' effectiveness (measured using user ratings). In addition, we found that apps aimed at promoting regional waste disposal, educating people of best waste management practices; commercial waste management and games, were the common kinds of waste management apps online. We discussed how each persuasive strategy was operationalized in waste management apps and offered recommendations for operationalizing persuasive strategies in apps that could potentially increase user engagement and experience, as well as persuade users to adopt sustainable waste management attitudes and protect the environment.

In our future study, we plan to explore user perceptions of persuasive strategies for waste management via large-scale studies in order to identify the most preferred strategy. We also plan to develop and evaluate the app for promoting waste management. We hope the design recommendations will be helpful to designers who would want to develop innovative apps for promoting waste management.

References

1. Adaji, I., Vassileva, J.: Evaluating personalization and persuasion in e-commerce. In: CEUR Workshop Proceedings (2016)
2. Almutari, N., Orji, R.: How effective are social influence strategies in persuasive apps for promoting physical activity? A systematic review. In: ACM UMAP 2019 Adjunct - Adjunct Publication of the 27th Conference on User Modeling, Adaptation and Personalization, pp. 167–172. Association for Computing Machinery, Inc (2019). https://doi.org/10.1145/3314183.3323855
3. Fogg, B.: A behavior model for persuasive design. In: ACM International Conference Proceeding Series (2009). https://doi.org/10.1145/1541948.1541999
4. Fogg, B.J.: Persuasive Technology: Using Computers to Change What We Think and Do (2003). https://doi.org/10.1016/B978-1-55860-643-2.X5000-8
5. Kelders, S.M., et al.: Persuasive system design does matter: a systematic review of adherence to web-based interventions (2012). https://doi.org/10.2196/jmir.2104
6. Matthews, J., et al.: Persuasive technology in mobile applications promoting physical activity: a systematic review. J. Med. Syst. 40(3), 1–13 (2016). https://doi.org/10.1007/s10916-015-0425-x
7. Nkwo, M.: Designing culturally-appropriate persuasive technology to promote positive work attitudes among workers in public workplaces. In: ACM UMAP 2019 - Proceedings of the 27th ACM Conference on User Modeling, Adaptation and Personalization (2019). https://doi.org/10.1145/3320435.3323465
8. Nkwo, M.: Mobile persuasive technology: promoting positive waste management behaviors in developing African nations. In: Conference on Human Factors in Computing Systems - Proceedings. Association for Computing Machinery (2019). https://doi.org/10.1145/3290607.3299071
9. Nkwo, M., et al.: Persuasion for promoting clean and sustainable environment. In: Proceedings of the Second African Conference for Human Computer Interaction on Thriving Communities - AfriCHI 2018, pp. 1–5. ACM Press, New York (2018). https://doi.org/10.1145/3283458.3283490
10. Nkwo, M., Orji, R.: Personalized persuasion to promote positive work attitudes in public workplaces. In: ACM UMAP 2019 Adjunct - Adjunct Publication of the 27th Conference on User Modeling, Adaptation and Personalization, pp. 185–190. Association for Computing Machinery, Inc (2019). https://doi.org/10.1145/3314183.3323858

11. Nkwo, M., Orji, R.: Persuasive technology in African context deconstructing persuasive techniques in an African online marketplace. In: ACM International Conference Proceeding Series, pp. 89–98. Association for Computing Machinery (2018). https://doi.org/10.1145/3283458.3283479

12. Nkwo, M., Orji, R.: Socially responsive ecommerce platforms: design implications for online marketplaces in developing African nation. In: ACM UMAP 2019 Adjunct - Adjunct Publication of the 27th Conference on User Modeling, Adaptation and Personalization (2019). https://doi.org/10.1145/3314183.3324984

13. Oinas-Kukkonen, H., Harjumaa, M.: A systematic framework for designing and evaluating persuasive systems. In: Oinas-Kukkonen, H., Hasle, P., Harjumaa, M., Segerståhl, K., Øhrstrøm, P. (eds.) PERSUASIVE 2008. LNCS, vol. 5033, pp. 164–176. Springer, Heidelberg (2008). https://doi.org/10.1007/978-3-540-68504-3_15

14. Omran, A., Gavrilescu, M.: Municipal solid waste management in developing countries: a perspective on Vietnam. Environ. Eng. Manag. J. 7(4), 469–478 (2008). https://doi.org/10.30638/eemj.2008.070

15. Orji, F.A., et al.: Personalized persuasion for promoting students' engagement and learning. In: CEUR Workshop Proceedings (2018)

16. Orji, R., Moffatt, K.: Persuasive technology for health and wellness: state-of-the-art and emerging trends. Health Inform. J. 24(1), 66–91 (2018). https://doi.org/10.1177/1460458216650979

17. Purity, N.-O.U., Ifeoma, A.R., Yusuf, A.E.: Waste management and sustainable development in Nigeria: a study of Anambra state waste management agency. Eur. J. Bus. Manag. 8 (2016)

18. Schiopu, A.-M., et al.: Solid waste in Romania: management, treatment and pollution prevention practices. Environ. Eng. Manag. J. (2018). https://doi.org/10.30638/eemj.2007.055

19. Supervisor, R.P., Kjeldskov, J.: Mobile Persuasive Technology » Promoting pro-environmental behaviour

20. How to Develop a Waste Management and Disposal Strategy - The Chartered Institute of Procurement and Supply. https://www.cips.org/en/knowledge/categories-and-commodities/facilities/waste-management/how-to-develop-a-waste-management-and-disposal-strategy/. Accessed 02 Nov 2019

Not (B)interested? Using Persuasive Technology to Promote Sustainable Household Recycling Behavior

Christina Bremer(✉)(ID)

School of Computing and Communications, Lancaster University, Lancaster, UK
c.bremer@lancaster.ac.uk

Abstract. In many recycling systems around the world, waste is separated at the source. Their success therefore depends on an active participation of households. However, especially young people have been found to not consistently follow their local recycling schemes. A promising approach to tackle such suboptimal household recycling behavior (HRB) is the use of persuasive technology. While existing studies have highlighted its potential, they also commonly relied on waste container augmentation. To better understand the requirements of augmentation-independent HRB-related persuasive technology, a two-phase study was carried out with young adults in Sweden. First, an online survey (N = 50) was used to establish the target users' recycling-related problems, attitudes and interests. Then, based on the survey results, a mobile phone application was designed and evaluated in an iterative manner. This led to the following design recommendations: (1) easy access to information about optimal household recycling behavior, (2) employment of several motivational strategies, (3) recognition of recycling scheme differences, (4) regard of users as equals and (5) use of a readily accessible technology channel. The technological format of persuasive technology interventions was found to spark the users' curiosity. Within a well-functioning recycling system and along with engaging content, it could encourage repeated use and elicit reflection to help break unsustainable household recycling habits.

Keywords: Household recycling behavior · Persuasive technology · User-centered design · Sustainable human-computer interaction

1 Introduction

With a growing population, increasing consumerism, urbanization and the intensive use of packaged products, the amount of waste that we as humans produce is steadily increasing. Particularly the waste that is not collected and recycled has a large negative impact on public health and contributes to environmental pollution and climate change [1]. Of the estimated 7–10 billion tonnes of urban waste that are produced annually, 2 billion stem from households. By 2050, this

© Springer Nature Switzerland AG 2020
S. B. Gram-Hansen et al. (Eds.): PERSUASIVE 2020, LNCS 12064, pp. 195–207, 2020.
https://doi.org/10.1007/978-3-030-45712-9_15

number is predicted to rise to 3.4 billion [2]. A key approach to reducing the negative impact of waste is recycling, which describes the general process of collecting previously used materials and reprocessing them into products, materials or substances [3]. However, for recycling to be effective, a well-functioning recycling system and the cooperation of citizens is required. Due to the environmental and economic benefits of recycling household waste, a policy goal in many countries, including Sweden, is to improve the household recycling behavior (HRB) of their citizens [4].

In sustainable human-computer interaction, a widespread approach for behavior change is the use of persuasive technology. This approach is sometimes called 'persuasive sustainability' and mostly applied to consumption behavior (related to energy, water, gas and solid materials), transportation, air quality and CO_2 emissions [5]. Recycling-related persuasive technology has received a moderate amount of attention. Several studies have introduced eco-feedback systems to highlight its potential [6–8]. However, gathering eco-feedback data commonly requires augmented waste containers or additional equipment, which can be costly and difficult to deploy on a larger scale. This paper aims to complement the existing literature by exploring the role and requirements of HRB-related persuasive technology that does not rely on augmentation of recycling bins or the home environment. It first reviews the relevant literature before going on to describe the survey and intervention methods used with the Sweden-based young adult participants. It then describes the iterative design of the prototype and concludes with key recommendations for HRB systems. These answer directly to the existing challenges of engaging users with digital interventions in recycling.

1.1   Household Recycling Behavior (HRB)

HRB comprises the collection, preparation and separation of waste at home. The extent to which citizens are asked to engage in these behaviors depends on the implemented recycling system. The higher the citizens' degree of involvement, the better quality waste materials can be extracted. HRB can be considered a habit as it occurs frequently, in a stable context and as an automatic response to a specific context [9]. This entails the need for awareness raising [10]. There is a consensus in the literature that young people tend to exhibit worse recycling habits than older people [11].

In 2013, Miafodzyeva and Brandt [12] conducted a meta-analysis of prior research that had investigated the determinants of HRB. The results revealed that the convenience of the recycling facility is the strongest predictor of HRB. It is closely followed by both moral norms, which are defined as personal concerns about recycling, and information. Miafodzyeva and Brandt [12] concluded that recycling needs to be portrayed as a pleasant yet meaningful activity and that citizens need to be encouraged to follow good recycling practices sufficiently and regularly. These findings are complemented by those of a 2017 meta-analysis in which Varotto and Spagnolli [13] reviewed HRB-related persuasive strategies and their effectiveness. They found that social modeling and environmental alterations are the most effective strategies, followed by combined interventions, prompts/information, incentives, commitment and feedback.

1.2 Sweden as the Study Context

Sweden provides a relevant study context as the responsibility for handling waste is divided between municipalities, producers, businesses and households [15]. This division in responsibility means that the initial sorting and disposal process is of particular importance. It also means that the recycling schemes for Swedish households differ depending on their geographic location. Across the country, the schemes rely on a basic separation of paper, plastic, metal and glass. Some municipalities have included economic incentives into their waste management policies to encourage a higher participation in their recycling schemes [14]. Between 2014 and 2018, Sweden recycled and composted around 50% of its household waste [15]. This stagnating percentage is a cause for concern, not only with regard to the European Commission's recycling target of 65% by 2030 [16].

1.3 Recycling-Related Persuasive Technology

Both within and outside of academia, technology has been used as a tool to address unsustainable recycling behavior. The most relevant found consist of four systems: (1) Weigh Your Waste, (2) BinCam/BinLeague, (3) the Trash Game and (4) the Sorteringsguide. These are described below.

Weigh Your Waste is a platform for users to monitor their waste charges and learn about related topics, including recycling, reuse and composting [7]. It consists of a digital weighing scale at the bottom of a wheelie bin and a touch screen monitor. The weight measurements of the waste are sent to the screen via WiFi technology. Weigh Your Waste can be integrated along with 'pay by weight' waste schemes or be used solely as an educational platform.

BinCam/BinLeague is a social persuasive system that aims to encourage reflection and promote sustainable HRB [6]. Instead of a normal kitchen refuse bin, users install a BinCam bin, which captures the bin's content via a camera and uploads the pictures onto a social media platform, where they are visible to all users of the BinCam system. The pictures are then sent to a crowd-sourcing service which identifies and counts the number of waste items. The numeric values that are generated this way can be used for the BinLeague application which visualizes and compares the recycling achievements and food waste savings of the participating households. In an evaluation study, 22 participants used the system for five weeks. Overall, the participants enjoyed using the system and said that it made them more aware of their recycling behavior. However, across households they also reported that it made them feel guilty or ashamed.

The Trash Game is a gamified system which aims to encourage better recycling behavior [8]. It consists of (1) several bins which are augmented with a camera to capture the waste and a screen to present feedback and (2) a mobile application designed as a game. In the game, the users manage a recycling company and one of their main activities is to sort waste in order to improve their revenue. The sorting choices of each user are evaluated against the choices made by all other users. The crowd feedback is also presented on the screens of the bins. In a preliminary evaluation study, the participants (N = 35) indicated that they liked the augmented bins and the application, but showed a tendency to focus more on the classification task rather than the game as a whole.

Finally, the Sorteringsguide is a web-based application that aids the categorization and disposal of waste [17]. Users can specify waste items and are given information about their category (e.g. garden waste) and where they should be disposed of (e.g. recycling center). The Sorteringsguide is only available in Swedish and can be found on the website of Uppsala Vatten.

Weigh Your Waste, the Trash Game and BinCam/BinLeague follow the popular eco-feedback approach, in which feedback is given on individual or group behavior to encourage more sustainable choices [18]. Hence, they rely on technologically augmented waste containers and even additional equipment like the stand-alone touch screen for Weigh Your Waste. In comparison, this study focuses on interventions without such augmentation. This makes it easier to apply the findings in different settings and reach a large audience. Similar to the Weigh Your Waste and Trash Game studies, this study adopts a user-centered approach in which the persuasive design is largely based on user input. It also places importance on the technology's role as an educational platform. The goal was to design an application on household recycling that users would be motivated to try out and ideally consult again if they had any questions on the topic. In order to achieve this, the gathered user input extensively covers the target users' recycling-related attitudes, interests, problems and design requests. An example of a purely educational approach from outside of academia is the Sorteringsguide.

2   Methodology

The study consisted of: (1) the design, implementation and analysis of an online survey and (2) iterative design work, including user evaluations. The results of the online survey were thereby intended to inform the design work. The chosen design methodology was Fogg's eight-step design process as it specifically targets persuasive technology [19]. The study phases linked to it as follows: literature work, steps 1–3; online survey, steps 2–4; iterative design work, steps 5–7. Step 8 would be a further expansion of the designed application. Based on a consensus in the literature that young people tend to exhibit worse HRB than older people, the study targeted young adults aged 18 to 30. As it was conducted in the context of the Swedish recycling system, participants were required to live in Sweden.

2.1   Online Survey

In the first phase of the study, an online survey was carried out among Sweden-based young adults aged 18 to 30. It was intended to provide insight into their recycling-related interests, problems and attitudes. In addition, participants were asked to assess their own HRB and state their requests and ideas for an HRB-related application. The survey contained multiple choice and ranking items, as well as open-ended questions. It was distributed via social media and accessible for a total of four weeks. Fifty participants (35 female and 15 male) filled in the survey. The average age of the participants was 24 years. The survey responses were analyzed using descriptive statistics. For the open-ended questions, a thematic content analysis was carried out, similar to the one described by Braun and Clarke [20].

2.2 Iterative Design Work

In the second phase of the study, a mobile phone application was designed and evaluated in an iterative manner. The aim was to complement the results from the online survey with findings from the design and evaluation process and to compare the survey responses with feedback from the evaluation sessions. The initial paper prototype was informed by the literature, findings from the online survey, existing technology and a set of design principles adapted from Preece, Rogers and Sharp [21]. It was improved in three iterations, each involving a task analysis and a short semi-structured interview with one or two participants. The participants were recruited via the author's university network. The evaluation sessions were audio recorded and lasted approximately one hour each. Based on the final paper prototype, a digital prototype was built. It was intended to reflect the obtained results and function as groundwork for future research.

3 Results

The results are divided into five subsections. Subsections 3.1–3.4 outline the survey outcomes, while Subsect. 3.5 describes the findings from the iterative design and evaluation of the mobile phone prototype.

3.1 HRB Self-evaluation and Difficulties

Sixty-eight percent of the survey participants agreed that they could improve how they prepare their household waste and 56% how they dispose of it. Linked to these results, 32% agreed that they are often unsure into which container they should put their waste items. Eighteen percent disagreed that they know how many waste containers there exist for their household waste. Of the five predefined response options, overflowing waste containers were reported as a problem by the largest number of participants (58%), followed by difficulties in dismantling waste (54%), difficulties in cleaning waste (32%), difficulties with inconvenient locations of waste containers (20%) and difficulties with unclear/no labelling of waste containers (18%). Fifty-four percent of the participants disagreed that it requires a lot of effort to prepare and dispose of their household waste correctly; 32% agreed. In the open-ended responses, one participant outlined their current work-around as: "At time when I don't know what to do with the item at hand I just put it in the brännbart [burnable waste] container, which I think is not good". Two participants expressed uncertainty about the location of recycling centers and waste containers ("finding where these damned containers are").

3.2   Recycling-Related Interests

Seventy-six percent of the survey participants disagreed that it does not make a difference whether they recycle and 84% disagreed that they do not really care about recycling. The participants wanted to learn about the impact of recycling onto the environment (72%), how to integrate good recycling practices into their daily life (64%), how different waste items get recycled (64%), the recycling efforts of other people in the community (60%) and the recycling system in their area (50%). A key theme in the open-ended responses was feedback. The participants wanted to know about the "impact that [their] personal contribution to recycling has on the environment" and if their HRB "made a difference", particularly in "reducing different environmental problems". It would be motivational for them to know that their HRB matters (e.g. "it would help motivate me to keep up if I knew I made a difference"). Related to the idea of feedback was the request to "monitor" or "track" recycling performances on a "weekly" or "monthly" rhythm. The participants wanted to see the development of their own HRB (e.g. "graphs of recycling habits over time") and compare it to the HRB of others (e.g. "everyone in the corridor I live in"). Other suggestions were to "make groups and monitor a consolidated performance" and to use an application as "something to talk about with other people and compare habits". As an additional step, goal-setting (e.g. "make people more aware about their optimum possible recycling performance against their current performance") and an achievement system with "points" or "rewards" were suggested, which might even "translate into something real in life". This opinion, however, was not shared by everyone as one participant preferred to have "no leader boards creating social pressure". After having disposed of their waste items, the participants were interested to know "what happens to [their] disposed items" and how they would be transformed into new products and materials (e.g. "showing what your recycled items become").

3.3   Use Context

Another key theme in the open-ended survey responses was the participants' wish for guidance when deciding which waste item they should put into which container and how they should prepare and dismantle the waste. Their wordings suggest that they require decision support "at the time" or "in situations" when they do not know what to do with a waste item. A particular focus was on uncommon waste items, like ceramics, and waste items that "need to go to a special station". The participants were also interested in learning about household waste recycling more generally (e.g. "showing basics how to recycle/what is

recycling" and "apps that show how to do the recycling in steps"). One participant asked for guidance when "making a choice on which product to buy (what
has a better chance of being recycled or what is easier to recycle, for example)".
Two groups that were specifically believed to benefit from a HRB-related application were people who changed their place of residence ("when you arrive at
the new place, or the people come from the place without recycling training")
and students ("especially in student housing it is often unclear how the recycling
system works and there is no real explanation except for from other students
who have lived there before").

3.4 Desired Platform, Content and Features

The survey participants were asked how interested they were in using an application that would help them improve their HRB. On a scale from 1 to 10 where
1 meant *not interested at all* and 10 meant *very interested*, the average response
was 5.8 and the median response 7.0 (26% of participants). The participants were
asked to rank five types of applications according to how interested they were
in using them. The weighted average scores were: (1) an application that gives
feedback (3.44), (2) an application that visualizes the recycling system (3.20),
(3) an application that sends reminders (2.94), (4) an application that lets the
users communicate with recycling providers (2.82) and (5) a game (2.60).

A common request in the participants' open responses were reminders
(e.g. "it would be nice to have something to teach me and remind me"). One
participant referred to the habitual nature of HRB, saying that they would
like "reminders for everyday habits to stabilise regarding recycling". Not everyone, however, shared this view as one participant asked for "no stressful alerts
and notifications". Another request was a platform to communicate with the
recycling provider(s). Specifically, the participants wanted to use the platform
to let the recycling providers know about problems ("when there are parts of
the recycling system that don't work well"), communicate "improvement ideas"
and ask questions ("then I could ask the people in charge right away"). To avoid
everyone asking the same questions, a Frequently Asked Questions section was
proposed.

Design-wise, a "well detailed" and "simple" design and "clarity" were seen
as important. Specific requests included "lots of pictures", "small movies" and
something similar to "tutorial videos on YouTube". One participant asked for
movies with "interesting facts about recycling". At the same time, the application should "not be patronising" or give the users the impression of being judged
(e.g. "anything that doesn't make me feel bad and blamed"). Two participants
suggested the use of games/game elements but to shift the focus from the com-
petitive aspects to the explorational and cooperational ones ("In the case of
a game, I would rather it either challenged me to do it or that it invited me
to explore the area, instead of any kind of social competition" and "Maybe add
some gamification and play not as an individual but as a community?"). Another
two participants liked the idea of presenting information on a map (e.g. "I would
also want to see some recycling place for electronics/paint etc on a map").

3.5   Design and Evaluation of the Prototype

The design of the mobile phone application was intended to incorporate the requests by the survey participants but still give its users the autonomy to use it in the way that would suit them best. It was also intended to encourage a dialogue between the users and the recycling providers. Table 1 summarizes the structure and features of the application and the changes made in response to the user feedback.

Table 1. Prototype structure and development.

Function	Content	Development
Sign-up	Opportunity to create a user profile; selection of location and local recycling scheme(s)	Several icons were revised; a *login* button was added
Home screen	A digital representation of the local recycling scheme, including relevant waste containers; a search function for waste items, similar to the Sorteringsguide [17]	The design of the container representations was altered; a link to the map was added
Map	A map with waste container locations and optional directions; the collection times for each container and a possibility to set reminders for them; the option to indicate when a container is full and statistics on such indications by other users	Most substantial design change: two screens and a map pop-up were merged into a map screen with various features
Communication platform	Frequently Asked Questions (FAQ); a chat function to ask questions or make suggestions to the recycling provider(s); a noticeboard for the recycling provider(s) to make announcements	The *questions* and *suggestions* tabs were merged; a search bar and private messaging feature were added
Background information	Links to additional recycling-related material and statistics	A *how to reduce waste* link was added
Settings	A menu to adjust the language, reminders and account settings	A *logout* menu item was added

Overall, the participants of the evaluation sessions seemed pleased with the design of the application. One participant positively mentioned the bottom navigation bar as he could see all menu items at the same time. The participant also described the design as "simple" and "to the point". Three of the four participants suggested independently of each other that the application could be beneficial for people who recently changed their place of residency. In the interviews, the participants reflected critically on their own HRB and how the application could help them overcome their current problems. These problems included a lack of knowledge on how to recycle milk cartons and waste containers that were only labelled in Swedish. The four participants differed as to which function of the application they found most useful: two participants liked the search function for waste items, one the visualization of the recycling scheme and one the waste container collection times. Screenshots of the final design (excluding the sign-up process and settings) can be seen in Fig. 1.

Fig. 1. Sample screenshots of the digital prototype.

4   Discussion

The research confirms the relevance of targeting HRB among young adults, with Sweden as a case study. The results show that a large majority of the participants believe that they can improve one or several aspects of their HRB, despite them being potentially more interested in recycling than the average member of the target population. The participants, however, also pointed out several issues that limit their ability to correctly dispose of their waste, the most common one being overflowing waste containers. These issues can be addressed by persuasive technology but must eventually be solved by the recycling providers. Overall, the survey participants showed a substantial interest in using persuasive technology to improve their HRB. This opens up the possibility to use the technological format of the interventions to attract interest.

The participants of the evaluation sessions highlighted the potential benefits of the designed application for people who recently changed their place of residence. After relocating, people might be especially receptive to the provided information as they are trying to settle in and look for guidance.

Together, the findings from the online survey and iterative design work led to five recommendations for the design of persuasive technology that is intended to improve their users' HRB. They are outlined in the following section.

4.1   Recommendations for HRB Intervention Design

Recommendation 1: Easy Access to Information About Optimal HRB.
This recommendation was supported by the results of the online survey and design evaluations. It confirms previous findings in the literature, notably those by Miafodzyeva and Brandt [12] and by Varotto and Spagnolli [13]. The survey participants indicated that they care about recycling but lack the knowledge to always dispose of their household waste correctly. In the evaluation sessions, the participants emphasized the usefulness of the application's educational elements. The easy access to the information was highlighted as most of the information that the target users require is already available but not sought out.

Recommendation 2: Employment of Several Motivational Strategies.
The study results show that different target users are motivated by different features. There does not exist a 'one-size-fits-all'. In the survey responses, the ranked average of the proposed types of applications were close together. The answers to the open questions were also diverse and sometimes even contradicting each other. Similarly, the participants of the evaluation sessions considered different parts of the application helpful. This is in line with the result by Varotto and Spagnolli [13] that combined interventions are among the three most successful strategies to improve people's HRB. Comparing the findings in [13] and the survey outcomes more closely, a large overlap regarding the role of information, prompts/reminders, moral norms and environmental concern can be seen. What stands out is the role of feedback. Varotto and Spagnolli [13] found feedback to be the least successful strategy while the survey participants considered it to be one of the most motivating features. Another interesting finding was the survey participants' lack of enthusiasm for the use of games as a persuasive strategy. It got the lowest ranked average of the proposed applications and was mainly supported by the participants in a non-competitive form. This is in line with the findings in [8] that the users of the Trash Game focused more on the classification tasks than the game scenario.

Recommendation 3: Recognition of Recycling Scheme Differences.
Due to a division in responsibility, the recycling schemes for Swedish households differ depending on their geographic location. As HRB can only be sustainable if it is in accordance with the local recycling schemes, persuasive technology needs to cater for these differences.

Recommendation 4: Regard of Users as Equals. The use of persuasive technology comes with a variety of ethical challenges, so much care is required of those who design and develop it. While they might consider sustainability a good cause, it is crucial that the developed systems are unobtrusive and transparent. Users should be made aware of the aims behind the persuasion and shown the researchers' underlying reasoning. Supporting the relevance of existing discussions on ethics [22], several survey participants stated that they did not want to use persuasive technology that was patronizing or would made them feel judged. As can be seen from the BinCam/BinLeague application [6], pressure can be an enticing tool to improve HRB. It should, however, be seen critically, not only because users who associate negative emotions with a persuasive system are unlikely to continue its use.

Recommendation 5: Use of a Readily Accessible Technology Channel. A readily accessible technology channel means that the technology channel should be accessible in the situations in which it is needed. By definition, HRB comprises several activities which do not necessarily take place in the same location. So if people want to consult an application as decision support, it should ideally be accessible in all of the relevant locations. A simple way to achieve this is by focusing on portable devices like mobile phones. The need for a readily accessible technology channel was supported by the survey outcomes: the participants asked for situational decision support, particularly when they had to decide what to do with a specific waste item.

5 Conclusion

For both economic and environmental reasons, countries around the globe aim to increase the recycling rates for household waste. Using Sweden as its research context, this study has established five recommendations for the design of persuasive technology which aims to promote sustainable HRB behavior without the need for waste container augmentation. It has also highlighted the importance of HRB as an area for future research. A key component of the study was the design of a mobile phone application. This design illustrates a way of implementing the established key elements in an artifact and can be used as a starting point for future HRB interventions.

Acknowledgments. I would like to thank Jon Back and Franck Tétard for their valuable advice, guidance and encouragement. I would also like to thank Bran Knowles, Mike Hazas, Oliver Bates, Kelly Widdicks and Matthew Marsden for their helpful and constructive feedback, and my participants for taking part in the study. The presentation of the described research was funded by the Leverhulme Centre for Material Social Futures Research (DS-2017-036).

References

1. Wilson, D.C., et al.: Global Waste Management Outlook. United Nations Environment Programme (2015)
2. Kaza, S., Yao, L.C., Bhada-Tata, P., Van Woerden, F.: What a Waste 2.0: A Global Snapshot of Solid Waste Management to 2050. World Bank (2018)
3. The European Parliament and of the Council of the European Union: Directive 2008/98/EC. Official Journal of the European Union, vol. 312, pp. 3–30 (2008)
4. Halvorsen, B.: Effects of norms and policy incentives on household recycling: an international comparison. Resour. Conserv. Recycl. **67**, 18–26 (2012)
5. Brynjarsdóttir, H., Håkansson, M., Pierce, J., Baumer, E., DiSalvo, C., Sengers, P.: Sustainably unpersuaded: how persuasion narrows our vision of sustainability. In: Proceedings of the SIGCHI Conference on Human Factors in Computing Systems, pp. 947–956. ACM (2012)
6. Thieme, A., et al.: "We've bin watching you" - designing for reflection and social persuasion to promote sustainable lifestyles. In: Proceedings of the SIGCHI Conference on Human Factors in Computing Systems, pp. 2337–2346 (2012)
7. Gartland, A.A., Piasek, P.: Weigh your waste: a sustainable way to reduce waste. In: CHI 2009 Extended Abstracts on Human Factors in Computing Systems, pp. 2853–2858. ACM (2009)
8. Lessel, P., Altmeyer, M., Krüger, A.: Analysis of recycling capabilities of individuals and crowds to encourage and educate people to separate their garbage playfully. In: Proceedings of the 33rd Annual ACM Conference on Human Factors in Computing Systems, pp. 1095–1104. ACM (2015)
9. Verplanken, B.: Beyond frequency: habit as mental construct. Br. J. Soc. Psychol. **45**(3), 639–656 (2006)
10. Prochaska, J.O., DiClemente, C.C., Norcross, J.C.: In search of how people change: applications to addictive behaviors. Addict. Nurs. Netw. **5**(1), 2–16 (1993)
11. Ojala, M.: Recycling and ambivalence: quantitative and qualitative analyses of household recycling among young adults. Environ. Behav. **40**(6), 777–797 (2008)
12. Miafodzyeva, S., Brandt, N.: Recycling behaviour among householders: synthesizing determinants via a meta-analysis. Waste Biomass Valoriz. **4**(2), 221–235 (2013). https://doi.org/10.1007/s12649-012-9144-4
13. Varotto, A., Spagnolli, A.: Psychological strategies to promote household recycling. A systematic review with meta-analysis of validated field interventions. J. Environ. Psychol. **51**, 168–188 (2017)
14. Andersson, C., Stage, J.: Direct and indirect effects of waste management policies on household waste behaviour: the case of Sweden. Waste Manage. **76**, 19–27 (2018)
15. Avfall Sverige: Swedish Waste Management 2018 (Report) (2018)
16. European Commission: Review of Waste Policy and Legislation. https://ec.europa.eu/environment/waste/target_review.htm. Accessed 05 Feb 2020
17. Uppsala Vatten: Sorteringsguide. https://www.uppsalavatten.se/sorteringsguide. Accessed 05 Feb 2020
18. Froehlich, J., Findlater, L., Landay, J.: The design of eco-feedback technology. In: Proceedings of the SIGCHI Conference on Human Factors in Computing Systems, pp. 1999–2008. ACM (2010)
19. Fogg, B.J.: Creating persuasive technologies: an eight-step design process. In: Proceedings of the 4th International Conference on Persuasive Technology. ACM (2009)

20. Braun, V., Clarke, V.: Thematic analysis. In: APA Handbook of Research Methods in Psychology: Vol. 2, Research Designs, pp. 57–71. American Psychological Association, Washington, DC (2012)
21. Preece, J., Rogers, Y., Sharp, H.: Interaction Design: Beyond Human-Computer Interaction, 4th edn. Wiley, Hoboken (2015)
22. Karppinen, P., Oinas-Kukkonen, H.: Three approaches to ethical considerations in the design of behavior change support systems. In: Berkovsky, S., Freyne, J. (eds.) PERSUASIVE 2013. LNCS, vol. 7822, pp. 87–98. Springer, Heidelberg (2013). https://doi.org/10.1007/978-3-642-37157-8_12

Persuasive Virtual Reality: Promoting Earth Buildings in New Zealand

Don Amila Sajeevan Samarasinghe[1(✉)], Nilufar Baghaei[1,2], and Lehan Stemmet[1]

[1] Otago Polytechnic Auckland International Campus, Auckland, New Zealand
dons@op.ac.nz
[2] School of Natural and Computational Sciences, Massey University, Auckland, New Zealand

Abstract. Earth built environments are popular around the world due to their health benefits, indoor environment quality, passive solar gains, aesthetics, thermal efficiency, weathertightness, low cost of building materials and high functionality. However, residential earth buildings are unpopular in New Zealand (NZ), despite their numerous benefits. Previous literature has shown that the lack of awareness of earth buildings and their benefits is one of the main barriers to earth construction. Persuasive technology is defined as the technology that is designed to change attitudes or behaviour of the users through persuasion. Previous studies looked at the applications of persuasive technology in enhancing student engagement and motivation in educational settings. The primary purpose of this paper is to apply Virtual Reality (VR) as a persuasive technology tool to promote residential earth buildings in NZ. The study initially explored the reasons why earth buildings are unpopular in NZ using Subject Matter Experts (SME) views combined with a review of past literature. We then designed and implemented a VR model of a sustainable earth building including earth walls, rainwater harvesting tank, dry toilet, solar panels, and green wall as a sustainable building model. The VR model incorporated the key design principles of persuasive technology proposed in the literature. This model was then showcased at Auckland Build Expo 2018 (ABE2018), for the public to view. The viewers who engaged with our VR model were educated on the benefits of living in earth buildings. We believe that this exploratory research will eventually contribute to making advancements in finding new ways to effectively promote earth buildings for living in NZ.

Keywords: Earth buildings · Persuasive technology · Virtual Reality · Sustainable buildings · Behaviour change

1 Introduction

Persuasive technology is defined as technology that is designed to change attitudes or behaviour of the users through persuasion and social influence [1]. Such technologies are used in sales & marketing, education, politics, military training, public health, lifestyle changes, management, and may potentially be used in any area of human-human or human-computer interaction. Most self-identified persuasive technology research focuses on interactive, computational technologies, including desktop computers, internet services, video games, and mobile devices [2]. Persuasive design principles have

© Springer Nature Switzerland AG 2020
S. B. Gram-Hansen et al. (Eds.): PERSUASIVE 2020, LNCS 12064, pp. 208–220, 2020.
https://doi.org/10.1007/978-3-030-45712-9_16

been classified into four main categories, namely, Primary Task Support, Dialogue Support, System Credibility Support and Social Support [2]. Each category has its own design principles. Previous studies looked at the applications of persuasive technology in enhancing student engagement and motivation in educational settings [3–5].

Virtual reality is a simulated experience that can be similar to or completely different from the real world [6]. VR in Persuasive Technology is an emerging and highly innovative field, as it has been used as a persuasive technology to change people's attitudes and behaviours [7]. For example, Chittaro and Zangrando [8] found that immersive VR can be an effective tool for changing attitudes concerning personal safety topics. VR is becoming more prevalent with the advent of affordable consumer head-mounted devices and has significant potential for influencing users' attitude and behaviour. In this exploratory study, we designed, implemented and preliminarily evaluated the effectiveness of VR models in promoting sustainable buildings (earth buildings with other sustainable features) in public. Firstly, we conducted a comprehensive literature review followed by SME interviews to understand why earth buildings should be promoted in NZ. Secondly, we created a VR model as a method of promoting and engaging earth buildings with the public. This VR model was exhibited at ABE2018 as the first step towards a comprehensive study of promoting earth-based sustainable construction in NZ.

2 Earth Buildings in NZ

Earth building is an 11000-year-old practice of architecture using unfired earth material [9]. It is well known that some of the oldest wonders such as ziggurats, aqueducts, monasteries, temples and the Great Wall of China were also made of earth [10]. In this widespread worldwide practice, earth is used to construct building components such as walls, floors and even roofs. Widely used earth building methods include structural walls made of earth (for example, mud bricks/adobe, pressed earth bricks, rammed earth and cob), timber structural infill made of earth (rammed earth, brick, cob), internal earth brick veneers, earth plasters and earth floors [9].

The NZ earth architecture has a history dating back to the mid-19th century. For example, the Pompallier House in Russell built in 1842, the Broadgreen Building in Nelson built in 1856 and Subritzky house (mud and stud-type construction) erected in about 1860–1862 [11, 12] are good examples of early earth buildings in NZ. The Indigenous Maori people have used earth to build their homes since long ago. For example, earth has been used to gather refined fortifications and for the floors of houses [13]. Europeans began building earth structures in the 19th century [14]. The British introduced a fence and adobe block structure to NZ and adjusted the regional soil and plant materials to suit the new environment [10]. Although this material was known to exist in NZ as early as 1902, there are no known records of use so far, which has many similarities with the situation in the United States [13]. In 1948, the Nelson area began a renaissance of earth buildings, which started with the earth building 30 km west of Nelson [15]. In 1971, benchmarking the history of earth buildings in NZ, Graeme North, an architect, built a rammed earth house near Whangarei. Through this project, he became an expert in earth building and straw bale architecture [15]. Graeme North is one of the founding members of the Earth Building Association of New Zealand (EBANZ).

In the 1990s, the use of the straw bale building technique was established, and since 1993 straw has been used in earth buildings. Another squashed earth house was built at Riverside community in 1975 and various houses utilising squeezed squares were built in Northland, Canterbury, and Marlborough during the 1970s and 1980s [16]. In the 1990s, NZ ushered in the golden period of earth buildings, during which a large number of earth buildings were built.

Currently, the highest number of earth buildings in NZ is found in Nelson. It has retained a considerable number of earthwork houses since 1945. A total of 144 earth buildings have been preserved so far, and Nelson's earth architecture laid the foundation for the historical background of NZ from 1945 to 2010. The preservation of these earth buildings shows that the earth building is suitable for construction in NZ. However, because of the rapid progress of science and technology and the development of colonial industry and infrastructure, society in NZ has primarily organised around the idea of progression [17]. Therefore, historical earth construction is no longer as popular with New Zealanders.

However, there are a few organisations who actively contribute to earth built environments in NZ. EBANZ is the leading organisation which promotes the art and science of earth and natural building [9]. Earthsong Eco Neighbourhood aims to design and construct a cohesive neighbourhood whose layout, buildings and services demonstrate the highest practical standards of sustainable human settlement [18]. Among the earth builders, Terra Firma Earth Building Company finds a sustainable, traditional way to build houses that will not damage the earth [19]. Bio Build specialises in healthy building for both people and the environment [20]. Solid Earth Adobe Buildings provide consultation and education on natural building techniques [21]. In order to research the current earth buildings in NZ, the primary researcher participated in the annual conference of EBANZ in Cromwell, NZ. Over three days, many earth buildings were observed (Fig. 1). Meaningful conversations happened with EBANZ members about the future of earth buildings.

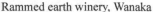
Rammed earth winery, Wanaka   Straw bale house, Luggate

Fig. 1. Examples of living earth buildings in NZ.

Earth buildings are characterised by the natural and excellent physical properties of the soil. The natural attributes include the ability to work as an insulator and the ability to conserve heat from within, sound and humidity adjustment and radiation protection

[22]. Earth buildings are environmentally friendly, and even after using the structure, the demolition does not have such a significant impact on the environment, because not all soil resources are modified and come from the environment [23]. Compared with concrete houses, earth building materials can reduce energy use by 85% during transportation. Studies have shown that using soil can reduce energy use by 62%, while during reinforced concrete frame structures construction energy can only be reduced by 45% [24]. Despite the numerous benefits of earth buildings, they have not been adequately utilised in the past due to lack of understanding of how they function in terms of health and safety and sustainability of the earth. This may have resulted in relatively few earth buildings at present. We believe that earth buildings can be effectively promoted by changing people's mind-set based on their perceptions of the numerous benefits of earth buildings.

3 Mitigating Errors in Behaviour Change Interventions

Changing mind-set and behaviour has received a lot of attention in the fields of health-care and marketing. Several important principles could be adapted within the context of applying VR in developing new mind-sets for using more sustainable building technologies. VR also offers a reasonable cost-effective method considering, for example, the cost of physically visiting some exemplars of sustainable building, media production costs to, for example, televise these types of initiatives.

In regards to the building industry, we can expect the challenge of behaviour change to be somewhat magnified given that the personal element is extended to an outward object that does not directly affect one's health in the short or long term in obvious ways. We also need to consider the reward mechanisms for changing behaviour and whether these rewards might be obvious in the short and longer-term.

It is useful to keep in mind the six major errors made by those who attempt to change behaviour. These six common errors largely ignore scientific evidence from psychology and sociology. It also helps us to develop new approaches incorporating behavioural science. The six common errors identified by Kelly and Barker [25] are listed below and also includes a summary description:

1. It is just common sense: In this context, common sense refers to the assumption that human behaviour is obvious and requires little or no thought, thereby ignoring the scientific evidence for positive behaviour change.
2. It is about getting the message across: This error assumes that getting the message out to people in some form will lead to behaviour change, specifically in instances in which messaging is the primary mechanisms used to impact on behaviour change.
3. Knowledge and information drive behaviour: Similar to the previous error, this assumes that people lack knowledge and information that can only be obtained from an expert source to help fill the gap in their own knowledge.
4. People act rationally: We often assume that people will do what is best once they have obtained the knowledge and information. In other words, they act sensibly upon rational appraisal of the evidence they have been given.

5. People act irrationally: We also often assume that people act all the time irrationally if they do not appear to change behaviour rationally based on the evidence provided to them.
6. It is possible to predict accurately: It is possible to predict behavioural outcomes to some extent, but we are not yet able to predict behavioural outcomes accurately or with any level of definitive certainty.

Unilever [26] have developed the Five Levers of Change as part of their sustainable living plan. These have been researched extensively and have formed a basis for changing the organisation from within, but also as part of their marketing strategy. According to the Unilever [26] behaviour change and sustainability plan, "successful change comes from a real understanding of people, their habits and their motivations." This is very much in line with the more individualised approaches also evident from the Kelly and Barker [25] article exploring alternative modes for effecting behaviour change. According to Unilever [26], fundamental changes in attitudes and behaviour are mandatory to create a sustainable future. A common challenge in behaviour change models is what might be referred to as a 'relapse' in medical and psychological terminology. This habit helps to reinforce and remind people that the change they are making is a positive change.

Drawing from the principles listed above, we can develop VR prototypes to test and improve in order to generate effective technology that could stimulate behaviour change cost-effectively and in a safe way. Safe both physically and economically as it requires limited access to actual construction sites for individuals and economically minimises the risk associated with potentially new building methods and materials people may not be familiar with. It also provides users with an immersive experience by stimulating more of their senses. These are discussed in the sections below.

4 The Project Process

This exploratory study aims to establish the fact that VR models could be used as a persuasive technology tool to encourage people to adopt sustainable living styles, such as residing in earth buildings. The project process comprises of four key phases. In the first phase, a comprehensive literature review was conducted to understand the popularity of earth buildings in NZ. Afterwards, SME interviews were conducted (see Table 1 for the profiles of the 7 research participants) to identify why earth buildings should be promoted in NZ. The third phase focused on designing and implementing a VR model of an earth building with other sustainable features. In the fourth phase, the VR model was exhibited at ABE2018 for the public's feedback.

Table 1. Research participants' profile.

Participant's profile	
P1	Has a Civil Engineering background. Researcher and Lecturer in earth architecture and timber structures at the University of Auckland

(continued)

Table 1. (*continued*)

Participant's profile	
P2	An earth building artisan who has 28 years' experience in earth construction. A member of EBANZ (www.earthbuilding.org.nz) and Solid Earth Adobe Buildings (www.solidearth.co.nz)
P3	Has a University degree in architecture. Coordinates the development and construction phases of Earthsong Eco Neighbourhood (www.earthsong.org.nz), including making sustainable visions and team decision making
P4	Has lived in earth architecture for 17 years. A member of Earthsong Eco Neighbourhood
P5	A lecturer (natural building specialised) from the Unitec Institute of Technology NZ. Institute of Architect (NZIA) award-winning registered architect with 30 years of experience in designing various buildings
P6	A builder from the Bio Build (www.biobuild.co.nz)
P7	A passionate architect who built a rammed earth house with fascinating architectural features in Auckland

In SME interviews, we asked the participants (P1–P7)' views on the unpopularity of earth construction and the reasons why we need to promote them. Table 2 presents a sample (P1–P4) of the responses received from SMEs.

Table 2. SME interview findings.

	Why are earth buildings not popular in NZ?	Why does the Earth Building need to be promoted?
P1	NZ Earth building is not popular because there is no good technical support	NZ doesn't have a lot of bad weather, so the earth building is very suitable for this country. Because the earth's building is very cool indoors during the day and warm at night
P2	In NZ, the market for earth building is smaller than that for traditional timber architecture. Although most people know the existence of earth building, they do not know enough about earth buildings	I often promote earth building around NZ. Because I think earth building is one of the most environmentally friendly buildings, all building materials are easy to obtain and are low-carbon materials. All the materials are non-toxic and recyclable
P3	Mainly because the wood structure is the mainstream building material in NZ, wood structure construction time is faster than earth buildings. In addition, NZ lacks the technical personnel for the construction of earth buildings	Courses related to Earth building are offered in universities to let more young people understand earth buildings
P4	Earth buildings take longer to build than timber structures, rising labour costs	Earth building is one of the most environmentally friendly buildings, without the addition of chemicals, all materials are natural materials

The study has collected substantial qualitative information on the reasons why earth buildings should be promoted for living in NZ. Earth buildings are non-toxic natural buildings which use materials that come from the earth [22]. Therefore, it helps to minimise environmental pollution caused by mining and burning coal to manufacture other materials such as concrete and steel. Ultimately, earth built environments would help to form a more synergistic and harmonious ecological effect. Earth buildings have the characteristics of energy-saving and carbon emission reduction [23]. Earth can be locally acquired, and a large amount of transportation cost and energy consumption processing costs can also be reduced. Having more earth structures could contribute towards reducing the negative effects of climate change and global warming. Soil can be safely reused after the building life span has expired. Earth is one of the well-known sustainable building materials. Earth buildings are characterised by good heat-insulating, good thermal stability and excellent heat storage capacity. They also have high fire resistivity and noise proofing qualities.

However, the total number of earth buildings in NZ is less than 1% of all entire buildings. Most of earth homeowners live privately in rural or semi-rural areas. The study found that many people share the same view that NZ earth architecture is unpopular primarily due to a lack of awareness [13]. In addition, another reason why earth architecture is not popular is because of a lack of technical capacity in NZ [27]. Large construction companies believe that the market for NZ earth architecture is too small to be profitable. In addition, the construction time of earth architecture is comparatively longer than that of traditional timber buildings. A majority of New Zealanders think earth construction takes significant time as opposed to conventional timber construction [13]. Therefore, we believe that there is a need and responsibility to actively work on increasing the awareness of constructing and living in earth built environments [28]. Previous literature has shown that tourists who have visited earth buildings would want to live in earth houses. In addition, people who have visited earth buildings generally appreciate them and actively recommend earth structures to their friends [13]. Therefore, promoting earth buildings would help increase people's understanding of earth architecture in the built environment. This would eventually promote earth buildings in NZ. The responses received from SME interviews further strengthened the significance of earth buildings. The responses revealed a need to change people's negative perceptions of living in Earth Buildings.

5 Design and Implementation of the VR Model

In order to address this, we design a project called Virtual Reality of Sustainable Living Styles. It was a collaboration between selected students from the Bachelor of Construction and the Graduate Diploma in Information Technology (IT) at Otago Polytechnic Auckland International Campus. The team's key objective was to create a virtual model of an earth house to showcase at the ABE2018. The virtual earth house included walls made of Rammed Earth, Cob, Mud Bricks, Straw Bale and compressed earth blocks. In addition, it consisted of dry toilets, rainwater harvesting tanks and solar panels to feature a sustainable building.

To design the VR model, we took three design principles, i.e. Physiological Comfort, Environmental Comfort & Ergonomics, proposed by Alger [29], Hudelson [30] and LaValle [31] into account. The VR model development process included gathering project requirements from the construction team, planning the model development process, model designing (with Auto CAD and 3D Max software), development of the VR model (using Google VR Architecture, Visual Studio IDE, C# language, JavaScript, CSS scripting language and.net framework) and model testing and verification [32].

We employed agile methods to develop the virtual earth building. The agile Software Development Life Cycle (SDLC) model is a combination of iterative and incremental process models with a focus on process adaptability and customer satisfaction by rapid delivery of working software product [33].

The first iteration of Proof of Concept (POC) was executed by providing a demo VR model to the construction team (a lecturer and selected students from the construction department) with minimum functionality. The POC was approved by the construction team, and then the concept was continued. The second iteration was the first phase of the actual development. In the second iteration, the interior parts of the earth building were focused. Hotspots were then introduced to pass the views which the viewer needs to open. In the third iteration, the exterior of the earth building was focused. In the exterior, solar panels, green roof, garden, fencing, gate and a rainwater harvesting tank were added. Figure 2 shows some screenshots of the exterior and interior of the virtual earth building. After the successful development of the VR model, the project was deployed (azure server was used) to the server. We also created five posters displaying earth wall construction techniques to assist our VR project showcase at ABE2018 [32].

Living room

Rear view with rainwater harvesting tanks

Bathroom and dry toilet

Kitchen

Fig. 2. The VR model.

After we exhibited the VR project at ABE2018, construction students were asked about their overall experience of being participants in this project. Firstly, students were asked about learning sustainable building features from VR models as opposed to learning from real construction projects. Even though most students commented that they like to learn from real projects on-site, other students suggested that learning through VR models would provide convenience and accessibility to sustainable building features. They expressed that good quality VR programmes would help to save cost and time of organising real construction site visits. Some students pointed out that VR models would enable seeing the detailed aspects and intuition of the sustainable features before they are installed on buildings.

Fig. 3. The VR project exhibition at ABE2018.

The feedback received from ABE 2018 revealed that VR of earth buildings would enable seeing the detailed aspects and intuition of the sustainable features before they are installed on buildings. The people who experienced our VR model said that since there are a few (<1% of total buildings) real earth buildings available in NZ, learning about earth buildings features through VR models would give more learning possibilities. Overall, the viewers said that they certainly enjoyed this experience. It was found that viewers liked the details displayed in the model, as they are hard to see from a single real building. A majority of the viewers expressed that the VR model was a realistic experience. One said:

"It looked real to me, and I felt like I was walking inside the rooms. I like the textured on the earth building walls, and it gives the real vibes exactly what we need".

We found that overall, this was a positive experience. We believe that this exploratory study can be further extended to a comprehensive project aiming to promote earth buildings through VR models.

6 Persuasive VR for Promoting Earth Buildings

We argue that our VR model is a persuasive tool. The virtual sustainable building we designed was based on the systematic framework proposed by Kukkonen and Harjumaa [2]. It addresses the below four categories of design principles (Table 3).

Table 3. Four categories of design principles.

Category 1 Primary task support	**Reduction:** System should reduce the effort that users spend in regard to performing their target behaviour. Our model shows examples of sustainable building features **Tunnelling:** System should guide users in the attitude change process by providing means for action that brings them closer to the target behaviour. Our model displays information about sustainable building features **Simulation:** Systems should provide simulations for persuasion. Our model will incorporate both sustainable and unsustainable building features to allow users to make a comparison **Rehearsal:** System should provide means for rehearsing a target behaviour. Our model allows for the navigation of a sustainable building
Category 2 Dialogue support	**Similarity:** System should imitate its users in some specific way. Our model imitates a typical house, but with sustainable features **Liking:** A system that is visually attractive for its users is likely to be more per-suasive. Our VR model has a look and feels that appeals to its users
Category 3 System credibility support	**Trustworthiness:** A system that is viewed as trustworthy (truthful, fair, and unbiased) will have increased powers of persuasion. Our model provides information that is informative, truthful and unbiased **Expertise:** A system that is viewed as incorporating expertise (knowledge, experience, and competence) will have increased powers of persuasion. Our VR model provides information indicating expertise **Surface credibility:** People make initial assessments of the system credibility based on a first-hand inspection. Our VR model has a competent look and feel **Verifiability:** Credibility perceptions will be enhanced if a system makes it easy to verify the accuracy of site content via outside sources. Our VR model provides the means of verifying the accuracy of the content
Category 4 Social support	**Cooperation:** A system can motivate users to adopt a target attitude or behaviour by leveraging human beings' natural drive to co-operate. Our VR model currently provides means for offline cooperation. The next version will include collaboration as part of navigating the building by presenting avatars **Competition & Recognition:** A system can motivate users to adopt a target attitude or behaviour by leveraging human beings' natural drive to compete and offer them public recognition. Our VR model will include quizzes about sustainable building features and will provide public attention for the users who do well on the quizzes

7   Recommendations and Conclusions

Due to the deterioration of the environment and global warming, human beings have begun to realise that it is crucial to protect the environment and the earth. In order not to damage the earth more seriously, human beings are starting to achieve a low-carbon economy, and the construction of low-carbon buildings has become a global consensus. Therefore, earth architecture has become one of the most mainstream sustainable buildings at present. In NZ, having an earth built environment has many advantages. Earth is a non-toxic natural material. It has a good heat retention capacity which suits the cold climate in NZ. Earth is readily available. Therefore, earth built environments help to minimise high Carbon emission due to small transportation. Since earth walls are thick and heavy, they have high noise and fireproofing performance. These characteristics are the reason why earth architecture should be rigorously promoted. It is crucial to increase the awareness of the enormous benefits of earth buildings and structures. We believe our research paves the way for systematic design and development of fully-fledged persuasive VR models dedicated to promoting such sustainable buildings. Through the application of VR, we intend to start addressing the challenges associated with behaviour change. VR offers a cost-effective method for people to be more fully immersed in earth built environments in order to expose them to sustainable technology. It could also potentially deal with issues around relapse into old habits by having multiple immersive earth built site visits until habits and attitudes change. In the near future, we hope to test our virtual sustainable building with people who work in the construction sector. Therefore, the next step is to progressively work towards developing a platform also to change the behaviour of the public who might purchase sustainable houses that incorporate earth walls and other energy-saving building features.

References

1. Fogg, B.J.: Persuasive Technology: Using Computers to Change What We Think and Do. Morgan Kaufmann Publishers, San Francisco (2003)
2. Oinas-Kukkonen, H., Harjumaa, M.: A systematic framework for designing and evaluating persuasive systems. In: Oinas-Kukkonen, H., Hasle, P., Harjumaa, M., Segerståhl, K., Øhrstrøm, P. (eds.) PERSUASIVE 2008. LNCS, vol. 5033, pp. 164–176. Springer, Heidelberg (2008). https://doi.org/10.1007/978-3-540-68504-3_15
3. Mintz, J., Aagaard, M.: The application of persuasive technology to educational settings. Educ. Tech. Res. Dev. **60**(3), 483–499 (2012)
4. Reddy, L., Baghaei, N.: Improving teacher behaviour in implementation of positive behaviour for learning (PB4L) pedagogy: persuasion via gamification. In: 13th International Conference on Persuasive Technology, Waterloo, Canada (2018). International Conference on Computers in Education (ICCE 2017)
5. Reddy, L., et al.: Designing mobile applications for improving positive behaviour for learning (PB4L) pedagogy. In: 25th International Conference on Computers in Education, Christchurch, New Zealand. Asia-Pacific Society for Computers in Education, New Zealand (2017). International Conference on Computers in Education (ICCE 2017)
6. Mihelj, M., Novak, D., Beguš, S.: Virtual reality technology and applications. Intelligent Systems, Control and Automation: Science and Engineering. Springer, Dordrecht (2013). https://doi.org/10.1007/978-94-007-6910-6. S.G. Tzafestas Editor

7. Tussyadiah, I.P., et al.: Virtual reality, presence, and attitude change: empirical evidence from tourism. Tour. Manag. **66**, 140–154 (2018)
8. Chittaro, L., Zangrando, N.: The persuasive power of virtual reality: effects of simulated human distress on attitudes towards fire safety. In: Ploug, T., Hasle, P., Oinas-Kukkonen, H. (eds.) PERSUASIVE 2010. LNCS, vol. 6137, pp. 58–69. Springer, Heidelberg (2010). https://doi.org/10.1007/978-3-642-13226-1_8
9. EBANZ. Natural building techniques (2019). http://www.earthbuilding.org.nz
10. Allen, M.: Out of the Ground: Earthbuilding in New Zealand. The Dunmore Press Ltd, Palmerston North (1997)
11. Burgess, L.: Historic Houses: A Visitor's Guide to 65 Early New Zealand Homes. Random House New Zealand, Auckland (2007). ed. R. Burgess
12. Salmond, J.: Old New Zealand Houses 1800–1940. Reed Methuen Publishers Ltd, Auckland (1986)
13. Jackson, E., Tenorio, R.: Accessibility of earth building in New Zealand. In: Sustainable Building Conference SB10: Innovation and Transformation. The University of Western Australia, Wellington (2010)
14. Williams, J., et al.: Development of the New Zealand earth system model: NZESM. Weather Clim. **36**, 25–44 (2016)
15. Hall, M.: Less and more in Aotearoa New Zealand: more houses and less CO_2 emissions. In: 51st International Conference of the Architectural Science Association (ANZAScA), Wellington, New Zealand. The Architectural Science Association (ANZAScA), Australia (2017)
16. Hall, M.: Earth and straw bale: an investigation of their performance and potential as building materials in New Zealand. In: School of Architecture - Te Kura Waihanga. Victoria University of Wellington, Wellington (2012)
17. Moyle, J.: Earth building history. Earth Building Association New Zealand (2019)
18. Earthsong. Earthsong Eco Neighbourhood (2019). https://www.earthsong.org.nz
19. Geraets, P.: Terra Firma Earth Building Company (2019). https://www.earthhomes.co.nz
20. Drayton, A.: BioBuild (2018)
21. Maeder, V., Davidson, S.: Solid Earth Adobe Buildings (2019). https://www.solidearth.co.nz
22. Bridge, M., North, G.: Passion for Earth: Earth Houses in New Zealand. David Ling Publishing Limited, Auckland (2000). ed. J. O'Brien
23. Ciancio, D., Beckett, C.: Rammed Earth Construction: Cutting-Edge Research on Traditional and Modern Rammed Earth. Taylor & Francis Group, London (2015). ed. D. Ciancio and C. Beckett
24. Ciancio, D., Beckett, C.: Rammed earth: an overview of a sustainable construction material. In: Third International Conference on Sustainable Construction Materials and Technologies, Kyoto, Japan (2013)
25. Kelly, M.P., Barker, M.: Why is changing health-related behaviour so difficult? Public Health **136**, 109–116 (2016)
26. Unilever: Unilever sustainable living plan. In: Inspiring Sustainable Living: Expert Insights into Consumer Behaviour and Unilever's Five Levers for Change. Unilever PLC, London (2011)
27. Langridge, R.M., et al.: The New Zealand active faults database. N. Z. J. Geol. Geophys. **59**(1), 86–96 (2016)
28. Jackson, E., Tenorio, R.: Accessibility of earth building in New Zealand. In: The New Zealand Sustainable Building Conference (SB07 and SB10). BRANZ, Wellington (2010)
29. Alger, M.: Visual design methods for virtual reality (2015). http://mikealger.com
30. Hudelson, B.: Designing for VR: A beginners guide (2017)
31. LaValle, S.M.: Virtual Reality. Cambridge University Press, Cambridge (2019)

220   D. A. S. Samarasinghe et al.

32. Samarasinghe, D.A.S., Latif, S.A., Baghaei, N.: Virtual reality models for promoting learners engagement in construction studies. In: IEEE Global Engineering Education Conference (EDUCON), Dubai, United Arab Emirates, United Arab Emirates. IEEE (2018)
33. Fowler, M.: Agile Software Guide (2019). https://martinfowler.com

On Security and Ethics in Persuasive Technology

PHISHER CRUSH: A Mobile Persuasive Game for Promoting Online Security

Chinenye Ndulue$^{(\boxtimes)}$ (ID), Oladapo Oyebode (ID), and Rita Orji (ID)

Faculty of Computer Science, Dalhousie University, Halifax, NS B3H 4R2, Canada
{cndulue,oladapo.oyebode,rita.orji}@dal.ca

Abstract. Phishing has become a major security threat in this Internet age. Dubious computer geeks and malicious hackers tend to make use of this mode of cyberattack due to the ability of phishes to deceive unsuspecting users without being prevented by various system security measures. The major reason why people fall for phishing attacks is that they are mostly unaware of how to detect them. This paper presents the design and implementation of a mobile persuasive game for promoting online security by teaching people how to detect and avoid phishing links. We also present the results and insights from the playability and persuasiveness evaluation of the game. The evaluators reported an overall high level of playability according to the Heuristic Evaluation for Playability (HEP). Above all, the results show that the game is highly persuasive, hence is expected to effectively motivate the desired behaviour of promoting online security. Based on our results, we provided some design consideration and insights from the evaluators' comments.

Keywords: Phishing · Persuasive games · Behaviour change · Heuristics for evaluating playability

1 Introduction

Internet security and cyberattacks have become very important technological issues in recent times. People have lost fortunes and even their lives due to a variety of cyberattacks. Phishing is one of the most popular media for malicious cyberattacks. It was reported to be "the number one infection vector employed by 71% of organized groups in 2017" [26]. *Cisco Systems* classifies it as an "increasingly common cyber threat" [5]. *Webroot* reported that "nearly 1.5 million new phishing sites are created each month" [10]. Furthermore, *PhishMe Inc.* reported that the average cost of phishing attacks for midsized companies is 1.6 million dollars [23]. Phishing mostly involves the use of spoof emails and dubious links to fool unsuspecting Internet users into divulging their personal information. This information is then used for a variety of criminal purposes like identity theft, financial theft, and other fraudulent purposes [28]. A variety of information can be collected by these criminals. They range from simple information like users' full names to critical information like users' bank account and credit card information. Unlike many other types of cyberattacks, phishing attacks do not focus on manipulating the victim's

© Springer Nature Switzerland AG 2020
S. B. Gram-Hansen et al. (Eds.): PERSUASIVE 2020, LNCS 12064, pp. 223–233, 2020.
https://doi.org/10.1007/978-3-030-45712-9_17

system resources. Instead, it focuses on manipulating humans, their behaviours, and their reactions to stimuli presented by the attacker through the victim's computer. These kinds of attacks are called semantic attacks. Developing effective system-centred interventions to curb this kind of security attack is almost impossible because so many human factors come into play when we discuss phishing threats. Some human factors that contribute to the ease of falling for phishing attacks include user fatigue, user's understanding level, relevance to users, human haste and errors [11, 12].

Although several attempts have been made towards developing automated tools to help curb this menace, an effective approach against phishing attacks is to ensure that internet users' behaviour towards internet activity and phishing is preventive rather than corrective. Persuasive gaming has become a very popular way of reinforcing or changing behaviours in diverse domains including Healthy Nutrition [13, 15, 21], Physical activity [3, 4, 7] and Disease Prevention [2, 18, 27]. The ability of Persuasive games to combine fun, excitement and persuasive strategies to engage users and promote the desired change in their behaviours makes it an attractive persuasive tool. Research has also shown that persuasive games can be effective tools for promoting behaviour change.

In this paper, we present the design and implementation of a mobile persuasive game called *'Phisher Crush'*, that teaches people how to identify and avoid phishing links and emails. *Phisher Crush* employed six persuasive strategies: *Simulation, Tunneling, Rewards, Praise, Feedback and Suggestion, and Liking* in its design to achieve the intended objective. We also present the results and insights from a playability and persuasiveness evaluation of the game. The results show that the game is highly persuasive, hence is expected to effectively motivate the desired behaviour of promoting online security. The evaluators reported a strong presence of the six persuasive strategies [20]. The results of the Playability Evaluation using the Heuristic Evaluation for Playability (HEP) [6] showed positive gameplay experience, adequate game mechanics, and a high level of usability. Based on our results, we provided some design consideration and insights from the evaluators' comments.

2 Literature Review

Gamified approach to educating people and creating awareness about phishing attacks has been employed by existing research, with only a few incorporating persuasive design principles to enhance knowledge acquisition and behaviour change. One of these few works is the *Phish Finder* mobile game designed by Misra et al. [17] to enhance users' confidence in dealing with phishing attacks. They adopted a theoretical model that combines conceptual knowledge and procedural knowledge to improve users' self-efficacy to mitigate phishing attacks. Arachchilage et al. [1] discussed a similar gamified app that aims to teach users the concept behind phishing attacks in addition to general knowledge about phishing.

Furthermore, Anti-Phishing Phil is an online game (developed by Sheng et al. [25]) that leveraged similar fish-worm concept used by Misra et al. and Arachchilage et al. to train users on how to identify fraudulent websites and find legitimate ones. The game's training content covers IP-based, subdomain-based and deceptive phishing URLs. However, they did not employ persuasive strategies in developing the game.

Rather than implementing a gamified anti-phishing concept, Kumaraguru et al. [14] delivered an embedded training system, called PhishGuru that delivers anti-phishing training messages during normal email use. In other words, users were sent a deliberate but malicious email message in the course of their normal activities, and instead of losing information when they ignorantly click on the phishing link(s) in that message, they receive preventive anti-phishing training content. PhishGuru, however, is not a persuasive system.

Finally, to evaluate game designs including mobile games, Desurvire et al. [6] developed the Heuristic Evaluation for Playability (HEP) which comprises of four game heuristic categories: *gameplay*, *game story*, *game mechanics* and *game usability*. The HEP authors argue that a heuristic approach to game evaluation can lead to highly usable and playable game designs. We employed the HEP to assess the playability our Phisher Crush game.

3 Phisher Crush Design Process

3.1 Early Design Phase

Before developing the persuasive game intervention, we had to fully understand the problem area and the behaviour that needs to be addressed to solve the problem [9]. One of the major causes of phishing attacks is clicking of phishing links and carelessly accessing emails from phishers. We researched the common forms that phishing links and emails appear as and also consulted with an online security expert. This enabled us to develop an adequate gaming objective for *Phisher Crush*. Some of these common forms include:

(a) Hyperlinks that begin with a number.
(b) Strange email addresses or hyperlinks from a popular domain.
(c) Badly spelt domain names of email addresses or hyperlinks.
(d) Meaningless emails addresses and hyperlinks.
(e) Email addresses with too many special characters.

We also had to decide on the gaming concept to use for the game. Prior research has shown that persuasive games are most likely to persuade if the gaming concept is engaging and if the controls for the game are easy and straightforward [1]. This is because if players focus all their cognitive power on trying to master the controls of the persuasive game, they may be less receptive to the persuasive strategies implemented in the game. We also wanted to pick a game that simulates the mental process that occurs when people encounter hyperlinks online. Therefore, we decided to use the concept of a matchup-memory game, which is a game genre that has one of the easiest controls.

We needed a list of real phishing links and emails for the game, therefore we downloaded a list of active phishing links from PhishFindR [22] for the malicious hyperlinks and we also downloaded a list of phishing email addresses from Samudrala's list of spammers' email addresses [24]. In total, we collected a list of 65,157 phishing links and 182 spamming emails addresses for the game's database. These hyperlinks and email addresses formed part of the basic elements of the game as discussed in the following section.

3.2 *Phisher Crush* Gameplay

Phisher Crush is modelled after the same engaging concept of traditional match-up memory games similar to MatchUp [16] and Remembery [8]. The primary task in this game is for the player to match pairs of correct hyperlinks or email addresses as fast as possible. When the game loads, a random array of malicious and unmalicious hyperlinks and email address are loaded. The links and email addresses are hidden under seeds represented by icons as shown in Fig. 1. Players are expected to click an icon to reveal the hyperlink or email address hidden under it. Whenever the player clicks a second icon, the player is prompted to confirm if the two exposed hyperlinks or emails addresses are a match or cancel if they are not. A match is correct if the two exposed hyperlinks or email addresses are both malicious or both unmalicious. A match is incorrect if one of the hyperlinks or email addresses is unmalicious and the other is malicious. Players are rewarded with points for matching two unmalicious hyperlinks or email addresses. They are also rewarded for matching two malicious hyperlinks or email addresses. The player loses points whenever he matches a malicious hyperlink or email address with an unmalicious hyperlink or email address respectively, and the selected icons are reset to allow the player to try another match. Each level of the game has a specific number of correct hyperlinks that a player is expected to match. There is no limit to the number of available levels in the game. The game has a countdown timer which begins at the start of each level. A player proceeds to the next level if he can complete all available matches before the specified time for the current level elapses. The higher the level, the lower the time allotted to complete the task. This serves as an incremental difficulty functionality as it urges players to make decisions fast. The game was implemented in the Unity Engine platform and was developed using C#. The game targets the Android mobile platform.

Fig. 1. Game seeds with hidden hyperlinks and email addresses attached to them in Phisher Crush

3.3 The Persuasiveness of *Phisher Crush*

From literature, we applied 6 popular persuasive strategies from persuasive technology research on our design [20] to make the game persuasive. They are:

Tunnelling. *"Using the system to guide users through a process or experience provides opportunities to persuade along the way"* [20]. We presented players with tutorials and tips on how to identify phishing hyperlinks and how to play the game before the actual gameplay (Fig. 2).

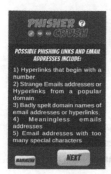

Fig. 2. Implementation of tunneling in Phisher Crush

Simulation. We simulated the cognitive process that occurs when people encounter links online. When people encounter hyperlinks or emails online, their brains try to match their mental models of phishing links or non-phishing links to the links they see, which helps them determine if they should click the hyperlink or not.

Rewards. *"Systems that reward target behaviours may have great persuasive powers"* [20]. Players are rewarded for correct matches with points. There are also badges for achieving different kinds of milestones. There is a badge for completing their first game, then there are also badges for every 500 points accumulated by the user. We believe this would engage and motivate the user to continue playing the game (Fig. 3).

Fig. 3. The reward badges in Phisher Crush

Praise. *"By offering praise, a system can make users more open to persuasion"* [20]. At different points during the gameplay, we praised the player for playing the game. After going through the tutorials, the player is praised for completion. After each game session, the player is also praised for playing when he wins (Fig. 4).

Fig. 4. Implementation of praises in Phisher Crush

Feedback and Suggestion. Before each gameplay, we provided *suggestions* on what phishing hyperlinks and email addresses look like. We also provided *feedback* on what links and email addresses are malicious or not at the end of each gameplay (Fig. 5).

Fig. 5. Implementation of suggestion in Phisher Crush

Liking. *"A system that is visually attractive for its users is likely to be more persuasive"* [20]. We tried to make the game as visually attractive as possible with the use of attractive colour combinations and animations.

4   Phisher Crush Heuristics and Persuasiveness Analysis

To ensure that the game was persuasive and user-friendly we ran a playability and persua-siveness evaluation of *Phisher Crush*. We recruited persuasive technology stakeholders to participate in the playability evaluation and persuasiveness evaluation of the game. They were invited to the Persuasive Computing Lab at Dalhousie University and were given a summarized description of a list of persuasive strategies. It consisted of a list of all the strategies that we actively implemented, combined with some other persuasive strategies that we did not implement. They were also given a summarized description of the list of heuristics under the HEP [6]. These lists were given to the evaluators before the game evaluation to study and familiarize themselves with them. After that, the evalu-ators played *Phisher Crush* for about 20 min and noted the occurrence of any persuasive strategy and also identified any of the HEP heuristics that was satisfied. After the gaming session, participants were asked to go through the summaries of the persuasive strategies and heuristics again to rate each item on a Likert scale of 1 to 5 (1 = Not Present and 5 = Strongly Present), while giving qualitative comments about any of their observations.

4.1 Selecting Evaluators

We recruited evaluators for Phisher Crush with the following criteria.

(a) They must have experience in either developing or evaluating mobile apps.
(b) They must be researchers in the field of Persuasive Technology.
(c) They must have experience of persuasive strategies, preferably the PSD Model.
(d) They must have experience in either developing or evaluating mobile games.

We recruited four (4) evaluators who matched these criteria. This is in line with Neilson's Heuristic evaluation standard which suggests that we use between 3 to 5 evaluators when running a heuristic evaluation [19].

4.2 Results of the Persuasiveness Evaluation

At the end of the evaluation, we analyzed the quantitative data collected to determine the persuasive strategies (PSs) the participants observed in Phisher Crush, as well as their disposition towards the game's functionalities. As shown in Fig. 6, out of the six PSs implemented in the game, the mean score (i.e., the "x" shape in the figure) of only five PSs were above the neutral mid-point of 3 for the 5-point Likert scale. In other words, participants were able to strongly identify five persuasive strategies in Phisher Crush, which are *tunnelling, simulation, praise, rewards and liking*. However, participants think *suggestion* is weakly implemented in the game. Table 1 summarizes the ranking of the PSs from the most observed to the least observed based on their mean values. *Praise*

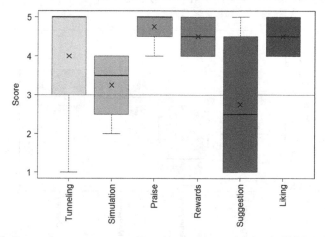

Fig. 6. Persuasiveness average rating observed by evaluators in Phisher Crush

Table 1. Ranking of persuasive principle in decreasing order of mean

Persuasive strategy	Mean (Standard deviation)
Praise	4.75 (0.50)
Rewards	4.50 (0.58)
Liking	4.50 (0.58)
Tunnelling	4.00 (2.00)
Simulation	3.25 (0.96)
Feedback and suggestion	2.75 (2.06)

ranked highest (mean = 4.75, sd = 0.50), closely followed by *rewards* (mean = 4.50, sd = 0.58) and *liking* (mean = 4.50, sd = 0.58). *Suggestion* has the lowest ranking (mean = 2.75, sd = 2.06).

An interesting point to note is that one of the persuasive strategies we intentionally implemented was not identified as a very strongly-obvious strategy. The *Feedback and Suggestion strategy* had a mean score of 2.75 which is below the midpoint of 3. This is because most of the evaluators felt that the absence of dynamic tips during gameplay would reduce the potency of the *strategy*.

4.3 Results of the HEP Playability Evaluation

Regarding the playability of *Phisher Crush*, the mean of all the four heuristic measures were above the neutral mid-point of 3, as shown in Fig. 7. Usability ranked highest (mean = 4.04, sd = 0.59) followed by mechanics (mean = 3.93, sd = 0.41) and gameplay (mean = 3.45, sd = 0.69). The game story has the least ranking (mean = 3.27, sd = 1.00) (Fig. 7 and Table 2).

Since all these measures of playability were well above the neutral rating, we can effectively say that *Phisher Crush* is optimally playable.

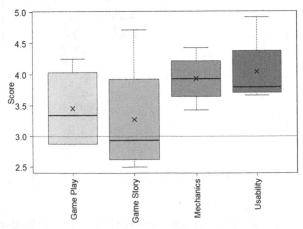

Fig. 7. Evaluators' disposition towards Phisher Crush's average rating observed by evaluators in Phisher Crush

Table 2. Ranking of game heuristics in decreasing order of mean

Game heuristics	Mean (Standard deviation)
Usability	4.04 (0.59)
Mechanics	3.93 (0.41)
Game play	3.45 (0.69)
Game story	3.27 (1.00)

4.4 Discussion: Design Considerations from Evaluators' Comments

We evaluated our persuasive game to assess its persuasiveness and playability. The results show that our game is persuasive enough and satisfies the game deign heuristics, hence it has the potential to motivate the intended behaviour of promoting online security on the users. Below, we discuss other insights from our evaluation in line with their implication for persuasive game design.

One of the evaluators made this comment, *"Simple game concepts make more sense for persuasive games"-P4*. This comment implies that it is better to make simple games for persuasion than highly complex games. Complex games require a lot of cognitive power to enjoy them. This places all the cognitive power of the player on the games itself with little to use for the processing of persuasion, on the other hand, simple games use less cognitive power. **Therefore, we recommend that persuasive game developers should make the game concepts simple and easy to understand.**

An evaluator also suggested that there should also be a form of praise when the player loses a level. In her words, *"When I lost, I encountered a scene that just outrightly told me that I lost. I felt bad and I believe users would feel bad too"-P2*. This implies that when implementing praise, persuasive technology developers should not only praise players for winning a challenge, they should also get some form of praise for attempting a challenge even if they lose. This would encourage the player to play more. **Therefore, we recommend that persuasive game designers employ praise irrespective of whether they are winning or losing**

Another evaluator pointed out the importance of a dynamic tutorial. In his words, *"I like the tutorial that occurs before the game, but it would be better if the tutorial happens as the first game is being played"-P1*. Humans tend to forget information if they are loaded with a huge quantity of it over a short span of time. Therefore, it would be better to have tips and instructions within the gameplay instead of having it before the gameplay. This would foster a progressive kind of learning instead of the cognitive overload that would occur if all information is given before gaming. **We recommend the use of dynamic real-time tips when developing persuasive games.**

An evaluator pointed out a need to appropriately inform players some seconds before ending the game after the time elapses. The game ends abruptly when the game time elapses and there is no warning for the player to realize when the time is almost up. This is an essential part of gaming. There is a need for *visual cues* for any significant action that is about to occur. He suggested a change in the colour of the timer text to signify the game is ending. Another evaluator suggested the use of sounds too. **We recommend** that persuasive game designers may employ the use of very significant visual or audio cues for important events that may impact the gameplay.

5 Conclusion and Future Work

In this paper, we presented the design of a persuasive game titled, *Phisher Crush*, to promote online security by teaching people how to identify phishing hyperlinks and email addresses. We also presented the results of a game heuristics and persuasiveness evaluation which shows that the game is highly persuasive hence is expected to be effective at achieving the desired behaviour of promoting online security. Based on our results, we provided some design consideration and insights based on the evaluators' comments.

The results of the Heuristic Evaluation for Playability (HEP) showed a high level of playability while the results of the Persuasiveness evaluation showed a strong presence of six persuasive strategies.

A limitation of our work is that evaluators played the game for only 20 min which may be a short time for an in-depth result. Also, hyperlinks and emails are not the only ways phishing attack, however, they are the common ones and accounts for a greater percentage of phishing attacks, hence our focus on them.

Future work will focus on evaluating the effectiveness of the game with respect to promoting actual online security awareness on a larger population and diverse audience. We also plan to extend the game eventually to account for other online security issues.

References

1. Brinol, P., et al.: Ease and persuasion: multiple processes, meanings, and effects (2013)
2. Brown, S.J., et al.: Educational video game for juvenile diabetes: results of a controlled trial. Med. Inform. (1997). https://doi.org/10.3109/14639239709089835
3. Chen, Y.-X., et al.: Opportunities for persuasive technology to motivate heavy computer users for stretching exercise. In: Spagnolli, A., Chittaro, L., Gamberini, L. (eds.) PERSUASIVE 2014. LNCS (LNAI), vol. 8462, pp. 25–30. Springer, Cham (2014). https://doi.org/10.1007/978-3-319-07127-5_3
4. Chittaro, L., Sioni, R.: Turning the classic snake mobile game into a location–based exergame that encourages walking. In: Bang, M., Ragnemalm, E.L. (eds.) PERSUASIVE 2012. LNCS, vol. 7284, pp. 43–54. Springer, Heidelberg (2012). https://doi.org/10.1007/978-3-642-31037-9_4
5. CISCO: Cyber Attack - What Are Common Cyberthreats? – Cisco. https://www.cisco.com/c/en/us/products/security/common-cyberattacks.html#~types-of-cyber-attacks. Accessed 31 Oct 2019
6. Desurvire, H., et al.: Using heuristics to evaluate the playability of games. In: Extended Abstracts of the 2004 Conference on Human Factors and Computing Systems - CHI 2004 (2004). https://doi.org/10.1145/985921.986102
7. Dickinson, A., et al.: UKKO: enriching persuasive location based games with environmental sensor data. In: CHI PLAY 2015 Proceedings of the 2015 Annual Symposium on Computer-Human Interaction in Play (2015). https://doi.org/10.1145/2793107.2810324
8. Dreamy Dingo: Matching games Memory games Pairs: Remembery. https://play.google.com/store/apps/details?id=ua.krou.remembery&hl=en. Accessed 21 Oct 2019

9. Fogg, B.: Creating persuasive technologies: an eight-step design process. In: Proceedings of the 4th International Conference on Persuasive Technology – Persuasive 2009 (2009). https://doi.org/10.1145/1541948.1542005
10. Webroot Inc.: Nearly 1.5 Million New Phishing Sites Created Each Month | Webroot. https://www.webroot.com/us/en/about/press-room/releases/nearly-15-million-new-phishing-sites. Accessed 01 Nov 2019
11. Jagatic, T.N., et al.: Social phishing. Commun. ACM (2007). https://doi.org/10.1145/1290958.1290968
12. Jakobsson, M.: The human factor in phishing. Priv. Secur. Consum. Inf. (2007). https://cofense.com/wp-content/uploads/2017/11/Enterprise-Phishing-Resiliency-and-Defense-Report-2017.pdf
13. Kadomura, A., et al.: Sensing fork and persuasive game for improving eating behavior (2013). https://doi.org/10.1145/2494091.2494112
14. Kumaraguru, P., et al.: School of phish: a real-world evaluation of anti-phishing training categories and subject descriptors. In: Proceedings of the 5th Symposium Usable Privacy Security - SOUPS 2009, p. 12 (2009). https://doi.org/10.1145/1572532.1572536
15. Lin, T., et al.: A persuasive game to encourage healthy dietary behaviors of kindergarten children. In: Adjunct Proceedings of the 8th International Conference on Ubiquitous Computing (2006)
16. Magma Mobile: MatchUp: Exercise your Memory. https://play.google.com/store/apps/details?id=com.magmamobile.game.MatchUp&hl=en. Accessed 12 Oct 2019
17. Misra, G., et al.: Phish phinder: a game design approach to enhance user confidence in mitigating phishing attacks (2017)
18. Ndulue, C., Orji, R.: STD PONG: an African-centric persuasive game for risky sexual. In: Adjunct Proceedings of the Persuasive Technology Conference (2018)
19. Nielsen, J., Molich, R.: Heuristic evaluation of user interfaces. In: CHI 1990 Proceedings of the SIGCHI Conference on Human Factors in Computing System (1990). https://doi.org/10.1145/97243.97281
20. Oinas-Kukkonen, H., Harjumaa, M.: Persuasive systems design: key issues, process model, and system features. Commun. Assoc. Inf. Syst. **24**(1), 485–500 (2009)
21. Orji, R., et al.: LunchTime: a slow-casual game for long-term dietary behavior change. Pers. Ubiquit. Comput. **17**(6), 1211–1221 (2013). https://doi.org/10.1007/s00779-012-0590-6
22. PhishFindR: Phishing Database. https://github.com/mitchellkrogza/Phishing.Database. Accessed 30 Sept 2019
23. PhishMe Inc.: Analysis of Susceptibility, Resiliency and Defense Against Simulated and Real Phishing Attacks (2017)
24. Samudrala, R.: List of spammers' e-mail addresses. http://www.ram.org/ramblings/philosophy/spam/spammers.html. Accessed 30 Sept 2019
25. Sheng, S., et al.: Anti-phishing phil: the design and evaluation of a game that teaches people not to fall for phish. In: ACM International Conference Proceeding Series (2007). https://doi.org/10.1145/1280680.1280692
26. Symantec: ISTR Internet Security Threat Report Volume 23 (2018)
27. Yoon, S., Godwin, A.: Enhancing self-management in children with sickle cell disease through playing a CD-ROM educational game: a pilot study. J. Pediatr. Nurs. **33**, 60–63, 72 (2007)
28. Yu, W.D., et al.: A phishing vulnerability analysis of web based systems. In: Proceedings - IEEE Symposium on Computers and Communications, pp. 326–331 (2008). https://doi.org/10.1109/ISCC.2008.4625681

GDPR and Systems for Health Behavior Change: A Systematic Review

Eunice Eno Yaa Frimponmaa Agyei(✉) and Harri Oinas-Kukkonen(✉)

Faculty of Information Technology and Electrical Engineering, University of Oulu, 90570 Oulu, Finland
{eunice.agyei,harri.oinas-kukkonen}@oulu.fi

Abstract. eHealth systems for behavior change need to cope with a wide variety of privacy requirements specified by governmental and other regulations. We conducted a systematic review of scientific articles. Analysis of the articles revealed General Data Protection Regulation (GDPR) compliant eHealth technologies, challenges posed by GDPR as well as early solutions for them. In addition, we highlight key GDPR issues to be considered when designing persuasive technologies.

Keywords: GDPR · eHealth · Persuasive technology · Persuasive features · Behaviour change

1 Introduction

eHealth technology seeks to enhance health care delivery [1]. It enhances the efficiency of healthcare by reducing cost, improving the quality of care, and empowering stakeholders by making personal electronic records readily accessible to them. It also provides a mechanism for collaboration between patients, health workers, and technology providers, and thus educates and facilitates information exchange between health practitioners and healthcare centers.

Persuasive eHealth technologies such as Behaviour Change Support Systems (BCSS) help users change their behaviour over time [2]. Despite their usefulness, eHealth systems are prone to ethical issues pertaining to informed consent, privacy breaches, and equity issues regarding who can have access to the resources and the opportunities it has to offer [3]. Privacy and security are a cause for concern due to the sensitive and personal nature of health data. Without addressing privacy related issues, the rate of adoption and use of eHealth applications and systems could to a significant manner be negatively impacted [4].

Privacy of health data presents serious concerns when health records are electronic [5]. Maintaining the privacy of health data involves ensuring confidentiality, integrity, and availability of the data, as well as securing the collection, transmission, storage and processing of the data. It further involves securing the technology itself, educating and increasing the awareness of privacy and security breach issues, as well as complying with policies and regulations to keep the data secured [6]. Two well-known legislations

S. B. Gram-Hansen et al. (Eds.): PERSUASIVE 2020, LNCS 12064, pp. 234–246, 2020.
https://doi.org/10.1007/978-3-030-45712-9_18

that regulate the handling of data are the Health Insurance Portability and Accountability Act (HIPAA) and General Data Protection Regulation (GDPR) [7].

In this paper, the following research contributions are made: (1) analysis of the influence GDPR has on the privacy requirements of eHealth systems, (2) identification of challenges GDPR possess to the development of eHealth systems and how these requirements can be fulfilled, (3) highlight key issues for designing persuasive features of eHealth systems. The terms eHealth systems, applications and technologies are used interchangeably in this paper.

2 Background

Although eHealth projects and applications do not always perform as anticipated [8, 9], one important issue to consider is the resistance to change attitude of health professionals which stems from the lack of reconciliation of their expectations and actual outcome of eHealth systems [8]. In the development of eHealth systems, attention is often given to the technical aspects leading to the neglect of the interdependencies that exist between the technology, people, and the environment to reap the full benefits of such systems [10]. This calls for the adoption of a comprehensive approach to the development of eHealth applications. One such approach is proposed by the Centre for eHealth Research and Disease Management (CeHRes) as the CeHRes Roadmap [10].

CeHRes Roadmap. The CeHRes Roadmap is an approach that serves as a guideline for eHealth development, implementation and evaluation. It adopts a holistic approach for the development of eHealth technologies using an iterative and dynamic 5-phase framework which encompasses participatory development, persuasive design techniques, and business modelling [10]. The phases of the framework are contextual inquiry, value specification, design, operationalization and summative evaluation. (1) *Contextual Inquiry:* The first phase focuses on gaining an in-depth understanding of the current state of the problem at hand, identifies and analyses the roles and needs of the various stakeholders who fall within the scope and context of the problem. (2) *Value Specification:* This phase involves the identification and elicitation of the specific benefits (values) of the technology based on stakeholder needs. These values can then be translated into end-user requirements. (3) *Design:* Here, the identification of user requirements of the system is followed by development mock-ups, prototypes, usability tests, technology development, and the addition of usability principles and persuasive features to the design are done [11]. (4) *Operationalization:* Plans regarding the operationalization of the technology are outlined. Concrete activities such as pilot programs, advocacies, and presentations are used to increase the awareness of the technology. (5) *Evaluation:* This phase involves a formative and/or summative assessment of the impact of the designed technology on the problem context and its stakeholders. Thus, the value added to the stakeholder's life should be apparent. The CeHRes Roadmap aids in the planning and execution of the development process of eHealth technologies and can be a valuable tool for the improvement of existing technologies.

General Data Protection Regulation (GDPR). The data protection regulation which emphasizes on the need to protect citizens of the European Union (EU) from privacy and data breaches and the consequences of non-compliance was enforced in May, 2018 [12]. GDPR is famous for the penalties associated with non-compliance and the rights of data subjects such as privacy by design, breach notifications, right to be forgotten, right to access, and data portability which was not the case in previous legislations. In the event of a breach or non-compliance, an organization can incur a fine to the tune of 4% of its annual global turnover or 20 million euros (whichever is greater). GDPR requires the data of people living within the EU to be processed within the EU regardless of the location of the company. This means that any business entity that seeks to process the data of EU citizens must have a representative within the EU. Consent is another requirement of GDPR. GDPR demands user consent be clear, informative, accessible, written in clear and plain language, and easy to withdraw from. GDPR also specifies requirements for proper record keeping of internal data operations. The implementation of GDPR in eHealth systems brings new design requirements, responsibilities, and expenditures leading to significant impact on eHealth organizations [13]. In this paper, the CeHRes roadmap will be used to identify the influence GDPR has on the development of eHealth systems.

3   Methodology

A systematic review was conducted to identify GDPR implementations in eHealth systems using data from the following databases: *Proquest, IEEE Xplore, Ebscohost, Web of Science*, and *ACM* using the following keyword combinations: GDPR AND (ehealth OR e-health OR mhealth OR m-health OR 'electronic health' OR 'digital health', OR 'digital interventions' OR 'online interventions' OR 'ehealth interventions' OR 'mobile intervention' OR 'e-health intervention' OR 'mhealth intervention' OR 'm-health intervention', OR 'mobile health' OR 'mobile app' OR 'mobile application').

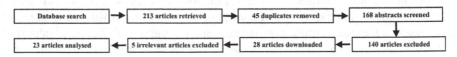

Fig. 1. Selection process

A total of 213 articles were found, of which 168 unique articles were obtained after deduplication. The titles and abstracts were screened for keywords and articles that did not have any of the keywords were excluded. A total of 28 articles remained for further analysis. Further screening was performed to exclude articles that were not relevant to our objective. Articles included were directly or indirectly related to eHealth and GDPR. 5 articles were not relevant for this study and hence excluded. A total of 23 articles were analysed. These articles can be found as publications [8, 14–35] in the reference list of this paper. See Fig. 1

4 Results

4.1 GDPR and Characteristics of eHealth Roadmap

The CeHRes roadmap employs participatory approach, persuasive design and business modelling [10]. Quite naturally, not all the analysed studies utilised all these principles, however, a number of characteristics of the roadmap were found in various studies. Table 1 shows how the CeHRes Roadmap characteristics were evident in the analysed studies.

Table 1. Characteristics of studies (N = 23)

	Number of studies (N = 23)	% addressed
Contextual inquiry	22	95%
Value specification	22	95%
Design	16	70%
Operationalization	4	17%
Summative evaluation	4	17%

Contextual Inquiry: A vast majority of the articles (22 out of 23) provided a detailed analysis of the current healthcare provision as well as a thorough description of the problem context, the strengths and weaknesses of the existing healthcare provisions (eHealth system in use) in the light of privacy and GDPR. The remaining article (1 out of 23) only analysed an existing system against GDPR requirements. The nature of the analysis was such that the phases of the CeHRes framework were unobvious and hence the roadmap was non-applicable to it. Some of the problems identified in the studies were centered around data privacy [14, 15, 19–21, 23], consent [21, 25, 31], ownership of user data [20, 27], right to data portability [27], security [19], right to be forgotten [25, 28], cyber insurance to cover eHealth assets [28], among others. Interestingly, only one article identified and analysed the stakeholders where surveys were used to collect privacy concerns of stakeholders which were then translated into user requirements [19].

Value Specification: Privacy related values of the technology were identified and translated into requirements. A clear and specific goal as well as the associated values of the technology were evident in 22 out of the 23 articles analysed. The values of the eHealth systems to be designed were clearly articulated by specifying the demands from the implementation context as well as how the set goals could be achieved. While some studies approached value identification from the stakeholder perspective [19], others sought to determine what could be improved or supported by means of an eHealth solution [14, 15, 18, 23, 25, 27, 29, 31, 33]. The identified privacy values thus formed the basis for the requirements of the design of the technology.

Design: The output of the contextual inquiry and value specification phases translated into a unified modelling language diagram [24], conceptual designs [14, 22], system architectures [15, 16, 18–20, 23, 25, 26, 28–32], and a high-fidelity prototype [17]. Persuasive features were identified from some of the studies. These include self-monitoring [16, 18], personalization [17, 29, 31], reduction [23, 26], rewards [26], reminders [29], and competition [29]. Gamification, a component of modern eHealth applications, which encompasses persuasive features was also identified [29]. Some of the studies went ahead to develop solutions [15, 18, 23, 28, 30] that solved the identified privacy issue (e.g. [21]) in the eHealth system.

Operationalization: A few studies (4 out of 23) implemented and tested their designs. Four studies piloted their eHealth technologies in different forms including in a real-world environment [18], a proof of concept [23], a field study [15], and an integration into an existing system [28].

Summative Evaluation: Only a handful of studies (4 out of 23) evaluated their eHealth technologies. Evaluation of the eHealth technologies were based on the values specified [30]. Two studies assessed the impact on system stakeholders [18, 23], while another evaluated the accuracy of a deep learning model that underpinned their privacy policy extraction system [15].

4.2 GDPR and System Requirements

eHealth technologies identified from the studies include web applications (e.g. [16]), Internet of Things (IoT) (e.g. [26]), cloud computing (e.g. [32]), artificial intelligence (AI) [24], mobile applications (e.g. [31]), big data [33], and blockchain-based solutions (e.g. [26]). These technologies varied in terms of application domain ranging from general solutions to specific solutions such as solutions tailored for monitoring heart conditions [31], well-being and fitness [7], human-disease infection [33], elderly care (e.g. [29]), and remote care [16].

Static healthcare data includes data that may not change during the lifetime of a person such as fingerprint and genome, whereas dynamic data includes data collected when a user engages in an activity (e.g. heartbeat rate) and the state of the user (e.g. blood test) [7]. Data is collected for an instance or continuously for both static and dynamic data depending on the purpose of the data collection and as such the frequency and size of the data collected, stored, and processed may require different methods and approaches. Typically, data is collected from web applications (e.g. [14]), mobile applications (e.g. [15]), IoT devices (e.g. [22]), or other health information systems [34], among others. These are stored on local or remote servers and/or cloud services.

The rights enjoyed by data subjects sit at the heart of GDPR with 19 out of the 23 articles reviewed addressing data subject rights. Nine articles discussed the right to access, five articles discussed the right to be forgotten, two articles addressed the right to rectification, three articles addressed data portability, while 18 articles addressed privacy by design. Interestingly, only one article addressed the issue of breach notifications. Clearly, there exist a need for a more solid and consolidated effort in implementing data subject rights in eHealth systems comprehensively to ensure compliance with GDPR requirements.

Table 2. Problems related to GDPR and proposed solutions

Theme	Problem	Implemented solution	Example study
Privacy	Privacy issues related to electronic health records such as data breaches	Privacy by design model for managing electronic health records	Bincoletto, 2019. [14]
	Issues related to readability of privacy policies of eHealth systems	A system to predict and extract privacy policies using privacy concerns of users	Chang et al. 2019 [15]
	Privacy issues caused by data leakage in remote digital health interventions	An architecture that secures remote transmission of sensor data	El Jaouhari and Bouabdallah, 2018 [16]
	Privacy issues in mHealth apps related to user-app interaction and transparency	Integrating GDPR requirements into app visualizations to enhance transparency	Muchagata and Ferreira, 2018 [17]
	Privacy issues associated with storing health records in the public cloud	Tokenization architecture to remove sensitive information from health records and encryption of the data	Paavola and Ekqvist, 2017 [18]
Privacy/Security	Vulnerability of electronic healthcare infrastructure to privacy and cybersecurity threats	A GDPR compliant platform for managing and transferring eHealth data	Diaz-Honrubia et al., 2019 [19]
	Privacy and security challenges related to IoT eHealth systems	An architecture for secured collection, storage and processing of data from IoT systems	Koutli et al., 2019 [29]
Ownership	The need to allow data subjects to control their own data	A GDPR controller to give full control of data to data subjects	Rhahla, Abdellatif, Attia, and Berrayana, 2019 [30]
Privacy/Ownership	Privacy challenges of healthcare data	Use of blockchain to enable users control their data	Mohammad Hossein, Esmaeili, Dargahi, and others, 2019 [20]

(*continued*)

Table 2. (*continued*)

Theme	Problem	Implemented solution	Example study
Trust/Ownership	Trust issues emerging during the exchange of healthcare data between institutions	A federated blockchain application to enable trust and allow users to own, control and exchange their data	Koscina et al., 2019 [25]
	Problems associated with ownership and control of health data	Blockchain based data sharing systems to enable users to control and own their data	Zheng et al., 2018 [26]
Ownership/Data Portability	The need for patients to own and control their data and data should be in a format that support interoperability	A GDPR compliant blockchain application to give control to the user	Stan and Miclea, 2019 [27]
Consent	Issues related to consent in eHealth systems	User-centered electronic consent system that incorporates data subject's rights	O'Connor et al., 2017 [22]
	The need for adequate management of consent in eHealth systems	Consent management framework to enable users of eHealth systems manage their own consent	Hyysalo et al., 2016 [23]
Consent/right to be forgotten	Issues related to knowledge management in artificial intelligence eHealth systems	A way to unlink (remove) user data from training samples	Lutze, 2019 [24]
Insurance	Data risks emerging from digital health data	A framework for risk assessment and insurance against risks	Hatzivasilis et al. 2019 [28]

The enforcement of the GDPR poses a significant amount of challenges to eHealth systems. GDPR gives a new dimension to issues of security and privacy, putting the user at the center of it all, with additional requirements that eHealth systems need to comply with. Interestingly, we identified several challenges which we have classified into high-level themes. These high-level themes represent the areas from which the reviewed articles identified GDPR-related problems and to which they proposed solutions. Privacy is a theme that a vast majority of the articles focused on. While some discussed privacy in eHealth systems in general, others were more specific, focusing on privacy of health data, privacy during data transmission and storage. Some of the themes however overlap with each other. A detailed description of the classification, the problems and challenges identified by the studies, and their suggested solutions can be found in Table 2.

4.3 GDPR and Persuasion for Behaviour Change

Behaviour change support systems are developed with persuasive features that enable and support users change their behaviour over time. From our analysis, only two persuasive features in eHealth systems were identified that targeted behaviour change: personalization and self-monitoring [29, 31]. Persuasion through personalization and self-monitoring is carried out based on the data of the information system. It is important that this data meets the GDPR requirements of the consent to collect, store and process data, the right to access data, the right to be forgotten, as well as privacy. These requirements must be properly incorporated into the design of behavioural change systems.

5 GDPR and Persuasive System Design

Persuasive System Design (PSD) is a model for designing and evaluating persuasive systems [35]. The PSD model specifies key issues that have the tendency to persuade a user. These include supporting the user to perform primary tasks of the eHealth system, supporting the interaction between humans and the system, supporting the credibility of the system and providing social support if necessary. Persuasion occurs via the content of the eHealth system, software features offered, the credibility of the system to function and privacy trust. For example, the content and software features have conflicting implications on the privacy of the user. Privacy issues are imperative because they act as barriers that influence the use of eHealth systems [5]. In Table 3, we summarize persuasive features according to support categories of the PSD model with examples of GDPR requirements and implementation for each.

Persuasive systems rely on user data such as goals, preferences, and lifestyle as well as objective data such as phone app usage, heart rate, etc. obtained from mobile and wearable device sensors [35]. The availability of such data enables persuasive systems to create and make better recommendations to users (e.g. to match the content with user preferences). Such user data is subject to GDPR requirements hence in building persuasive systems, it is important to consider how the various data subject rights can affect the performance of the system (e.g. the right to be forgotten).

Often, software features in persuasive systems are tailored for user segments and hence not truly unique for an individual user [36]. Unique software features for an individual user would require personal data and may raise privacy concerns. The possibility of providing truly unique persuasive features to match an individual's preferences provides an interesting research opportunity but it is very complex [37]. Such features could perhaps sustain behaviour change and/or equip users to commit to their set goals. Such a feature is analogical to human gratitude when another human or creature demonstrates thoughtfulness. As we aim to closely mimic human ways in human-computer

Table 3. Persuasive principles and GDPR requirements

Category	Example GDPR requirement	Example GDPR implementation
Primary task support	• Systems should protect the privacy of its users • Systems should allow users to control their own data • Systems should seek the consent of users when collecting and processing their data • Systems should limit data collection to what is needed for persuasion to be effective • Data collection and processing should be recorded for accountability	• The app limits the amount of data to what is needed for the functioning of the app • The app allows users to rectify incorrect information
Dialogue Support	• Systems should provide feedback in a way that does not reveal private or sensitive information	• The app displays important information but not information that compromises the privacy of the user • The app allows users to use pseudonyms or avatars instead of their real names
System credibility support	• Systems should demonstrate compliance with GDPR rules	• The app displays the contact details of the Data Protection Officer (DPO) to enable users to request information about their data • The app provides a means for users to configure privacy settings • The app shows the logo of privacy rules complied to
Social support	• Systems should preserve the privacy of users in social settings	• The app informs and seeks the consent of users before sharing data with other users

interaction, unique and meaningful persuasive features in eHealth systems cannot be overemphasized. Providing such unique features requires a large amount of user data and huge computational capabilities which may not be possible with the current fourth generation (4G) telecommunication networks. Perhaps the introduction of fifth generation (5G) and subsequent telecommunication networks could create this possibility. We call for research into individualized persuasive features and encourage debates on the perceived persuasiveness of unique features based on the preferences of an individual.

6 Discussion

Research has shown that privacy remains a concern for electronic health records produced from eHealth systems [38]. Persuasive strategies such as monitoring, tracking, and personalization affect the privacy of users. Not only is health data sensitive, it may also trigger placebo effect [39] and/or undesired outcomes which may lead to coercion [40] and falsification of information (by the user) [41]. These issues have the tendency to affect the efficiency of an eHealth application particularly for systems that offer personalization and recommendations. As such, the designers and developers of persuasive technologies should aim to protect the privacy of users as their own. This also applies to third party data collectors [42].

This systematic review was conducted to identify the requirements of GDPR in eHealth systems and technologies particularly those that persuade users. The results obtained shows that lingering privacy concerns can be addressed when GDPR requirements are factored in the design and development of eHealth systems. The study confirms that there is a relationship between privacy and GDPR requirements. Although GDPR presents a tall list of requirements which may seem overwhelming or even impossible to implement, we beg to differ. We argue this can be simplified if developers carefully analyse the data required for persuasive software features, identify the privacy issues and address them with the corresponding GDPR requirement (See examples in Table 3). This analysis should be carried out at the onset of the software project. Using approaches such as the CeHRes Roadmap as a guide, the privacy concerns of stakeholders can be identified in the contextual inquiry phase. Privacy values can be specified and incorporated into the design and development of the eHealth system. Also, privacy requirements of the technology such as frequency of data collection, storage and data processing activities (e.g. anonymization, encryption) must be specified and incorporated into the design and development of the system. The knowledge obtained from privacy concerns of stakeholders and privacy requirements of the system can be useful information for crafting meaningful and informed privacy policies. After the development, concrete plans must be made to test and prepare the system for use. The plan must include benchmarks which will be used to assess the functionality, privacy and security aspects of the system by stakeholders in the evaluation phase. We advocate involving stakeholders as much as possible from the contextual inquiry phase through to the evaluation phase of the CeHRes Roadmap or any similar holistic eHealth development framework. This will help address the privacy concerns of users and fulfil the requirements of privacy legislations like GDPR.

Notwithstanding, some GDPR requirements such as the right to be forgotten [27] and accountability requirement for artificial intelligence (AI) based technologies may be challenging to implement [43–45]. While a data subject can request to be forgotten, this request can also be rejected based on public interest. These critical issues must be factored into the design. New fields of research such as explainable AI [45] seek to make transparent the AI. This is a step in the right direction to ensure transparency and accountability of 'AI-powered' eHealth systems. It can therefore be assumed that adherence to GDPR requirements in eHealth technologies will significantly increase trust and transparency between developers of eHealth applications and its users which may ultimately affect its adoption and use.

7 Conclusion

In this study, we investigated how GDPR is implemented in eHealth systems as addressed in literature. The relevance of a holistic approach to the development of eHealth systems cannot be overemphasized especially when it addresses privacy concerns of stakeholders and fulfils GDPR requirements. As the literature review shows, there is a missing anchor in terms of the implementation of data subject rights. Only a few studies extensively addressed data subject rights in the reviewed papers. To address such shortcomings, we advocate an all-encompassing agenda that will empower and enable both researchers and practitioners to work together to guarantee compliance of eHealth systems to GDPR requirements. This can be done by ensuring that not only privacy but also data subject rights, and system evaluation become a fundamental value anchored in eHealth systems; particularly behaviour change systems and persuasive technologies.

The need for a human-centric viewpoint to the implementation of GDPR is yet to be exhaustively discussed within the scope of eHealth systems. We hope that our study is in itself a call to action concerning these issues.

References

1. Oh, H., Rizo, C., Enkin, M., Jadad, A.: What is eHealth (3): a systematic review of published definitions. J. Med. Internet Res. **7**(1), e1 (2005)
2. Oinas-Kukkonen, H.: A foundation for the study of behavior change support systems. Pers. Ubiquitous Comput. **17**(6), 1223–1235 (2013)
3. Eysenbach, G.: What is e-health? J. Med. Internet Res. **3**(2), e20 (2001)
4. Slamanig, D., Stingl, C.: Privacy aspects of ehealth. In: 2008 Third International Conference on Availability, Reliability and Security, pp. 1226–1233 (2008)
5. Raychaudhuri, K., Ray, P.: Privacy challenges in the use of eHealth systems for public health management. In: Emerging Communication Technologies for E-Health and Medicine, pp. 155–166. IGI Global (2012)
6. Sahama, T., Simpson, L., Lane, B.: Security and privacy in eHealth: is it possible? In: 2013 IEEE 15th International Conference on e-Health Networking, Applications and Services (Healthcom 2013), pp. 249–253 (2013)
7. Braghin, C., Cimato, S., Della Libera, A.: Are mHealth apps secure? A case study. In: 2018 IEEE 42nd Annual Computer Software and Application Conference, vol. 02, pp. 335–340 (2018)
8. Granja, C., Janssen, W., Johansen, M.A.: Factors determining the success and failure of eHealth interventions: systematic review of the literature. J. Med. Internet Res. **20**(5), e10235 (2018)
9. Greenhalgh, T., Russell, J.: Why do evaluations of eHealth programs fail? An alternative set of guiding principles. PLoS Med. **7**(11), e1000360 (2010)
10. van Gemert-Pijnen, J.E.W.C., et al.: A holistic framework to improve the uptake and impact of eHealth technologies. J. Med. Internet Res. **13**(4), e111 (2011)
11. van Gemert-Pijnen, L., Span, M.: CeHRes Roadmap to Improve Dementia Care. In: van Hoof, J., Demiris, G., Wouters, E.J.M. (eds.) Handbook of Smart Homes, Health Care and Well-Being, pp. 133–146. Springer, Cham (2017). https://doi.org/10.1007/978-3-319-01583-5_15
12. GDPR Archives - GDPR.eu. https://gdpr.eu/tag/gdpr/. Accessed 10 Feb 2020

13. Shao, X., Oinas-Kukkonen, H.: How does GDPR (General Data Protection Regulation) affect persuasive system design: design requirements and cost implications. In: Oinas-Kukkonen, H., Win, K.T., Karapanos, E., Karppinen, P., Kyza, E. (eds.) PERSUASIVE 2019. LNCS, vol. 11433, pp. 168–173. Springer, Cham (2019). https://doi.org/10.1007/978-3-030-17287-9_14

14. Bincoletto, G.: A data protection by design model for privacy management in electronic health records. In: Naldi, M., Italiano, Giuseppe F., Rannenberg, K., Medina, M., Bourka, A. (eds.) APF 2019. LNCS, vol. 11498, pp. 161–181. Springer, Cham (2019). https://doi.org/10.1007/978-3-030-21752-5_11

15. Chang, C., Li, H., Zhang, Y., Du, S., Cao, H., Zhu, H.: Automated and personalized privacy policy extraction under GDPR consideration. In: Biagioni, E.S., Zheng, Y., Cheng, S. (eds.) WASA 2019. LNCS, vol. 11604, pp. 43–54. Springer, Cham (2019). https://doi.org/10.1007/978-3-030-23597-0_4

16. El Jaouhari, S., Bouabdallah, A.: A privacy safeguard framework for a WebRTC/WoT-based healthcare architecture. In: 2018 IEEE 42nd Annual Computer Software and Applications Conference (COMPSAC), vol. 02, pp. 468–473 (2018)

17. Muchagata, J., Ferreira, A.: Translating GDPR into the mHealth practice. In: 2018 International Carnahan Conference on Security Technology, pp. 1–5 (2018)

18. Paavola, J., Ekqvist, J.: Privacy preserving and resilient cloudified IoT architecture to support eHealth systems. In: Fortino, G., et al. (eds.) InterIoT/SaSeIoT-2017. LNICST, vol. 242, pp. 134–143. Springer, Cham (2018). https://doi.org/10.1007/978-3-319-93797-7_15

19. Diaz-Honrubia, A.J., et al.: An overview of the CUREX platform. In: 2019 IEEE 32nd International Symposium on Computer-Based Medical Systems (CBMS), pp. 162–167 (2019)

20. Mohammad Hossein, K., Esmaeili, M.E., Dargahi, T., et al.: Blockchain-based privacy-preserving healthcare architecture (2019)

21. Neame, R.L.B.: Privacy protection in personal health information and shared care records. J. Innov. Health Inform. 21(2), 84–91 (2014)

22. O'Connor, Y., Rowan, W., Lynch, L., Heavin, C.: Privacy by design: informed consent and internet of things for smart health. Procedia Comput. Sci. 113, 653–658 (2017)

23. Hyysalo, J., Hirvonsalo, H., Sauvola, J.J., Tuoriniemi, S.: Consent management architecture for secure data transactions. In: ICSOFT-EA, pp. 125–132 (2016)

24. Lutze, R.: Digital twins in eHealth – : prospects and challenges focussing on information management. In: 2019 IEEE International Conference on Engineering, Technology and Innovation (ICE/ITMC), pp. 1–9 (2019)

25. Koscina, M., Manset, D., Negri, C., Kempner, O.P.: Enabling trust in healthcare data exchange with a federated blockchain-based architecture (2019)

26. Zheng, X., Mukkamala, R.R., Vatrapu, R., Ordieres-Mere, J.: Blockchain-based personal health data sharing system using cloud storage. In: 2018 IEEE 20th International Conference on e-Health Networking, Applications and Services (Healthcom), pp. 1–6 (2018)

27. Stan, O.P., Miclea, L.: New Era for Technology in Healthcare Powered by GDPR and Blockchain. In: Vlad, S., Roman, N.M. (eds.) 6th International Conference on Advancements of Medicine and Health Care through Technology; 17–20 October 2018, Cluj-Napoca, Romania. IP, vol. 71, pp. 311–317. Springer, Singapore (2019). https://doi.org/10.1007/978-981-13-6207-1_49

28. Hatzivasilis, G., et al.: Cyber insurance of information systems. In: 2019 IEEE 24th International Workshop on Computer Aided Modeling and Design of Communication Links and Networks (CAMAD), pp. 1–6 (2019)

29. Koutli, M., et al.: Secure IoT e-Health applications using VICINITY framework and GDPR guidelines. In: 2019 15th International Conference on Distributed Computing in Sensor Systems (DCOSS), pp. 263–270 (2019)

30. Rhahla, M., Abdellatif, T., Attia, R., Berrayana, W.: A GDPR controller for IoT systems: application to e-health. In: 2019 IEEE 28th International Conference on Enabling Technologies: Infrastructure for Collaborative Enterprises (WETICE), pp. 170–173 (2019)

31. Mustafa, U., Pflugel, E., Philip, N.: A novel privacy framework for secure m-health applications: the case of the GDPR. In: 2019 IEEE 12th International Conference on Global Security, Safety and Sustainability (ICGS3), pp. 1–9 (2019)

32. Ducato, R.: Cloud computing for s-health and the data protection challenge: getting ready for the General Data Protection Regulation. In: 2016 IEEE International Smart Cities Conference (ISC2), pp. 1–4 (2016)

33. Kostkova, P.: Disease surveillance data sharing for public health: the next ethical frontiers. Life Sci. Soc. Policy **14**(1), 16 (2018)

34. Sousa, M., et al.: OpenEHR based systems and the general data protection regulation (GDPR). In: Building Continents Knowledge in Oceans of Data: The Future of Co-Created eHealth (2018)

35. Oinas-Kukkonen, H., Harjumaa, M.: Persuasive systems design: key issues, process model, and system features. Commun. Assoc. Inf. Syst. **24**(1), 28 (2009)

36. Oinas-Kukkonen, H.: Personalization myopia: a viewpoint to true personalization of information systems. In: Proceedings of the 22nd International Academic Mindtrek Conference, pp. 88–91. ACM (2018)

37. Pratt, W., Klasnja, P., Consolvo, S.: How to evaluate technologies for health behavior change in HCI research. In: CHI 2011 (2011)

38. Meingast, M., Roosta, T., Sastry, S.: Security and privacy issues with health care information technology. In: Annual International Conference of the IEEE Engineering in Medicine and Biology - Proceedings, pp. 5453–5458 (2006)

39. Beun, R.J., et al.: Improving adherence in automated e-coaching. In: Meschtscherjakov, A., De Ruyter, B., Fuchsberger, V., Murer, M., Tscheligi, M. (eds.) PERSUASIVE 2016. LNCS, vol. 9638, pp. 276–287. Springer, Cham (2016). https://doi.org/10.1007/978-3-319-31510-2_24

40. Cheng, R.: Persuasion strategies for computers as persuasive technologies (2003)

41. Raybourn, E.M., et al.: Data privacy and security considerations for personal assistants for learning (PAL). In: International Conference on Intelligent User Interfaces, Proceedings IUI, 29 March 2015, pp. 69–72 (2015)

42. Davis, J.: Design methods for ethical persuasive computing (2009)

43. Wachter, S., Mittelstadt, B., Floridi, L.: Transparent, explainable, and accountable AI for robotics. Sci. Rob. **2**, eaan6080 (2017)

44. Guarda, P.: Essays "Ok Google, am I sick?": artificial intelligence, e-health, and data protection regulation. BioLaw Journal-Rivista di BioDiritto **15**, 359–375 (2019)

45. Samek, W., Wiegand, T., Müller, K.-R.: Explainable artificial intelligence: understanding, visualizing and interpreting deep learning models, August 2017

Author Index